Jacob and the Divine Trickster

Siphrut
Literature and Theology of the Hebrew Scriptures

Jacob and the Divine Trickster

A Theology of Deception and Yʜᴡʜ's Fidelity to the Ancestral Promise in the Jacob Cycle

John E. Anderson

Winona Lake, Indiana
Eɪsᴇɴʙʀᴀᴜɴs
2011

www.eisenbrauns.com

Library of Congress Cataloging-in-Publication Data

Anderson, John Edward, 1981–
    Jacob and the divine trickster : a theology of deception and YHWH's fidelity to
        the ancestral promise in the Jacob cycle / John E. Anderson.
            p.   cm. — (Siphrut : literature and theology of the Hebrew Scriptures ; 5)
        Includes bibliographical references and indexes.
        ISBN 978-1-57506-219-8 (hardback : alk. paper)
        1. Deception in the Bible.   2. Truthfulness and falsehood—Religious
    aspects—Judaism.   3. Bible. O.T. Genesis—Criticism, interpretation, etc.
    I. Title.
        BS1238.D42A53   2011
        221.6—dc23
                                                                                                2011030414

The paper used in this publication meets the minimum requirements of the American National Standard for Information Sciences—Permanence of Paper for Printed Library Materials, ANSI Z39.48-1984.

לאבן בכרי

To Evan, my firstborn.
You are truly a blessing from God.
I love you.

And Jacob erected a pillar on the place where He spoke to him,
a pillar of *stone*,
and he poured upon it a drink offering,
and he poured upon it oil.
And Jacob called the name of the place
where God had spoken with him Bethel.
Gen 35:14–15

Contents

Preface and Acknowledgments

This book is the result of a long and unexpected journey. It is nearly impossible to acknowledge with thanks all those who have contributed to this project. There are indeed many individuals to thank for their help, encouragement, and support.

While perhaps unconventional, I must first thank my great-grandmother, Ann Anderson, who first introduced me to the Bible. I still vividly recall her taking me on her lap and reading to me from the book of Genesis. My journey began with her. She was the first theologian to incline my mind and heart to the importance, beauty, and power of the Bible. I miss her dearly.

A number of former teachers have been instrumental in shaping this book in ways of which they are probably unaware. Murray Haar continued this journey for me by opening up the academic world of biblical studies and showing me that it is not the pursuit of answers but rather the asking of thoughtful and probing questions that breathes life into the text. It is because of him that I entered this field. Richard Swanson taught me always to use imagination and creativity in interpreting biblical texts. The seeds for this project were first planted in the spring of 2006 during a seminar on Genesis with Anathea Portier-Young at Duke University. My proposal to investigate the connection between deception and blessing in the Jacob cycle was met with great interest. The present book is markedly different from my original proposal nearly five years ago, and I thank Thea for her engaging questions during that initial foray, which have been of tremendous assistance in helping me to refine both my method and my argument.

This book is a revision of my Ph.D. dissertation, completed at Baylor University (2010), and I am deeply indebted to my supervisor, W. H. Bellinger Jr. As a constant source of encouragement and confidence, he graciously and with great interest accepted the task of directing a dissertation on the divine trickster! He has instilled in me a passion for the task of Old Testament theology. He has exemplified encouragement, confidence, and care in shaping both this project and me as a scholar. Always an important advocate of my work, Dr. Bellinger has been both a mentor and a friend, never allowing me to settle for easy conclusions and always pressing me harder. I have learned from him the value and transformative power of theological inquiry of the biblical text, but also so much more that transcends academia. His interest in my scholarship and my family and me during my time at Baylor have taught me more than books ever could.

Countless others at Baylor are deserving of great thanks. First among them is James D. Nogalski, who served as my second reader. His keen eyes prevented me from making many a mistake or claiming more than the evidence allows. He generously gave freely of his time, honoring my "interruptions" on more than one occasion. His careful reading, thoughtful remarks, and genuine interest in the project have ensured that the ambiguities remain in the Jacob cycle and not in my own writing. My additional examiners—Luke Ferretter, Lidija Novakovic, and Bill Pitts—asked thoughtful and probing questions that have improved this work. I am also grateful to my former colleagues in the Baylor University Religion Department, who have been supportive of my studies in this area and have sharpened many of my thoughts through worthwhile and enjoyable conversations. The Baylor University Graduate School generously provided funding for travel to various regional and national meetings of the Society of Biblical Literature, at which I was able to present parts of the larger work.

I must also extend my deepest thanks to a number of scholars who have taken a keen interest in this project and have freely offered of their time and expertise in Genesis. Laurence Turner, whose own work on Genesis I am extremely grateful for, has been a wonderful dialogue partner through e-mail and at SBL meetings. Christopher Heard, whose *Dynamics of Diselection* first piqued my interest in literary approaches to Genesis, has become a colleague and friend. My sincerest appreciation goes to Walter Brueggemann, who has read and commented on the manuscript and has offered strong words of encouragement, appreciation, and advocacy. It has been a joy to dialogue with him on this topic. His vision of Old Testament theology, coupled with an ardent desire to underscore the unsettling nature of ancient Israel's God, informs this study in innumerable ways. His own work has been generative for my own, and he has paved much of the way for me to be able to offer this contribution. It is truly humbling to walk in his footsteps, but—to paraphrase something he once wrote to me—I am glad we are at the same task.

I would be remiss not to thank Eisenbrauns, especially Jim Eisenbraun for his expertise, professionalism, and guidance throughout the publishing of this book, and Beverly McCoy, for her careful and thoughtful editorial work in helping to bring this book into being. Special thanks also go to the editors of the Siphrut series—Stephen Chapman, Tremper Longman III, and Nathan MacDonald—for accepting my manuscript for this new, exciting, and vibrant series. On the publishing side, my appreciation also goes to the editors of *Perspectives in Religious Studies*, who have graciously given permission to use previously published material in this book. Parts of my article ("Jacob, Laban, and a Divine Trickster? The Covenantal Framework of God's Deception in the Theology of the Jacob Cycle," *PRSt* 36 [2009] 3–23), with some modification and significant expansion, appear in chap. 3 and a small part of chap. 4.

My friends and family have provided unfailing support and encouragement. I must thank especially my parents for modeling the type of love and devotion to one another and to God that I can only hope to achieve. I am certain they never would have thought the child pretending to sleep late on Sunday mornings would ultimately choose the field of religion as his profession! Truly, the Lord works in mysterious ways! To my parents I owe more than I can say.

Last, but by no means least, the largest praise goes to my wife, Taryn, and son, Evan. Both have sacrificed in countless ways so that I may bring this work to completion. Words are inadequate to express the level of appreciation, gratitude, and love I have for them. They have kept me sane and grounded throughout this process. Every day, I have known that I would walk in the door and be greeted by a big hug and the exuberant shout of "Daddy!" which transforms even the least productive days into happy and worthwhile days. This has truly been the ultimate system of encouragement and support. Taryn has been at my side always. It is one thing to say you support someone, but it is quite another to embody it with patience, steadfastness, understanding, faith, and love. Without either of them, I could not have completed this work. And, my little Evster, who is all-too-quickly becoming my big Evster, this book is for you.

Abbreviations

General

ASV	American Standard Version
B.C.E.	Before the Common Era
C.E.	Common Era
ed(s).	edition, edited by, or editor(s)
JPS	Jewish Publication Society Version
KJV	King James Version
LXX	Septuagint
MT	Masoretic Text
NIV	New International Version
NJB	New Jerusalem Bible
NRSV	New Revised Standard Version
SBL	Society of Biblical Literature
trans.	translated by or translator(s)
v(v).	verse(s)
vol(s).	volume(s)

Reference Works

AB	Anchor Bible
BDB	F. Brown, S. R. Driver, and C. A. Briggs. *A Hebrew and English Lexicon of the Old Testament.* Oxford, 1907
BSac	*Bibliotheca Sacra*
BN	*Biblische Notizen*
BRev	*Bible Review*
BTB	*Biblical Theology Bulletin*
BZ	*Biblische Zeitschrift*
BZAW	Beihefte Zeitschrift für die alttestamentliche Wissenschaft
CBQ	*Catholic Biblical Quarterly*
COS	*Context of Scripture.* Edited by W. W. Hallo. 3 vols. Leiden, 1997
ETL	*Ephemerides theologicae lovanienses*
FOTL	Forms of the Old Testament Literature
GKC	*Gesenius' Hebrew Grammar.* Translated by A. E. Cowley. Edited by E. Kautzsch. 2nd ed. Oxford, 1910
GOTR	*Greek Orthodox Theological Review*
HALOT	L. Koehler, W. Baumgartner, and J. J. Stamm, *The Hebrew and Aramaic Lexicon of the Old Testament.* Translated and edited under the supervision of M. E. J. Richardson. 4 vols. Leiden, 1994–99
HSM	Harvard Semitic Monographs
HTR	*Harvard Theological Review*
HUCA	*Hebrew Union College Annual*
ICC	International Critical Commentary

IJT	Indian Journal of Theology
Int	Interpretation
JANES	Journal of the Ancient Near Eastern Society
JAOS	Journal of the American Oriental Society
JARCE	Journal of the American Research Center in Egypt
JBL	Journal of Biblical Literature
JBQ	Jewish Bible Quarterly
JETS	Journal of the Evangelical Theological Society
JJS	Journal of Jewish Studies
JNES	Journal of Near Eastern Studies
JSOT	Journal for the Study of the Old Testament
JSOTSup	Journal for the Study of the Old Testament Supplement Series
JSS	Journal of Semitic Studies
JSSSup	Journal of Semitic Studies Supplements
JTS	Journal of Theological Studies
LHBOTS	Library of Hebrew Bible / Old Testament Studies
MdB	Le Monde de la Bible
MKAW Letterkunde	Mededeelingen der koninklijke Akademie van Wetenschappen Letterkunde
NAC	New American Commentary
NCBC	New Cambridge Bible Commentary
NICOT	New International Commentary on the Old Testament
OBT	Overtures to Biblical Theology
OTG	Old Testament Guides
OTL	Old Testament Library
PRSt	Perspectives in Religious Studies
RBL	Review of Biblical Literature
ResQ	Restoration Quarterly
SBLSymS	Society of Biblical Literature Symposium Series
ST	Studia Theologica
TWOT	Theological Wordbook of the Old Testament. Edited by R. L. Harris and G. L. Archer Jr. 2 vols. Chicago, 1980
TZ	Theologische Zeitschrift
UF	Ugarit-Forschungen
VT	Vetus Testamentum
VTSup	Vetus Testamentum Supplements
WBC	Word Biblical Commentary
WMANT	Wissenschaftliche Monographien zum Alten und Neuen Testament
ZAW	Zeitschrift für die alttestamentliche Wissenschaft
ZTK	Zeitschrift für Theologie und Kirche

Chapter 1

Introduction

The Jacob cycle (Gen 25:19–35:29) is one of the most engaging yet troubling texts in all of the Hebrew Bible. Jacob is brazenly and unequivocally depicted as a character who has no qualms about deceiving another person. Indeed, the three objects of his deceptions are his own family: his brother Esau, father Isaac, and uncle Laban. Deception in the Jacob narratives also extends well beyond the character of Jacob himself; his mother, Rebekah, and favored wife, Rachel, also actively deceive. Scholars have responded to these deceptive tendencies in Jacob's character—and the individuals around him—in a variety of ways.

One position is to regard Jacob as a character in transformation—in a way, "earning his stripes" as patriarch and thus being made a worthy recipient for the promise (Gen 12:1–3; 26:2–5; 28:13–15) that accompanies this title. The Jacob that emerges from the wrestling match at Peniel in Gen 32 is, this view argues, utterly distinct from the wily and deceptive Jacob of Gen 25 and 27; his change in character is evidenced by his change in name. A second position views the human actors negatively—for example, citing the unrelenting struggle that epitomizes Jacob's life after the deception of his father. Another view seeks to exonerate Jacob from complicity in any wrongdoing, often by transferring the blame for his deceptions to other actors in the text. Each of these views, however, in addition to having its own difficulties, fails to address the questions that arise from the readings, primarily: What role does God then play in relation to the deceptions that pervade the Jacob cycle? What has not been investigated is the way that God may factor into this deceptive activity. How is one to reconcile Jacob as trickster with Jacob as elect patriarch (25:23), recipient of the ancestral promise (28:13–15), namesake for the people Israel (32:28; 35:10), chosen, accompanied, and protected *by God*? This is the central theological issue raised in the Jacob cycle. It is this gap that I seek to fill in this book.

I contend that God is intimately involved in and at times complicit in Jacob's deceptions—a notion that gives rise to an issue that is theological in nature. What does this deception reveal about God? In the analysis that follows, I will seek to understand the ways in which divine deception in Genesis contributes to a richer and under-appreciated theological portrait of both God and the Genesis narratives. In the Jacob cycle, God is not *deus*

1

absconditus;[1] rather, God's presence is often associated with or is literarily proximate to scenes of deception.[2] These moments of theophany appear within the Jacob cycle at crucial junctures; they are the "pillars" of the narrative, supporting it and holding it together.[3] The prenatal divine oracle in Gen 25:23 governs the entire cycle, yet it also anticipates the deception of Isaac in Gen 27. The appearance at Bethel in Gen 28 functions both to corroborate the previous deceptions and to set the stage for the deceptions that ensue in Gen 29–31. Jacob's prolonged stay with Laban and subsequent dream theophany in 31:9–16 provides the justification for his escape with Laban's daughters and property, an event that Laban clearly interprets as a deception (31:27). Likewise, the numinous אִישׁ of Gen 32 presages the further deception of Esau in Gen 33, and at the outset of Gen 35 God again appears, this time on the heels of a deadly act of deception in Gen 34.

This recognition of divine culpability, however, need not necessitate a negative evaluation of God's character. As will become clear in what follows, matters of ethics and morality are not at the fore here in the original utterance of these texts. Similarly, it is not as easy as appealing to contemporary sensibilities that automatically equate deception with something negative. Within Genesis, deception appears to function in a much different, much more robust way, for, when read in the proper context of promise and blessing that typifies the ancestral narratives broadly and Jacob's existence more specifically, God's purpose in engaging in trickery appears intimately tethered to God's concern for the perpetuation of the ancestral promise (Gen 12:1–3). I do not intend by this manner of reading to communicate a timeless moral or ethical truth but, rather, to look at the issue of divine deception theologically. This is a necessary precursor to making any absolute statements regarding God and/or deception. Read within this context, divine deception attests to God's faithfulness to the ancestral promise. I have dubbed this phenomenon of God's role and complicity in Jacob's shenanigans a *theology of deception.*

---

1. Amelia Devin Freedman (*God as an Absent Character in Biblical Hebrew Narrative: A Literary-Theoretical Study* [Studies in Biblical Literature 82; New York: Peter Lang, 2005] 1–3) argues that, while God is the central character of the Hebrew Bible, God is absent from many stories and at times is involved only "indirectly." She contends, however, that regardless of God's seeming absence from much of the biblical text, various "stand-ins" are often used for God. Moreover, she maintains that a number of literary methodologies—narrative criticism, reader-response criticism, intertextuality, and feminist literary criticism—can assist readers in better understanding the character of God in the Hebrew Bible.

2. Elmer A. Martens (*God's Design: A Focus on Old Testament Theology* [Grand Rapids, MI: Baker, 1981] 32) notices a similar pattern in relation to the wife-sister stories in Gen 12, 20, and 26, where the narrative tempers deception by prefacing the act with a reference to the promise of descendants.

3. Terence E. Fretheim, *The Pentateuch* (Interpreting Biblical Texts; Nashville: Abingdon, 1996) 87.

It will be helpful to begin this investigation with a survey of the secondary scholarly literature on the topic of deception in Genesis and divine deception more broadly. These discussions will serve as a useful orientation for the reader who may be unacquainted with the subject. These discussions will also inform the perspective offered in the subsequent chapters, as well as situate it in the wider context of extant scholarship. In what follows, I will summarize and analyze the diverse approaches to and understandings of divine deception in the Jacob cycle, organized according to the following categories: traditional views on God and deception in the Jacob cycle; divine deception in Genesis: implicit references; divine deception in Genesis: explicit references; and divine deception elsewhere in the Hebrew Bible.

Divine Deception in Genesis: A Scholarly Gap

Traditional Views on God and Deception in the Jacob Cycle

Scholars have clearly noted the ubiquity of deception in the Jacob cycle. What the secondary literature lacks, however, is a sustained treatment of the role of Yнwн in the deceptions. To be sure, there are those who seek to negotiate the delicate relationship between Yнwн and trickery, yet these readings largely depict God as either set over and against deceptive activity or as entirely absent from the narrative scene during an act of deception. Two extended examples serve as sound representatives.

Laurence A. Turner's *Announcements of Plot in Genesis* provides a fine example of the former. Turner argues that human meddling in areas of divine jurisprudence can and does lead only to trouble. Within the Jacob cycle, Turner analyzes three "announcements" that turn out to be unreliable indicators of the way the plot will unfold: Yнwн's oracle to Rebekah (25:23), Isaac's blessing of the disguised Jacob (27:27b–29), and Isaac's blessing of Esau (27:39b–40).[4] Jacob and Rebekah's impatience and presumption in bringing about the fulfillment of 25:23 through deception directly results in the nonfulfillment of both the oracle and Isaac's blessing of Jacob; Jacob becomes servant (עבד) and Esau lord (33:1–15), and Jacob later reflects upon his life as all-too-short and difficult (47:9).[5] It is Yнwн alone who will

---

4. Laurence A. Turner, *Announcements of Plot in Genesis* (JSOTSup 96; Sheffield: JSOT Press, 1990) 119–20.

5. Ibid., 179. See also Nahum M. Sarna (*JPS Torah Commentary: Genesis* [Philadelphia: Jewish Publication Society, 1989] 397–98), who argues that scenes such as Laban's giving of Leah before Rachel and Jacob's assessment of his life here reflect a narratorial condemnation of Jacob's chicanery. John G. Gammie ("Theological Interpretation by Way of Literary and Tradition Analysis: Genesis 25–36," in *Encounter with the Text: Form and History in the Hebrew Bible* [ed. Martin J. Buss; Philadelphia: Fortress, 1979] 128, 132) sees Jacob's providential success as offset by the theme of retribution, an assumption this study

bring about the fulfillment of these "announcements," but YHWH is also free to rescind or modify any part of them, which Turner argues he has done with Jacob and Esau.[6] For Turner, there exists a causal relationship between Jacob's activity in regard to the announcements and his life as being one typified by service.[7] Turner sums up his reading: "human attempts to frustrate the Announcements tend to fulfil them; human attempts to fulfil the Announcements tend to frustrate them."[8]

Turner has produced a thoughtful and provoking argument, yet it has several difficulties. The primary difficulty lies in his conclusion that YHWH responds punitively to Jacob's (and Rebekah's) deceptions on only this one occasion. Jacob by no means ceases to deceive after these events, and elsewhere when he deceives he reaps great benefit, as is evident in his prolonged stay with Laban in Gen 29–31. Why would YHWH not respond in a similar castigatory manner in this instance? Strikingly, YHWH does appear to play a role during Jacob's time in Haran, but it is a role that ensures Jacob's wealth and protection after several deceptions, as chap. 3 will show. What differentiates these deceptions from those carried out by Jacob and Rebekah, from the divine perspective? Very little, it seems. Rather, it is precisely through Jacob's "service" (עבד) to Laban that Jacob acquires great wealth as well as multiple children, evincing a movement toward the promise of a "great nation" recounted in Gen 12:2.[9]

A second difficulty exists in the fact that, despite Jacob's later claim that his life has been long and hard, he is and remains the child of the prom-

---

will challenge. Most recently, Robert R. Gonzales, Jr. (*Where Sin Abounds: The Spread of Sin and the Curse in Genesis with Special Focus on the Patriarchal Narratives* [Eugene, OR: Wipf & Stock, 2009] 163–192) sees the Jacob cycle (indeed, the entirety of Genesis) as continuing the theme of human sin and divine curse that originates in the Fall. As I will argue in the course of this study, partitioning out deception and God into separate categories is a misreading of the text. I also wonder if the language of "sin" as Gonzales uses it is anachronistic and overly informed by New Testament conceptions.

6. Turner, *Announcements of Plot*, 181–82.

7. Ibid., 179. Turner writes: "it is precisely *because* of Jacob's efforts to secure his destiny as lord that he actually becomes the servant" [emphasis original].

8. Ibid.

9. Turner (ibid., 126, 135–37) notes this very point, but he emphasizes that Jacob's acquisition of this wealth occurs only *after* God has opened the "hated" wife Leah's womb and closed the loved wife Rachel's womb. God, however, remembers Rachel, and she too conceives (30:22) and bears Joseph, yet this scene occurs *before*, not after Jacob receives great wealth with the help of YHWH. To see Rachel's barrenness as both a punishment for Jacob's attempt to realize the oracle through deception and a prerequisite for his attaining wealth with YHWH as his benefactor is without textual merit. Similarly, Turner's claim that the announcement in 27:39b–40 concerning Esau leads the reader to expect that Jacob will meet an "impoverished individual" rests solely on Turner's reading of Esau's announcement as a curse. As I will argue in chap. 2, this understanding is unnecessary; Esau also receives a blessing from his father, which differs in one vital component: God is not mentioned in Esau's blessing.

ise. Yʜᴡʜ never threatens to withdraw his allegiance to Jacob. In fact, as Jacob is journeying with his family to Egypt—in the scene immediately before Jacob shares these words Turner notes with Pharaoh—Yʜᴡʜ affirms for a third time that he is the bearer of the ancestral promise (46:3–4). Whether Jacob is servant to Esau or not is ultimately of little consequence for understanding the Jacob/God dynamic. Turner interestingly treats the Abrahamic Announcement (Gen 12:1–3) separately from the other three Announcements specific to the Jacob cycle. And even Turner must admit there is movement in the Jacob cycle toward the eventual fulfillment of the Announcement/promise.[10] It is almost as if the success of the Abrahamic Announcement/promise is not contingent upon the success or failure of the three Announcements in the Jacob cycle. Therefore, despite the outcome of Jacob and his mother's earlier deceptions, Jacob's life from beginning to end is one intimately bound up with and blessed by God, deceptions and all.

More recently, W. Lee Humphreys' *The Character of God in the Book of Genesis: A Narrative Appraisal* has presented a case for the latter position mentioned above, accentuating not God's complicity but human duplicity in reference to Jacob's deceptions. Humphreys is interested in the literary characterization of God in Genesis. For Humphreys, God is not to be found in the narrative at these crucial junctures.[11] God plays no part in Jacob's acquisition of the right of the firstborn (25:29–34), and God is inconspicuous in the deception of Isaac (27:1–45).[12] In this second scene, Humphreys asserts that God is present only in the speech of deceivers, Rebekah and Jacob (vv. 7, 20), and the deceived, Isaac (v. 28). None of their testimony can be taken as a trustworthy representation of the characterization of God, argues Humphreys, because it involves speech from others about God rather

---

10. Turner sees this fulfillment specifically concerning the promise of nationhood. He is incorrect that the promise of land experiences little in the way of even partial fulfillment in the cycle, and he maintains that the strained relationships between Jacob's family and the nations preclude the possibility of this family's serving as a source of blessing for the nations. I will challenge Turner's reading in greater detail in chap. 3.

11. On this point see also Gerhard von Rad (*Old Testament Theology* [2 vols.; trans. D. M. G. Stalker; New York: Harper & Row, 1962–65] 1: 171), who claims that "the reader completely loses sight of God and his action in the jungle of unedifying manifestations of human nature."

12. W. Lee Humphreys, *The Character of God in the Book of Genesis: A Narrative Appraisal* (Louisville: Westminster John Knox, 2001) 158, 163. See also Kevin Walton (*Thou Traveller Unknown: The Presence and Absence of God in the Jacob Narrative* [Carlisle: Paternoster Press, 2003] 1–2, 217–224), who sees the Jacob cycle as typified by a paradox between distinctive moments of divine presence and absence. Walton groups the narratives into two large blocks: those communicating "points of divine disclosure" and those which emphasize "the human story of Jacob." See also Samuel Terrien (*The Elusive Presence: Towards a New Biblical Theology* [San Francisco: Harper & Row, 1978]), who regards the motif of divine presence as primary and covenant as secondary; these motifs span both Testaments.

than God's own speech or the narrator's explicit comment.[13] Therefore, what Jacob, Rebekah, and Isaac say *about* God is given little credence and contributes nothing to Humphreys' characterization of God. He contends that at Bethel God seems entirely disinterested in Jacob's life thus far.[14] God has uttered a divine word prior to the twins' birth and has now withdrawn, allowing the divine will to come about however it may, even at the cost of dissolution of this family. Similarly, God is absent during the extended stay with Laban, replete with its deceptions (Gen 29–31), and Jacob's reported dream theophany in Gen 31 associating Yʜᴡʜ with the trickery of the previous chapter is unattested elsewhere. Absent any narratorial comment speaking to its authenticity, Jacob's speech here cannot be afforded a great level of reliability, a view I will challenge explicitly in chapter three.

One difficulty with Humphreys' analysis is the *a priori* assumption built in to his methodology that a character's speech about her/himself is automatically more trustworthy than any other character's speech. One may just as legitimately ask whether the narrator can and should be trusted. Must the narrator be a disinterested party? Within literary criticism this appears to be a most unsafe assumption to make.[15] To privilege the narrator's speech prejudices a particular reading of God's character. Such a practice is especially problematic when Humphreys does not identify the narrator. Is it ancient Israel or a particular group within Israel? Such distinctions matter. Would ancient Israel truly depict God's relationship with its namesake, Jacob, in such an unflattering light without adequate reason?

---

13. Humphreys, *The Character of God in the Book of Genesis*, 163. Central to Humphrey's methodology is his scale of textual indicators for characterization, a distillation of Robert Alter's six points into three pairs: (1) external descriptions and what other characters say; (2) actions and speech; (3) inner thoughts and the narrator's evaluation. At the beginning of this short spectrum the information is far less trustworthy, and as one moves along it one begins to encounter material that can be taken with far greater confidence. See Robert Alter, *The Art of Biblical Narrative* (New York: Basic Books, 1981) 114–30.

14. Humphreys, *The Character of God in the Book of Genesis*, 168, 172.

15. Most recently, Jerome T. Walsh (*Old Testament Narrative: A Guide to Interpretation* [Louisville: Westminster John Knox, 2009] 98–102) points out that while the narrator may be "reliable" this does not require the narrator to reveal everything he knows about a given character. The narrator's omniscience need not be shared with the reader. At the same time, the author's omniscience need not be shared with the narrator; the former may limit what the latter knows. This relationship between author and narrator is an important one that often goes unappreciated. The author, says Walsh, could also create the narrator and his viewpoint as a foil to the author and the argument he is trying to make. The author may disagree with the "opinions and values" of the narrator and thus set out to "subvert the narrator's point of view in subtle ways." These are all possibilities that a reader must consider, making the assumption that the narrator is the bastion of truth a problematic view to maintain without adequate weighing of the various options. As a further example that the narrator need not be entirely trustworthy in ancient literature, see Scott Richardson, "The Devious Narrator of the 'Odyssey,'" *The Classical Journal* 101 (2006) 337–39.

Both Turner and Humphreys create an additional, perhaps unintentional, problem given their respective readings. Insuring God is far removed from the narrative scene during a deception ends up drawing too sharp a dichotomy between the divine and human. God's transcendence is emphasized at the expense of divine immanence, the latter of which this study will demonstrate is a vital and irrefutable aspect of the ancestral narratives broadly and the Jacob cycle more specifically. What ultimately emerges in these characterizations of God in the Jacob cycle are portraits tending toward deism. Distancing God from instances of deception in the interest—implicit or explicit—of addressing one theological problem (divine deception) lays the groundwork for another, equally troubling theological problem: a transcendent God that ultimately does not square with the role and activity of God depicted in the ancestral narratives.

Divine Deception in Genesis: Implicit References

There are those who have conversely argued that the Jacob cycle is highly theological and thus God occupies a much more prominent role vis-à-vis the other characters. Yet even these treatments do not connect God with Jacob's deceptions explicitly. In many instances, though, the connection is implicit and, regrettably, undeveloped (or unrecognized?) by the author. This section will survey the work of five scholars: J. P. Fokkelman, Allen Ross, Gerhard von Rad, David Carr, and Victor Matthews and Frances Mims.

J. P. Fokkelman's *Narrative Art in Genesis* reads the entire Jacob cycle through the lens of "Providence," which he sees as evident in the prenatal oracle in 25:23.[16] By employing such language, Fokkelman implies a divine hand at work guiding matters to their proper conclusion. He later goes so far as to call this "a rare specimen of predestination."[17] As a result, he holds that Jacob and Rebekah's actions are amoral; they are unwitting pawns accomplishing Yhwh's desire, their capacity to choose between proper and improper behavior removed.[18] With this interpretation in place, Fokkelman then awkwardly and unexpectedly transitions to challenge this reading he has just presented. He now claims that Jacob and Rebekah act of their own volition and are thus morally culpable and "independent in their sins."[19]

---

16. J. P. Fokkelman, *Narrative Art in Genesis: Specimens of Stylistic and Structural Analysis* (Eugene, OR: Wipf & Stock, 1991) 94.

17. Ibid., 116.

18. Fokkelman (ibid., 117) writes: "Once his [God's] main characters are in the service of predestination, they are puppets, dummies. They have been deprived of their responsibilities, thus of their dignity and their credibility. Jacob and Rebekah do what they cannot help doing. They perform God's will and so they act in a morally right way—or rather, they do not; as unfree vehicles of predestination their actions are neither right nor wrong for the tension between right and wrong, thus morality itself, has been extinguished, taken away."

19. Ibid., 120.

The reason for this sudden transition is not entirely clear, yet one plausible rationale becomes all the more potent when Fokkelman states: "Their independence consists in their high-handedness."[20] Fokkelman's final analysis has the feel of an apologetic attempt to exonerate God from any role in deception. This discussion undermines his treatment of the Jacob cycle; the reader remains unclear with regard to whether predestination is an operative interpretive category for these texts or not. What makes this transition even more puzzling is that Fokkelman continues to discuss the remainder of the Jacob cycle through the lens of Providence, going so far as to admit that God, not Jacob, is the one who deceives Laban in Gen 30–31.[21] Despite Fokkelman's equivocation, his treatment of the Jacob cycle highlights the possibility of seeing divine deception in Genesis.

Similarly, Allen Ross in his *Creation and Blessing* makes the general statement that, while YHWH may use human deception to further YHWH's own purposes, YHWH in no way agrees with this behavior.[22] This sort of view, however, at the very least implicates YHWH, giving Jacob's actions the sheen of divine approval. More germane to the topic at hand, Ross advances the argument that YHWH orchestrates Laban's deceptive giving of Leah prior to Rachel to demonstrate to Jacob that deception is unpalatable to God.[23] An argument of this sort is counterintuitive for a variety of reasons, not least of which being that YHWH is said to use something he despises, deception, to show that the very thing he despises is worthy of being despised! Ross, however, limits YHWH's role in deception to but a few instances, not advancing a thoroughgoing analysis of the deceptions in the Jacob cycle, and I will challenge his view that YHWH uses deception only punitively. However, might not Ross's claim belie the possibility that YHWH's role in trickery has an altruistic motivation? It appears so; this possibility will serve as an object for further exploration, especially in chap. 2. For now, however, Ross's notice further supports the viability of viewing YHWH as trickster in Genesis.

What remains latent in Ross's discussion is given potent voice in the final analysis of Gerhard von Rad. Von Rad muses over the question whether in Gen 27:1–45 the narrator purposefully communicates the idea that human deception fulfills God's intended plans.[24] To this question, von Rad

---

20. Ibid.

21. Ibid., 160–61.

22. Allen P. Ross, *Creation and Blessing: A Guide to the Study and Exposition of Genesis* (Grand Rapids, MI: Baker Academic, 1998) 451, 478. See also R. Christopher Heard (*Dynamics of Diselection: Ambiguity in Genesis 12–36 and Ethnic Boundaries in Post-exilic Judah* [Semeia Studies; Atlanta: Society of Biblical Literature, 2001] 100), who appears to dismiss a particular reading of the oracle in 25:23 at least in part because this reading runs the risk of implicating God in Jacob's acquiring the right of the firstborn and blessing from his blind father.

23. Ross, *Creation and Blessing*, 497.

24. Gerhard von Rad, *Genesis* (rev. ed.; trans. J. H. Marks; OTL; Philadelphia: Westminster, 1973) 280.

responds with a resounding yet troubling yes. The narrator, he argues, exhibits no moral qualms or pronouncements of guilt because of God's decree (25:23). Rather, the narrator desires to inculcate in his readers a "sympathetic suffering for those who are caught up mysteriously in such a monstrous act of God and are almost destroyed in it."[25] By "monstrous act," von Rad appears to mean not only the oracle delivered to Rebekah, announcing a preference for Jacob over Esau, but also God's employment of *human* deception in Gen 27 to advance God's own purposes. Von Rad never explicitly deems God culpable in these matters of deception, nor does he ever accuse God of acting deceptively. He simply notes the mystery and enigma of the scene and its positive results.

This thoroughly honest treatment, however, is tempered by von Rad's emphasis on pentateuchal source criticism. To continue using Gen 27:1–45 as an illustration, von Rad designates this narrative as an artistic interweaving of the traditionally defined J and E sources, comprising a single, sustained episode.[26] The narrative that follows in Gen 27:46–28:9 he attributes to P and considers it to be a separate and unique understanding of the story of Jacob and Esau.[27] According to von Rad, P has here "purified" the earlier tradition in 27:1–45 by expunging any and all problematic elements, evidencing a later time in ancient Israel, in which these sorts of depictions of the ancestors (and presumably God, though von Rad makes no mention of God here) became more disconcerting than before.[28] Therefore, von Rad presupposes an evolutionary view of Israelite society, so foundational to the Documentary Hypothesis, by which the disturbing possibility of God's mysterious role in deception may be remedied by appealing to a later, different, "moralizing" source.

The Documentary Hypothesis, as assumed by von Rad, is no longer a convincing way to speak of pentateuchal composition.[29] That approach

---

25. Ibid., 281.
26. Ibid., 276.
27. Ibid., 281–82.
28. Ibid., 282.
29. In this brief space, I cannot hope to articulate a full dismissal of the classical Documentary Hypothesis, nor can I adequately attend to the depth and variety that currently pervades pentateuchal scholarship. More recent works evidence a shift away from the classically defined sources, preferring instead to speak of tradition history as a more accurate and viable alternative. On the fatal flaws of the Documentary Hypothesis, one may wish to consult the thoughtful and convincing treatments of Rolf Rendtorff (*The Problem of the Process of Transmission in the Pentateuch* [JSOTSup 89; Sheffield: JSOT Press, 1990]), whose volume deftly demonstrates the incompatability between tradition history and source criticism as practiced by documentarians; and R. N. Whybray (*The Making of the Pentateuch: A Methodological Study* [JSOTSup 53; Sheffield: JSOT Press, 1987]), who offers the most systematic denunciation of the Documentary Hypothesis to date. Admittedly, by the time his Genesis commentary appeared, von Rad had already begun to move away from traditionally defined source criticism, yet his volume is replete with its language, employing the designations JEDP. See his "Form-Critical Problem of the Hexateuch," *The Problem*

deals with the final form of the text, but does so in an artificial way. It is still a diachronic analysis, segmenting the text into independent literary units, and not an attempt to make sense of the text as a cogent literary whole with its own narrative integrity. Rather, in the earlier tradition, certain issues he identifies are troubling, while in another, later tradition, the attempt has been made to eradicate these difficulties. What remains unexpressed here, however, is that the final form of the text preserves both of these "sources" alongside each other, thus also creating a tension in the text that a synchronic approach needs to address. Von Rad's understanding of 27:1–45 is very fine indeed, and he raises many of the questions I will address in this book. He does not, however, struggle with the implications of this reading in relation to what follows and in the context of the final form of the text.

More recently, David Carr's *Reading the Fractures of Genesis* takes a similar approach yet succeeds in underscoring the inherent difficulty latent in diachronic analyses. Carr employs both diachronic and synchronic methodologies with the aim of isolating the various fractures (doublets, contradictions) or seams between narrative units.[30] Unlike von Rad, Carr believes one can speak confidently about only one source, P, and about non-P material. In the development of Genesis, P stands as a later source based on and attempting to stand against and replace non-P.[31] The final form of the text, fractures and all, results from the work of a redactor who merged P and non-P in the interest of preservation. Concerning the Jacob cycle more specifically, Carr conjectures that Jacob's deceptions have undergone a reinterpretation based on this convergence of dissonant sources.[32] One may notice already a strong affinity with von Rad's view of a later textual stratum recasting an earlier one. Carr, however, appears more restrained in postulating that recognition of these various layers eliminates the problem entirely. He writes:

> The trickster has not been completely tamed. As a result, the reader is left with the task of making sense out of a subversive Jacob, on the one hand, and Jacob the divinely supported and morally justified ancestor of Israel, on the other.[33]

What emerges in the final form of the text is a tension, not a resolution. Carr demonstrates both the way in which von Rad's explanation remains incomplete and the importance of readers in adjudicating a text's meaning.

---

of the Hexateuch and Other Essays (trans. E. W. Trueman Dicken; London: SCM, 1984) 1–78. His analysis assumes much of what is assumed by documentarians and still seems implicated in the tethering of tradition history and source criticism challenged by Rendtorff.

30. David M. Carr, *Reading the Fractures of Genesis: Historical and Literary Approaches* (Louisville: Westminster John Knox, 1996) vii, 3–4.

31. Ibid., 47.

32. Ibid., 299.

33. Ibid., 300.

The agenda of the present book is to propose a way to understand this tension in the final form of the text.

Last, Victor Matthews and Frances Mims's article "Jacob the Trickster and Heir of the Covenant: A Literary Interpretation" identifies an older trickster motif undergirding the theological nature of the Jacob cycle.[34] For Matthews and Mims, Jacob is a patriarch-in-the-making whose experiences with Esau, Laban, and God refine his character into one worthy to receive the covenant.[35] Jacob's interactions with God are thus seminal to his transformation. Unfortunately, this overarching metanarrative that Matthews and Mims see as being operative in the Jacob cycle cannot be sustained under a close scrutiny of the text. Jacob has already received the ancestral promise from God in Gen 28:13–15; there is no reason to presume that he is on a spiritual pilgrimage toward becoming an acceptable recipient of something he already possesses. Moreover, it is not entirely clear that Jacob undergoes the sort of spiritual and moral transformation that Matthews and Mims describe. In fact, in the reconciliation with Esau, he very much appears to act in accordance with the cerebral and tricky Jacob that the reader has seen all along. I will discuss and develop these difficulties with Matthews and Mims's reading more fully at the outset of chap. 4. Their emphasis on a theological reading of trickery is, however, an important insight that I will develop in the chapters that follow.

Divine Deception in Genesis: Explicit References

The question of divine deception in Genesis has been raised surprisingly few times within the last century, with Hermann Gunkel being the earliest proponent of the view that God engaged in deception, yet it is only fairly recently that the issue has begun to be addressed in any meaningful way. Investigation remains inchoate and embryonic. Works by three scholars warrant more thorough mention: Hermann Gunkel, Walter Brueggemann, and Michael James Williams.

Perhaps the earliest explicit scholarly treatment on the topic is by Hermann Gunkel in his classic 1901 *Genesis* commentary. Gunkel takes special notice of God's apparent role in Jacob's deceptions, deeming God's complicity at various points in the narrative as "especially offensive."[36] He further notes that Jacob's deceptions neither cease nor recede; instead, Jacob continues to perfect his craft with the help of God.[37] A proper comprehension

---

34. Victor H. Matthews and Frances Mims, "Jacob the Trickster and Heir of the Covenant: A Literary Interpretation," *PRSt* 12 (1985) 186.

35. Ibid., 187, 193.

36. Hermann Gunkel, *Genesis* (trans. Mark E. Biddle; Macon, GA: Mercer University Press, 1997) 301.

37. Ibid., 300. While Gunkel regards Jacob's deceptions as intentionally humorous episodes that possess no moral concerns in their original form as old legends, he also sees the necessity of allowing contemporary readers to react as they may to these texts. It is in this context that Gunkel couches his statements about God's complicity. He concludes: "The

of these matters emerges for Gunkel only if one addresses them historically. Two points are foundational here for Gunkel: (1) these texts belong to a period in ancient Israel's history during which religion and morality had not yet been linked; (2) the "god" referenced is not Yhwh but "a much more primitive figure" with no misgivings about using deception.[38] Moreover, Gunkel avers that it is feasible to speak of the "religious element" as a secondary addition to these texts of deception.[39] While Gunkel is correct that God has a part in Jacob's deceptions, he is incorrect in his assessment that one should thereby interpret God's role negatively. Gunkel's emphasis placed on reconstructed history is also done only to the detriment of the final literary form of the text, which sees a continuity between the God of the ancestors and Yhwh.[40] At bottom, Gunkel fails to interpret the text in its final form, which by his reading connects Yhwh deeply with Jacob's deceptions, and instead he attempts to remedy a literary problem with historical speculation. How his literary reading functions in the final form of the text remains an unexplored area of inquiry.

Walter Brueggemann in his *Genesis* commentary treats the Jacob cycle under the heading "The Conflicted Call of God." Brueggemann argues that the text is concerned primarily with the God of Jacob.[41] God inaugurates a life of conflict for Jacob as the son of the promise. The character God is thus not neat and tidy. Brueggemann writes: "Jacob is a scandalous challenge to his world because the God who calls him is also scandalous. . . . At many points the narrative presents the inscrutable, dark side of God."[42] Contributing further to Brueggemann's portrayal of God as scandalous is the recognition that God's purposes are advanced through the "self-serving cleverness of human desire."[43] One may recall the previous discussions of Ross and von Rad, both of whom implied that God felt free to avail himself of human trickery to further the divine purpose. Brueggemann agrees, but his view is different in that the impetus behind human trickery lies in God's enigmatic call of Jacob. This call tethers God and Jacob together in

---

exegete should not allow his moral sensibilities to be confused by these narratives. On the other hand, however, he should also have enough respect for antiquity not to paint over these old legends with modern colors."

38. Ibid., 301.

39. Ibid., 301–2.

40. In the revelation of the divine name in Exod 3:1–22, Yhwh identifies himself as "the God of Abraham, the God of Isaac, and the God of Jacob" (vv. 6, 15). Similarly, in Exod 6:2–9 God declares that he appeared to the ancestors yet did not make known to them the divine name. Further complicating Gunkel's view that the deity is not Yhwh are the multiple occurrences of the divine name throughout Genesis, including the scenes of deception in the Jacob cycle.

41. Walter Brueggemann, *Genesis* (Interpretation; Atlanta: John Knox, 1982) 204, 209.

42. Ibid., 209.

43. Ibid., 212.

a deeply intimate way. God is and will remain a formidable presence and assurance throughout Jacob's life.[44]

Brueggemann is rightly nonapologetic in regard to the characterization of God in the Jacob cycle. His consistent and trenchant claims that the divine plan is being fulfilled through measures such as trickery, coupled with the intimate relationship between God and Jacob that he sees buttress the present argument in a most meaningful way. What Brueggemann leaves unspoken, however, is a clear articulation of *how* the God who wrought a life of conflict and deception for Jacob actually figures into the scenes of deception. The biblical narrative allows for the possibility of greater precision in describing God's role and purposes beyond the numinous adjectives such as "inscrutable" and "hidden" that Brueggemann prefers. I will seek in the chapters that follow to give voice to the *how* of divine deception in the Jacob cycle.

The most sustained engagement of deception in Genesis of which I am aware is Michael James Williams's *Deception in Genesis: An Investigation into the Morality of a Unique Biblical Phenomenon*. Williams offers a catalog of deceptive events in Genesis, outlining the perpetrator, victim, type of deception, motive, specific vocabulary, pentateuchal source, and narrative evaluation in the hopes of systematizing the deceptions in Genesis. At no point does Williams identify God as either perpetrator or victim in Genesis's deceptions. Upon further analysis, Williams concludes that the Genesis narratives evaluate deception positively when the perpetrator has previously been a victim; this retaliation, he holds, restores the status quo or what he calls "*shalom.*"[45] Conversely, a negative evaluation is given when a deception causes a breach in *shalom*.

Outside Genesis, however, matters are quite different. Williams notes that God is said to deceive elsewhere in the Hebrew Bible for various reasons. He further claims that the narrative provides no ready evaluations of God's deceptive activity, but the mere fact that God is the perpetrator means that one should evaluate these scenes positively.[46] This avowal leads Williams to posit the fascinating hypothesis that among the primary differences between deceptions inside and outside Genesis is the fact that God has no part in the Genesis deceptions. Accordingly, outside Genesis God's purposes in deception serve to "keep Israel within the covenant relationship he has established with them."[47]

---

44. Brueggemann (ibid., 205) speaks of the "commitment" that God has made to Jacob, a commitment that both introduces conflict and at the same time ensures a resolution of the conflicts "in [Jacob's] favor."

45. Michael James Williams, *Deception in Genesis: An Investigation into the Morality of a Unique Biblical Phenomenon* (Studies in Biblical Literature 32; New York: Peter Lang, 2001) 56, 221.

46. Ibid., 73.

47. Ibid., 75.

Williams's study is careful and judicious, but I register disagreement with him on several crucial items: (1) that God plays no role in Genesis's deceptions; (2) that the narrative evaluations of deception are as decisive and consistent as he claims; (3) that deceptions in Genesis are of an entirely different kind from deceptions outside Genesis. I will address the first and second of these points throughout this study. Regarding the third, one could make a case that deception both within and outside Genesis may plausibly serve a quite similar function: the protection and perpetuation of the ancestral promise. This sort of comparative investigation, however, lies beyond the bounds of the present book, yet my reading of the Jacob cycle will hopefully begin to the lay the groundwork for just this sort of analysis. For the beginnings of this discussion, see the concluding section, on "Trustworthy Deception" (pp. 177–186), in which I advance the argument that deception and promise are intimately bound up with one another throughout the Hebrew Bible.

Some scholarly treatments tether God and deception yet take the form of a brief sentence or two, made almost in passing, and remain frustratingly undeveloped. For example, Matthews and Mims label Yʜᴡʜ as Rachel's "fellow trickster" in her stealing of Laban's household gods.[48] They do not expound on the potential implications, which are numerous, of this label for Yʜᴡʜ. Similarly, Susan Niditch states that the traditional trickster figure as it exists in both the Bible and other literature is sometimes aided by a divine benefactor.[49] She unfortunately offers no further elaboration as to the implications of this divine assistance. And more recently, Joel Kaminsky has contributed a tantalizingly brief statement, reading Jacob's election against the backdrop of his deceptions. He writes:

> The notion that human action may be required to bring the chosen one's election to consummation is here further reflected upon as well as morally complicated. It appears that at times even deceitful actions can be employed in bringing God's purposes to pass. While such deceit may lead to family strife and may result in the deceiver himself being deceived in hurtful ways, in this instance, the elect status of Jacob is further reinforced through his morally questionable behavior.[50]

These cursory statements signify the viability of speaking of Yʜᴡʜ as trickster in Genesis. They also, however, highlight a seeming uneasiness regarding what one is to do with the association of Yʜᴡʜ with trickery/deception. It is not adequate to leave this connection unexplored. There is much in the way of theological profundity to be gained.

---

48. Matthews and Mims, "Jacob the Trickster," 189.
49. Susan Niditch, *A Prelude to Biblical Folklore: Underdogs and Tricksters* (Urbana: University of Illinois, 2000) 45.
50. Joel S. Kaminsky, *Yet I Loved Jacob: Reclaiming the Biblical Concept of Election* (Nashville: Abingdon, 2007) 57.

Divine Deception in the Garden?
Moberly and Barr on Genesis 2–3

One extended discussion of divine deception in Genesis deserves further attention in its raising of the issues of both God and trickery and how readers are to adjudicate the issue theologically. R. W. L. Moberly and James Barr have had a spirited discussion in the pages of *The Journal of Theological Studies* spanning some 20 years.[51] The text under consideration is Gen 2–3, more specifically investigating the potential ramifications of the failure of God to enact the death sentence imposed on anyone who eats the fruit of the tree of the knowledge of good and evil (2:17). Does God's mind change? Is God mistaken or even wrong about the result? Is the punishment carried out in another way? Or might God's prohibition against eating the fruit be an instance of divine deception, with God tricking the first couple about the true ramifications of their eating the forbidden fruit?

The initial article by Moberly, "Did the Serpent Get It Right?" wrestles with the issue of the purported authenticity of the serpent's words in Gen 3:1–5 juxtaposed with the seemingly unreliable speech of Yhwh in Gen 2:17.[52] God says that death will follow eating the fruit, whereas the serpent says the humans will instead become like God. As Moberly writes: "Everything happens exactly as the serpent had said."[53] The apparent truthfulness of the serpent's speech as opposed to God's dictum is the central theological issue raised by the text for Moberly.[54] Moreover, Moberly muses, since Gen 2:15–17 contains the first words spoken by God to humanity, should readers regard them as "normative" for the entirety of the Old Testament?[55] Moberly suggests a single viable line of interpretation to address these central issues: the death sentence is carried out, albeit in a different way. Put most simply, Moberly argues that the death should be interpreted "in a non-literal, metaphorical way to signify something other than the termination of physical existence," that is, death as arising from disobedience to Torah.[56] In the end, for Moberly, the serpent may speak rightly and God wrongly, but appreciating this point reveals more about the ambiguous

---

51. There remains much in the way of rich and fertile theological ideas in the conversation between Moberly and Barr that cannot be reproduced here. The debate between the two revolves around a number of exegetical, hermeneutical, and theological issues; my treatment here focuses on and highlights one particular aspect related to the topic of divine deception. For a recent, more exhaustive survey of Moberly and Barr's exchange, see Robert P. Gordon, "The Ethics of Eden: Truth-Telling in Genesis 2–3," in *Ethical and Unethical in the Old Testament: God and Humans in Dialogue* (ed. Katharine J. Dell; LHBOTS 528; New York: T. & T. Clark, 2010) 11–33.

52. R. W. L. Moberly, "Did the Serpent Get It Right?" *JTS* 39 (1988) 1–27.

53. Ibid., 8.

54. Ibid., 9

55. Ibid., 13.

56. Ibid., 16, 17.

correlation between human disobedience and divine judgment than it does about divine deception.[57]

Barr's rejoinder addresses the issue of divine deception much more acutely. On the matter of the serpent specifically, Barr says the serpent is both right and wrong: the serpent speaks truth but with the purpose of committing evil.[58] This, however, raises the attendant issue of divine deception in Gen 2–3. Barr shows how Moberly's own concern with avoiding making God a liar actually achieves this very result.[59] Moberly's twin affirmations that God employs the statement "you will surely die" metaphorically and that Adam and Eve understand the phrase to connote a literal death still mean for Barr that God deceives, albeit in a way that many theologians—Moberly included—deem pardonable.[60] Barr also challenges Moberly's imprecision in defining what constitutes a lie; Barr claims that "statements may be untrue without being lies."[61] Thus, understanding God's speech as a "lie" is unsuitable to the context of Gen 2–3. This failure of nuance compels Barr to regard Moberly's God as a liar.

Another important facet of Barr's critique of Moberly is the former's raising of "the liar argument," which Barr defines as follows:

> The Liar Argument is any argument that criticizes a biblical interpretation on the ground that it implies that God, in uttering or supporting some biblical utterance, was lying.[62]

Barr suggests the liar argument is an a priori belief that may underlie and prejudice Moberly's interpretation. Barr goes on to conclude, upon surveying a number of examples elsewhere in the Hebrew Bible, that God may indeed have spoken falsely in Gen 2:17, a notice that is hardly irreconcilable with other portrayals of God in the Hebrew Bible.[63]

Two years after Barr's death in 2006, Moberly published a final response.[64] Moberly appears to concede Barr's point about the inappropriateness of the terminology of "lying," yet he shifts the discussion to emphasize the potential *unreliability* (שׁקר) of the divine word.[65] God's *trustworthiness* thus becomes central for Moberly. This new stress, Moberly says, supports his original thesis: "*the apparent non-realization of God's warning leads the reader to reread and rethink the meaning of the story and only thus to construe 'die'*

---

57. Ibid., 18.

58. James Barr, "Is God a Liar? (Genesis 2–3)—and Related Matters," *JTS* 57 (2006) 1–22, esp. p. 13.

59. Ibid.

60. Ibid., 15.

61. Ibid., 6.

62. Ibid., 1.

63. Ibid., 21.

64. R. W. L. Moberly, "Did the Interpreters Get it Right? Genesis 2–3 Reconsidered," *JTS* 59 (2008) 22–40.

65. Ibid., 31.

metaphorically."[66] Genesis 2–3 is thus a text that underscores the difficulty for humanity at any moment in trusting and living as God would have us live.

Moberly concludes his essay with reflections on "theological preunderstandings" in interpreting the Bible, which clearly is a response to Barr's accusation concerning the liar argument. At bottom, Moberly rightly affirms that no interpreter is entirely disinterested, whether s/he admits it or not, and that all interpreters cull from what is beyond the text, including "one's sense of what is meaningful in life today as we know it."[67] On this front, writing from an unabashedly Christian perspective, Moberly advocates "a constant dialectical sifting of preunderstanding and proposed interpretation alike, in the attempt to articulate an understanding of the text that may rightly be found persuasive."[68]

This debate raises a number of important methodological and theological considerations for the present book. I will briefly highlight three. Foremost among them is the liar argument. The assumption that God can and should be exempted from lying based on the theological presupposition of a given interpreter not only skews the text but also fails to account for other instances in the Hebrew Bible where God deceives. Yet I must echo Barr's own caution in his response to Moberly. I am not implying that any of the interpreters surveyed above propound the liar argument as a way to make sense of or even avoid the issue of divine deception. Some may, and others may not; I am not in the business of psychologizing about the views of biblical interpreters! My point is that judging the viability of a particular biblical portrait of God solely against one's own preexistent theological convictions is inherently flawed. Most recently, John Collins has evaluated the practice of theological readings of Genesis, using Gen 22 (the near-sacrifice of Isaac) as an example; Collins concludes that scholars engaged in the theological enterprise of reading Genesis are all too often implicated in the apologetic tendency to "lie for God" as opposed to honest wrestling with and questioning of the biblical text.[69] This proclivity toward apologetics, he argues, is injurious to the genuine theological task. Put most simply, to say that God does not deceive because a reading of this sort is dissonant with conventional theological principles for many is not an acceptable rationale for dismissing or avoiding this thorny and complex issue. It is perhaps, therefore, more advisable to call God a liar than to "lie for God" and say God is not. Second (a counterbalance to this first point), extreme care must be taken in adjudicating the presence and nature of divine deception. This survey of the exchange between Moberly and Barr above indicates

---

66. Ibid., 35–36 (italics original).

67. Ibid., 38.

68. Ibid., 40.

69. John J. Collins, "Modern Theology," in *Reading Genesis: Ten Methods* (ed. Ronald Hendel; Cambridge: Cambridge University Press, 2010) 214.

that a number of factors must be considered: literary and narrative insights, theological constructions elsewhere in the Hebrew Bible, the assumptions of the reader as well as the integrity of the text, and accuracy in language and terminology in constructing one's case. I also readily heed Moberly's caution against ignoring the fact that interpreters play a role in the creation of meaning. Third, if God indeed has spoken deceptively in Gen 2:17, regardless of the reason, is it not significant and formative for subsequent texts—as Moberly rightly recognizes—that the first exchange in the Bible between God and humanity involves (the potential of) the former's deceiving the latter?

Divine Deception Elsewhere in the Hebrew Bible

Despite the relative dearth of scholarship on divine deception in Genesis, scholars have more readily acknowledged the presence of divine deception elsewhere in the Hebrew Bible. My discussion here will offer a brief survey of these instances as scholars have noted their occurrence in the Pentateuch, the Deuteronomistic History, and the Prophets. This section will also include succinct treatment of the potential functions of divine deception as limned by extant scholarship.

The Pentateuch

Within the Pentateuch, scholars have seen divine deception as most clearly evident in the book of Exodus. The most common example cited occurs in Exod 3:16–22, God's initial instructions to Moses regarding the divine plan of the exodus.[70] God clearly outlines to Moses that he is to tell Pharaoh that the duration of the journey is a mere "three days," and the purpose is sacrifice (v. 18). Immediately prior, in v. 17, however, God had promised deliverance from Egypt and arrival in "the land of the Canaanites, the Hittites, the Amorites, the Perizzites, the Hivites, and the Jebusites, a land flowing with milk and honey." Divine deception is clear. Moses follows God's plan perfectly, repeating to Pharaoh the request intimated to him by God (5:3). Williams notes that Pharaoh receives no indication of God's true intent.[71] W. H. Propp sees the scene as "an enjoyable story," attesting a tradition in which the Israelites "and their god" deceive, attributable to the allure of "trickster tales" within ancient Israel.[72] And Ken Esau's thorough analysis argues that the scene evidences deception, in which Mo-

---

70. Most recently, see the treatment of Dean Andrew Nicholas (*The Trickster Revisited: Deception as a Motif in the Pentateuch* [Studies in Biblical Literature 117; New York: Peter Lang, 2009] 63–68), who argues that the entire exodus event is laden with deception. He concludes: "The clear contradiction between the plan to deliver the people from Egypt and the instructions to ask for a mere three-day journey is not an editorial slip or an opening gambit. Rather, it is essential to a deceptive plot that would eventually release Israel, giving them the wealth of Egypt and destroying the enemy in the process."

71. Williams, *Deception in Genesis*, 62.

72. William Henry Propp, *Exodus 1–18* (AB 2; New York: Doubleday, 1999) 207.

ses is "backed by divine command."[73] Esau further elaborates, advancing the notion that divine deception here should be read as a requisite aspect of wartime, during which even God is free to ignore traditional ethics.[74] Williams also cites God's instruction to Moses in Exod 14:1–4 to have the Israelites feign confusion in the wilderness so that Pharaoh will believe they are lost or disoriented as an example of divine deception.[75]

The Deuteronomistic History

Divine deception in the Deuteronomistic History occurs most frequently in the context of battle. Richard D. Patterson labels this phenomenon a *ruse de guerre*.[76] He elucidates four specific passages that show God as being active in deception during battle: 2 Sam 17:14; 1 Kgs 22:19–23; 2 Kgs 6:15–20; 7:6–7.[77] Among these four, 1 Kgs 22:19–23 has received the most attention.[78] Here King Ahab asks the prophet Micaiah's advice about the prospects for success were the king to attack Ramoth-gilead. After his favorable report is met with a challenge by Ahab, Micaiah relates a heavenly dialogue in which YHWH asks for a volunteer to 'deceive' (פתה) the king into attacking Ramoth-gilead, which, the reader learns, will result in Ahab's death. Both Robert Chisholm and J. J. M. Roberts, respectively, point out that the 'lying spirit' (רוח שקר, lit., 'spirit of falsehood') placed in the mouth of Ahab's prophets has its origin with YHWH, the perpetrator of this deadly deception.[79] Both of these scholars also deem YHWH's resorting to deception as being in line with YHWH's justice. For Roberts, God is trustworthy as long as the believer is obedient, and for Chisholm, divine deception is used solely to punish sinners.[80]

R. W. L. Moberly, however, suggests that the text is ultimately about "speak[ing] truth to power."[81] The text is less about divine deception and

---

73. Ken Esau, "Divine Deception in the Exodus Event?" *Directions* 35 (2006) 8. Esau provides helpful summaries of previous scholarly attempts to make sense of this scene, among them the claim that the Israelites never stated that they would return or that the three-days request was meant to serve as the first stage in a series of negotiations between Moses/God and Pharaoh.

74. Ibid., 15.

75. Williams, *Deception in Genesis*, 62.

76. Richard D. Patterson, "The Old Testament Use of an Archetype: The Trickster," *JETS* 42 (1999) 387.

77. Ibid., 393.

78. See Evangelia G. Dafni, "RWH SQR und falsche Prophetie in I Reg 22," *ZAW* 112 (2000) 365–85.

79. Robert B. Chisholm, Jr., "Does God Deceive?" *BSac* 155 (1998) 14, 16; J. J. M. Roberts, "Does God Lie? Divine Deceit as a Theological Problem in Israelite Prophetic Literature," in *Congress Volume: Jerusalem, 1986* (ed. J. A. Emerton; VTSup 40; Leiden: Brill, 1988) 216–17.

80. Roberts, ibid., 219–20; Chisholm, "Does God Deceive?" 28. I will discuss and engage the respective views of Roberts and Chisholm in more detail in chap. 5.

81. R. W. L. Moberly, "Does God Lie to His Prophets? The Story of Micaiah ben Imlah as a Test Case," *HTR* 96 (2003) 3.

more about Yhwh's gracious offer to bring about repentance from King Ahab. Moberly sums up his argument: "If the message is that the king will die, it is given so that the king may not die."[82] The prophetic word originating with God serves a compassionate, not catastrophic end: to bring about a change of heart and mind for the king.[83] While it will press too far afield to offer a full evaluation of Moberly's arguments, it is enough to say that divine deception (which Moberly has essentially argued away in this specific text) is still in fact present, yet Moberly has raised the important idea that divine deception may in some circumstances have altruistic motivations.

The story of Micaiah ben Imlah is also crucial for identifying additional texts that implicate the deity in deception. Esther Hamori has recently argued for the presence of a much more robust tradition in the Hebrew Bible associated with the 'spirit of falsehood' (רוח שקר).[84] She isolates a complex of eight texts—five of which directly refer to the tradition (1 Kgs 22:19–23; 1 Sam 16:14–23; 18:10–12; 19:9–10; Judg 9:23–24; 2 Kgs 19:7; Isa 19:13–14) and three of which evoke the tradition or display knowledge of its existence (Isa 29:9–10; Job 4:12–21; Hos 4:12–5:4)—that depict the 'spirit of falsehood' as coming from Yhwh, often in the form of a deceiving messenger from the heavenly court.[85] Out of this aggregate of texts, seven of the eight see the spirit of falsehood as originating from God.[86] Hamori has deftly shown that the biblical tradition equating the deity with falsehood and deception is more widespread than many interpreters have recognized. I am appreciative of Hamori's insights and aim to extend the appreciation of divine deception in the biblical canon even further.

A final example within the Deuteronomistic History is noted by Williams. He recognizes a deception in Yhwh's instruction to a concerned Samuel in 1 Sam 16:1–5 that the purpose of the journey is to offer a sacrifice when in reality it is to anoint a new king from among Jesse's sons.[87] Saul is the victim of this divine deception.

The Prophets

In the prophets, one encounters perhaps the most palpable instances of divine deception. These occur largely in the context of false prophecy, much akin to 1 Kgs 22 discussed above. Jeremiah gives voice to many examples. Roberts cites the prophet's accusatory speech in Jer 4:10 that Yhwh had

---

82. Ibid., 9.
83. Ibid., 11–12. Foundational for Moberly's argument is the recognition that the heavenly court—replete with deception in this case—is meant to shed light on the reality of the king's earthly court. Micaiah's message is not deceptive itself but, instead, aims to break through to the king and reveal that Ahab and his prophets are the true purveyors of deception.
84. Esther J. Hamori, "The Spirit of Falsehood," *CBQ* 72 (2010) 15–30.
85. Ibid., 18, 30.
86. Ibid., 28.
87. Williams, *Deception in Genesis*, 62.

'utterly deceived' (הִשָּׁא הִשֵּׁאת) the people and Jerusalem into a false sense of security when in fact destruction was looming.[88] Chisholm highlights the intensifying evident in the infinitive absolute construction and deems this instance yet another example of Yʜwʜ's using deception to attain his own objectives.[89] Jeremiah 15:18 sees the prophet comparing Yʜwʜ to a "deceitful brook, like waters that fail."[90] James Crenshaw has argued that Jer 20:7 portrays the prophet again as accusing God of deception.[91] While William Holladay is correct to caution against the assumption that Jeremiah's accusations are statements of fact that Yʜwʜ did indeed deceive the prophet, the prevalence of material concerning divine deception in Jeremiah attests to the veracity of seeing it as a possible theme in the Hebrew Bible.[92]

Most recently, Israel Knohl has sought to expand upon Roberts's earlier study on whether God lies. Knohl looks specifically at the *seraphim* vision in Isa 6 and the *topheth* ('burning place') vision in 30:26–33, maintaining that the theme of "consuming divine fire" predominates in the book.[93] He draws a connection between these two scenes and 1 Kgs 22, concluding:

> Just as Ahab is led to his end by the false enticement of the spirit of the Lord, in the seraphim vision, the prophet leads Israel to its doom by means of deceptive promises that stay their return to the Lord. In the Topheth vision, the spirit of the Lord acts in similar fashion as it guides the nations with the deceiving bridle to perdition.[94]

Yʜwʜ, argues Knohl, deceptively orchestrates the people's inability to repent in Isa 6 and does the same for the nations in 30:26–33.

One example is worthy of more sustained treatment: Nancy Bowen's 1994 dissertation *The Role of Yahweh as Deceiver in True and False Prophecy*. Bowen examines three passages in which Yʜwʜ is the subject of the verb פתה 'to deceive' (1 Kgs 22:1–38; Jer 20:7–13; Ezek 14:1–11). My analysis has already addressed the first two texts. In Ezek 14:1–11, Yʜwʜ has revoked from the people the possibility for prophetic intermediation because of the people's breaking of the covenant. The victim of the divine deception, notes Bowen, is the prophet who presumes to utter the divine word. This instance of divine deception shows Yʜwʜ as ultimately concerned with

---

88. Roberts, "Does God Lie?" 217.

89. Chisholm, "Does God Deceive?" 18.

90. Roberts, "Does God Lie?" 218.

91. James L. Crenshaw, *A Whirlpool of Torment: Israelite Traditions of God as an Oppressive Presence* (OBT; Philadelphia: Fortress, 1984) 41, and his *Defending God: Biblical Responses to the Problem of Evil* (Oxford: Oxford University Press, 2005) 90.

92. William L. Holladay, *Jeremiah 1: A Commentary on the Book of the Prophet Jeremiah, Chapters 1–25* (Hermeneia; Philadelphia: Fortress, 1986) 552.

93. Israel Knohl, "Does God Deceive? An Examination of the Dark Side of Isaiah's Prophecy," in *Mishneh Todah: Studies in Deuteronomy and Its Cultural Environment in Honor of Jeffrey H. Tigay* (ed. N. S. Fox, D. A. Glatt-Gilad, and M. J. Williams; Winona Lake, IN: Eisenbrauns, 2009) 291.

94. Ibid., 291.

being known, evident in the presence of the identification formula "then you shall know that I am Yʜᴡʜ" in v. 8. It is through deception of the prophet that Yʜᴡʜ makes his name known, argues Bowen.[95]

By way of conclusion, Bowen maintains that each of these three texts depicts Yʜᴡʜ's deception in unique theological terms. In 1 Kgs 22, Yʜᴡʜ is the sovereign king-breaker who responds fittingly to disobedience. Jeremiah 20:7 challenges the reliability of Yʜᴡʜ and Yʜᴡʜ's promises. And Ezek 14:1–11 highlights deception as a means by which Yʜᴡʜ is made known.[96] She proposes that Yʜᴡʜ as deceiver functions in each of these texts as an agent of social change, pushing against the status quo.[97] This function parallels one of many characteristics of the trickster that Bowen isolates that are known from other literature. Bowen elaborates, noting that Yʜᴡʜ's portrayal in these texts exemplifies several other traditionally-defined characteristics of the trickster—ambiguity and anomaly, working inversion, creativity, and moral ambiguity—and belies ancient Israel's borrowing of the divine trickster motif from elsewhere in the ancient Near East.[98]

With this history of research in mind, I conclude that the lack of a sustained scholarly treatment of divine deception in Genesis is palpable. Scholars have adequately addressed the viability of the topic; what remains inchoate is a specific focus on Genesis from a theological trajectory. Before moving forward, however, I will show that it is helpful to broaden the horizon beyond the biblical text—only briefly—and look at the presence of divine deception in the wider cultural context of ancient Israel and in anthropological literature. This survey will corroborate the history of scholarship offered here from a historical perspective, showing that divine deception was indeed a fixture in the literature of the wider ancient Near Eastern milieu.

Precursors to Divine Deception: The Ancient Near East and Anthropological Evidence

This theme of divine deception is not endemic to the Hebrew Bible alone. Within the wider ancient Near Eastern context, divine deception appears to be a prominent motif. Both gods and goddesses are complicit in deception and trickery. Their deceptions also know no geographical boundaries; instances of divine deception appear in Mesopotamian, Egyptian, Hittite, and Greek texts alike. More recently, modern anthropological literature has demonstrated evidence of the existence of trickster deities. In the pages that follow, I will discuss the various places where divine de-

---

95. Nancy R. Bowen, *The Role of Yahweh as Deceiver in True and False Prophecy* (Ph.D. Dissertation, Princeton Theological Seminary, 1994) 113, 117.

96. Ibid., 123–24.

97. Ibid., 133–34.

98. Ibid., 131–35.

ception appears in texts from the ancient Near East as well as, briefly, in modern anthropological literature.

Ancient Near Eastern Examples of Divine Deception

Deceptive deities appear frequently in the literature of the wider ancient Near East, providing a context within which to interpret Yhwh's role in deception in the biblical text. Perhaps the most thorough study to date on the divine deceiver is that of W. B. Kristensen in his 1928 Dutch article, "De goddelijke bedrieger."[99] Therein Kristensen identifies specifically Babylonian Ea (Enki) and Greek Hermes, along with a brief mention of Egyptian Seth as deceptive deities. Kristensen also draws a distinction between the classical trickster and the divine deceiver, the latter of which is a wholly inscrutable and ambiguous figure.[100] Subsequent scholarship has taken upon itself the task of expanding upon Kristensen's seminal contribution. A few examples should suffice, from Mesopotamian, Egyptian, and Hittite texts.

Mesopotamian

Within Mesopotamian texts, Ea (Enki), god of great wisdom and cunning, often plays the role of trickster. Thorkild Jacobsen describes him as follows:

> It is not his nature to overwhelm; rather, he persuades, tricks or evades to gain his ends. He is the cleverest of the gods, the one who can plan and organize and think of ways out when no one else can. He is the counselor and adviser, the expert and the troubleshooter, or manipulator of the ruler; not the ruler himself.[101]

Ea is a crafty and clever deity whose trickery comes to the fore most often in his dealings with humanity.

In *Atrahasis*, an Akkadian myth of human origins dating between 1850 and 1500 B.C.E., Enki shows his mettle as a trickster largely in the context of circumventing Enlil's attempts to reduce the noisy and disturbing human

---

99. William Brede Kristensen, "De goddelijke bedrieger," Mededeelingen der Koninklijke Akademie van wetenschappen. Amsterdam, Afdeeling Letterkunde. Deel. 66, Serie B no. 3 (1928) 63–88.

100. More recently, and in an entirely different vein, Michael Dolzani ("The Ashes of the Stars: Northrop Frye and the Trickster-God," *Semeia* 89 [2002] 59–73) traces the idea and development of a "trickster-God" in the thought and writings of Canadian literary theorist Northrop Frye. This discussion goes beyond the bounds of the present study as it involves analysis of much of Frye's own works, along with the works of seminal authors like William Blake who very much influenced Frye. Dolzani, though, interestingly notes a development in Frye's thought on the topic of the trickster God across all his works, moving from a view that this understanding of the deity as "ambiguous" and typified by the book of Job may give way to seeing a "positive trickster-God" that is a liberating force in people's lives (59).

101. Thorkild Jacobsen, *Treasures of Darkness: A History of Mesopotamian Religion* (New Haven, CT: Yale University Press, 1976) 116.

population.[102] Enlil seeks to diminish the human population on four separate occasions. First, he plans to send a plague, but Enki advises the human, Atrahasis, to placate the plague god with worship and offerings. Second, a drought is unsuccessful for much the same reason. Third, in response to a famine Enki, although the text is fragmentary at this point, presumably communicates with Atrahasis in a dream, resulting somehow in an abundance of fish. Fourth and finally, Enlil becomes aware of Enki's shenanigans and requires that all the deities—Enki included—swear by an oath not to reveal Enlil's master plan: a flood. Enki cleverly outwits Enlil again, pretending to speak to a reed wall within earshot of Atrahasis and instructing him to build a boat (III i 11–35).[103]

Ea is depicted as a trickster in another text involving a flood: the *Epic of Gilgamesh*. In the pertinent scene (XI 36–47), Utnapishtim, the boatman, relates to Gilgamesh how it is that he survived the flood in a scene having several echoes with *Atrahasis*. Upon receiving the instructions from Ea to build a boat, Utnapishtim asks the deity how he should explain his hasty departure to his neighbors. Ea responds by commanding Utnapishtim to inform them that he is leaving the city because of Enlil's displeasure with him, when in reality it is to escape the flood.[104] This divine deception is all the more troubling because Ea encourages Utnapishtim to reassure the populace by stating that Ea will "rain down abundance" of birds, fish, bread, and harvest, when in reality it is the rain that will obliterate the population.

A final example of Ea/Enki's role in deception occurs in *Adapa*. In *Adapa*, the main character of the same name is summoned before Anu to explain why he fractured the wing of the south wind.[105] Ea, who appears to have a special relationship with Adapa, offers advice to help prepare Adapa for the meeting and to ensure success. He suggests that Adapa do two things, specifically. First, Adapa is to clothe himself in the attire of a mourner, claiming that he is mourning the disappearance of two gods, Tammuz and Gizzida, when in fact these are the two deities he will encounter at Anu's door; as a result, Ea claims that they will speak a favorable word on Adapa's behalf to Ea. Second, Ea advises against Adapa's accepting the bread and water *of death* from Anu, if they are offered. Nearly everything happens as Ea describes, except for the curious fact that Anu offers Adapa the bread and water *of life*, not death. Adapa adheres to Ea's command, declining the

---

102. See Benjamin R. Foster, *Before the Muses: An Anthology of Akkadian Literature* (3rd ed.; Bethesda: CDL, 2006) 227–80, for the text of *Atrahasis* used here.

103. The god Ea does precisely the same thing in the parallel account in the *Gilgamesh Epic*.

104. Most recently, Nicholas (*The Trickster Revisited*, 117–18) has interpreted Ea's deception in the *Gilgamesh Epic* as a "humorous example," despite its murderous results. See also Williams (*Deception in Genesis*, 159), who describes the results of this deception as "catastrophic."

105. See Foster, *Before the Muses*, 525–30, for the translation of *Adapa* used here.

offer. The text breaks off at this point, but another version preserved on a fragment shows Anu laughing uncontrollably at Ea's plan, asking, "Who else, of all the gods of heaven and netherworld, could d[o] something like this?" (frg. D 6–7). Anu's laughter appears to betray the fact that Ea is acting as the trickster here, yet this point has been debated. Giorgio Buccellati, however, provides a helpful survey of the possible interpretations of this episode, noting that the common denominator in nearly all of them is that Ea intends through his words to trick Adapa.[106] The divine deception, then, entails Ea's convincing Adapa to forego the chance for eternal life by leading him to believe that the bread and water of life that Anu will offer will in fact result in death.

Ea/Enki is the prototypical trickster in the ancient Near East. The texts surveyed here are but a few of the instances in which this deity employs deception, often for the benefit of a certain individual, but taking Adapa into consideration, perhaps also to the detriment of the individual.[107] Within the wider ancient Near East, Ea seems to be the trickster par excellence.[108] He is not, however, the only trickster.

Carole Fontaine has presented compelling arguments that goddesses may also deceive, such as Inanna in the Sumerian myth *The Transfer of the Arts of Civilization*.[109] The story runs as follows: the goddess Inanna visits her grandfather Enki in Eridu. Shortly after her arrival, the two begin drinking beer together, and a drinking challenge ensues. An intoxicated Enki offers a series of toasts to the goddess; after each toast, he gives her groups of the *me*, divine ordinances that govern matters from the high priesthood and godship to judgment-giving and decision-making. After 14 of these sorts of exchanges, Enki orders that Inanna be given free and safe passage to Uruk. Taking the *me* with her, she embarks for Uruk. Meanwhile, Enki at last sobers up and inquires 14 times about the *me's* whereabouts. He dispatches Isimud and various creatures to retrieve the *me*, but they are ultimately unsuccessful. Upon reaching Uruk, Inanna discovers that there are more *me* on the boat than she had originally received from Enki.

---

106. Giorgio Buccellati, "Adapa, Genesis, and the Notion of Faith," *UF* 5 (1973) 62–63.

107. I must admit that it does remain unclear who serves as the object of Ea's deception in *Adapa*. Is it Adapa himself or the god Anu? Given that Ea seldom if ever tricks to harm humanity, coupled with the recurrent theme of him as a trickster of other gods, one may make a compelling case that Ea intends Anu to be the object of his deception.

108. For additional examples of Ea as trickster, see the recent article by Keith Dickson ("Enki and Ninhursag: The Trickster in Paradise," *JNES* 66 [2007] 1–32, esp. pp. 7, 9, 22, 27, and 32), who argues that Enki is a character undergoing a transformation "into a suffering male trickster" identified by "exuberant sexual and culinary hunger, . . . his violence, his deception, his knowledge, his bellyache, his ridiculous and magical pregnancy, his status as simultaneously sacred and cursed" (p. 32). For additional examples of Sumerian trickster deities, see Williams, *Deception in Genesis*, 155–56, 160–61.

109. "Inanna and Enki" (trans. Gertrud Farber; *COS* 1.161: 522–26).

He eventually admits defeat, and the two reconcile. The *me* are allowed to remain in Uruk.

The divine deception in this story, argues Jacobsen, is evident in Inanna's seizing the opportunity when Enki, a master trickster himself as the aforementioned texts make clear, appears most susceptible.[110] Fontaine advances another possibility, holding that Inanna demonstrates not only her "craft" but also her "courage" in challenging the traditional boundaries placed on females, goddesses included.[111]

Egyptian

In Egyptian literature, four deities engage in deception: Re, Isis, Horus, and Seth. In *The Destruction of Mankind* Re, the sun-god, formulates a plan to placate the goddess Hathor and in effect to put a stop to her murderous destruction which, ironically, Re had instigated.[112] A surviving papyrus extols Isis's aptitude for deception:

> Now, Isis was a wise woman. Her heart was more devious than millions among men; she was more selective than millions among the gods; she was more exacting than millions among the blessed dead.[113]

This praising of her deceptive abilities, Williams notes, immediately precedes and likely legitimates the goddess's creation of a snake that bites Re, leading Isis to claim that she alone can heal him in exchange for Re's sharing his secret "name of power."[114] Williams provides a fine summary of Isis's and Horus's respective deceptions, each of which involves "disguises": Isis conceals her identity in order to trick "Seth into validating the claim of her son, Horus," and Horus deceives Seth in a boat-building competition by covering his own pine boat with gypsum to give it the look of stone, resulting in Seth's losing the contest when his own concrete boat sinks.[115]

Seth does not, however, always play the fool. In Egyptian literature, H. Te Velde argues, Seth also functions as a trickster. Te Velde cites five specific ways in which Seth's activities parallel what is known of the trickster from other primitive cultures. First, Seth presents a challenge to *maat* 'ethical and cosmic order', in that in Egyptian the word meaning 'confusion' (*khenenu*) is determined in hieroglyphics with the symbol for the Seth-animal.[116] More fittingly, the Egyptian verb 'to deceive' may also be

---

110. Jacobsen, *The Treasures of Darkness*, 114–15.

111. Carole Fontaine, "The Deceptive Goddess in Ancient Near Eastern Myth: Inanna and Inaraš," *Semeia* 42 (1988) 92–93.

112. "The Destruction of Mankind" (trans. Miriam Lichtheim; *COS* 1.24: 36–37).

113. "The Legend of Isis and the Name of Re" (trans. Robert K. Ritner; *COS* 1.22: 33–34).

114. Williams, *Deception in Genesis*, 167.

115. Ibid.

116. H. Te Velde, "The Egyptian God Seth as a Trickster," *JARCE* 7 (1968) 37.

written with the symbol for the Seth-animal.[117] Second, Seth is described as a *shed-kheru*, which means essentially 'to make mischief' or 'stir up strife', a hallmark of the trickster.[118] Third, Seth's trickery leads to the murder of the netherworld god Osiris, when Seth promises a chest (which is in reality a coffin) to the individual who fits into it. Each deity takes a turn, and when Osiris discovers that he is a fit, "Seth unexpectedly runs up, closes the chest, and throws it into the water without any funeral ceremonies," resulting in Osiris's death by drowning.[119] Seth, says Te Velde, had offered eternal life through the coffin, because an Egyptian mind would see a coffin as ensuring life after death, but through deception, Seth gave only death.[120] Fourth, Seth's engagement in homosexual activity with his nephew Horus evidences a crossing of sexual boundaries that often identifies the trickster.[121] And fifth, Seth is a "slayer-of-the-monster"—serving as an intimidating presence through natural phenomena, such as thunder—who keeps chaos at bay.[122]

Hittite

One Hittite text preserves an instance in which a goddess deceives with the aid of a human. In *The Myth of Illuyankaš*,[123] the goddess Inaraš kills the Illuyankaš dragon through trickery with the help of the human Hupašiyaš. Similar to the story of Inanna and Enki in *The Transfer of the Arts of Civilization* mentioned above, the goddess Inaraš gets the dragon intoxicated and takes advantage of the situation. She hides Hupašiyaš, who suddenly appears and binds the drunken dragon. The Storm-god then emerges and slays the dragon.

Greek

Recent tendencies in scholarship are to view the ancient Near Eastern context more broadly than in the past; Greek parallels are thus also important in looking at the larger cultural world of ancient Israel. I intend here only to offer a sample from the Greek world. Four figures deserve to be

---

117. Ibid. See also Te Velde's *Seth, God of Confusion: A Study of His Role in Egyptian Mythology and Religion* (trans. G. E. van Baaren-Pape; Probleme der Ägyptologie 6; Leiden: Brill, 1977) 25, where the determinative for the Seth-animal is discussed in relation to the "divine joker."

118. Idem, "The Egyptian God Seth as a Trickster," 38.

119. Ibid. Te Velde further states that this episode was viewed by the Egyptians as especially heinous, and therefore, "it is never depicted, and the Egyptian texts only refer to Seth's deed in veiled terms." On this point, see also *Seth, God of Confusion*, 82–84, where Te Velde labels Seth "a divine murderer and deceiver" in the murdering of Osiris (p. 83).

120. Ibid.

121. Idem, "The Egyptian God Seth as a Trickster," 39.

122. Ibid.

123. "The Storm-God and the Serpent (Illuyanka)" (trans. Gary Beckman; COS 1.56: 150–51).

mentioned, though there are certainly others: Athena, Prometheus, Zeus, and Hermes.

The *Odyssey* itself is a book replete with deception. Odysseus is perhaps the most notable trickster in Greek literature, much akin to Ea/Enki in the Mesopotamian texts. Odysseus, however, is hardly the only figure involved in deception in the *Odyssey*. The goddess Athena, Odysseus's divine benefactor and protectress throughout the story, is complicit on numerous levels. She disguises Odysseus so that he is unrecognizable to the suitors, and when she first appears to Odysseus in Book 13, it is in the guise of a young shepherd boy to compound the hero's confusion about his location and to set her plan in motion. Odysseus responds with a deceptive story, recounting his adventures; prefacing his answer is the statement that Odysseus "did not speak the truth, and made up a lying story in the instinctive wiliness of his heart" (13.256). Athena's rejoinder affirms and praises Odysseus's skill as a trickster, as she calls him a "shifty, lying fellow" who is "full of guile, unwearying in deceit" and one who has an "instinctive falsehood" (13.291–302). Athena disguises Odysseus as an aged beggar, another instance of her stealth in deception, and dispatches him to Eumaeus's residence, where he will engage in a litany of deceptions of Eumaeus, the suitors, and his own wife, Penelope. C. R. Trahman remarks that Odysseus's elaborate lies in Books 13–19 are not mere poetic digressions but are fully integrated into the fabric of the story and help to hold the narrative together. [124] It is the goddess Athena who conceals Odysseus's identity at first, and each of the deceptions just discussed center on his identity. Camouflaging Odysseus's true identity is necessary if the suitors are to be killed, which is precisely what happens—with Athena's help—after Odysseus successfully strings his own bow and shoots it through a dozen axe heads to win Penelope again. Athena had prompted Penelope to hold the contest knowing full well that Odysseus would be successful. [125]

---

124. C. R. Trahman, "Odysseus' Lies (*Odyssey*, Books 13–19)," *Phoenix* 6 (1952) 43.

125. The figure of Odysseus presents another interesting example. While he is not divine, he is said to have divinity included in his lineage. His maternal great-grandfather was Hermes, messenger of the gods and guide to the underworld in Greek literature. Nonetheless, the boundaries between the categories of divine and human are by no means distinct sets in Greece, and Odysseus is clearly portrayed as a human being with an aptitude for deception. He is described as *polymeteis* 'one who knows a lot of tricks'. R. Z. Burrows ("Deception as a Comic Device in the Odyssey," *The Classical World* 59 [1965] 33) calls Odysseus's fluency in deception an "intellectual trademark" for the character that Homer wanted established. He is a trickster par excellence, deceiving even his own wife, Penelope (19.165–202, 221–48, 262–303), with immaculate skill—Homer commends Odysseus's proficiency in deception, writing, "[H]e kept his eyes as hard as iron without letting them so much as quiver, so cunningly did he restrain his tears" (19.203)—by concealing his identity from her, all the while speaking of having met Odysseus during his journeys and forecasting that he would return home to Ithaca soon. His lie to Penelope is one among many concerning his identity that occur in Books 13–19 of the *Odyssey*; therein Odysseus will also deceive Eumaeus (14.192–352) and the suitors (17.419–44).

In Hesiod's *Theogony*, Prometheus, the son of a Titan (gods who had challenged the sovereignty of Zeus), engages in a battle of wits with the supreme deity Zeus. Prometheus is described at birth as "clever Prometheus, full of various wiles" (lines 510–11) and elsewhere as "wily" (line 545) and the perpetrator of a "cunning trick" (line 547). The trick occurs at a banquet at Mekone (lines 545–57). Playing the role of advocate for humanity, Prometheus agrees to separate the things that are for the gods from the things that are for humans, in order to demarcate clear boundaries; Zeus clearly has much to gain here.[126] Prometheus divides the sacrificial ox in two, as suggested, yet things are not as they seem outwardly. In one of the piles, Prometheus arranges the ox's bones, covered by the fat of the animal to make this choice appealing; in the other pile, he places all the meat and covers it with the animal's stomach. Zeus, however, will not be the butt of the deception, because the text records that in his infinite wisdom he discerns the trick and plots punishment for humanity as a result (lines 550–55). Zeus's choice of the hidden pile of bones thus transforms a deception *of* Zeus into a deception *by* Zeus.[127] Zeus retaliates by taking fire from humanity, which Prometheus summarily retrieves by theft. Deception and counterdeception in the struggle between (semi-)divine beings pervade and unite the Prometheus myth.[128]

Odysseus is perhaps most interesting because of his relationship with the goddess Athena. The relationship between patron deity and human hero is well known in ancient literature. Despite Odysseus's being a human, his deceptions at numerous points are hatched with the assistance of his divine protectress, Athena, with whom Odysseus shares a desire for the suitors' destruction and the peace of Ithaca. Understood in this way, the Odysseus-Athena relationship functions in a similar way to the Jacob-YHWH relationship in Genesis. The divine and human work and move together—in, through, and amidst deception—toward what becomes a common cause. Moreover, Athena is complicit in Odysseus's deceiving of his wife, Penelope, much as I will argue that YHWH has a hand in Jacob's deceptions of various members of his family. This similarity tied up in the notion of patron deity and human trickster is an intriguing and potentially worthwhile point of comparison for one's reading of Jacob, yet it is not a point that I wish to pursue in this book. Doing so casts the net more widely than I would like; my concern in this book is entirely bound up with the phenomenon of trickster deities.

126. Eliot Wirshbo ("The Mekone Scene in the *Theogony*: Prometheus as Prankster," *Greek, Roman and Byzantine Studies* 23 [1982] 107) argues to the contrary that Prometheus's trick "is not motivated by any far-sighted plan to aid mankind" but instead "is simply following impish impulse and aiming at causing a disturbance," much as tricksters are prone to do. It is not until later that altruistic intentions attach themselves to Prometheus's actions.

127. Zeus is also known as a skilled divine deceiver, for instance on the many occasions that he disguises himself in order to engage in sexual liaisons with fair maidens.

128. Klaus-Peter Koepping, "Absurdity and Hidden Truth: Cunning Intelligence and Grotesque Body Images as Manifestations of the Trickster," *History of Religions* 24 (1985) 205, 206.

Hermes also plays the role of a trickster deity. The messenger of the gods, Hermes is also the god of, among other things, thieves and cunning.[129] William G. Doty isolates a number of characteristics traditionally associated with the trickster that are also relevant for Hermes: marginality, erotic and relational aspects, a role as creator and restorer, deception and thievery, comedy and wit, and the role given to him in hermeneutics, from which his name derives.[130] This final insight is especially pertinent to my argument in chap. 2, where Yʜwʜ selectively and ambiguously presents a divine message to Rebekah (Gen 25:23). Similarly, Hermes as messenger of the gods often feels free to "select or adapt what he alone chooses to present . . . and when" to the recipient.[131] As it pertains to deception explicitly, Hermes is seldom the object of a return-deception, and his tricks are often benevolent.[132] One of the finest examples of Hermes as divine deceiver appears in the Homeric *Hymn to Hermes*, which celebrates Hermes' arrival and initiation as a god. At birth he is described as "a wily boy, flattering and cunning, a robber and cattle thief" (lines 11–12). True to his name, almost immediately after his birth he leaps from his mother's arms with the purpose of stealing his brother Apollo's herds (line 22). Hermes is also careful to cover his tracks, steering the herds in a zigzag pattern and then driving them backward in order to confuse Apollo when he follows, while Hermes himself walks in a straight line (lines 66–70). Crafty Hermes also fashions large wicker sandals to disguise his own footprints (lines 71–74). There also remains some ambiguity as to whether Hermes' so-called coming of age as a god attains any sort of completion. Judith Fletcher argues that, while the *Hymn to Hermes* portrays the god as moving from tricky and unsworn oaths to oaths of ritualized friendship, it is not at all clear that Hermes completes the ceremony and transition, thus shedding his old trickster ways.[133] Similarly, I will argue in chap. 4 against the traditional interpretation that Jacob comes of age as a patriarch after the nocturnal struggle (Gen 32:23–33) but, rather, persists as a deceiver of his brother, Esau.

---

129. Norman O. Brown, *Hermes the Thief: The Evolution of a Myth* (Madison: University of Wisconsin Press, 1947).

130. William G. Doty, "A Lifetime of Trouble-Making: Hermes as Trickster," in *Mythical Trickster Figures: Contours, Contexts, and Criticisms* (ed. William J. Hynes and William G. Doty; Tuscaloosa: University of Alabama Press, 1993) 46. While I do not share Doty's confidence in the universality of the trickster figure and comparisons across cultures, as will become evident, this list does encompass a number of features that convincingly inform Hermes' deceptions.

131. Doty, ibid., 62. I do not mean to suggest that the Gen 25:23 text has Hermes in mind at all but, rather, that the idea that a deity could shape a message and offer the response with great liberty and freedom is attested elsewhere among divine tricksters.

132. See ibid., 57, 59, for several examples.

133. Judith Fletcher, "A Trickster's Oaths in the 'Homeric Hymn to Hermes,'" *American Journal of Philology* 129 (2008) 19–46.

Summary and Implications

This survey of divine deception in texts from the ancient Near East is in no way meant to be exhaustive; it is, rather, representative. Several important themes emerge from this survey. First, divine deception testifies to the unique freedom of a given deity to act in accordance with the deity's purpose in and through deception. Second, divine tricksters are often in relationship with a human counterpart; their deceptions include a human partner or are for the benefit of a human. Third, these deceptions often occur within the context of the (divine) family. All of these elements are present in and relevant to the Jacob cycle.

These examples also support the present study by noting the ubiquity of divine deception within ancient Israel's wider cultural context. These textual traditions had a great staying-power in the ancient Near East and survived over the course of several centuries. They constitute part of the milieu of the ancient Near East, and it is quite likely that ancient Israel would have been aware of such a prevalent theme.[134] To make this connection all the more explicit, Fontaine argues that the image of the deceptive goddess treated above provides an apt parallel to biblical women deceivers, such as Rebekah and Tamar.[135] She calls the deceptive goddess "the divine sister" of the female trickster and rightly notes that these mythic texts emerged and developed "in the same thought world" as the biblical text.[136] One should not then be surprised to discover this very same motif of divine deception to be prevalent within the Hebrew Bible, Genesis included.

Modern Anthropological Examples of Trickster Deities

Modern anthropological literature also evidences the existence of trickster deities. I will be quite brief in this section for a variety of reasons. First, in terms of methodology, in this book I am not concerned with cross-cultural parallels or readings of the biblical text but with a literary-theological approach to the biblical text. Second, comparisons of this sort quickly become too restrictive. The very nature of the trickster is to transcend simplistic definitions and comparisons. Moreover, the separation of time, culture, and literary impetus in the use of the trickster figure means that it is ultimately unhelpful and perhaps even misleading to compare ancient materials with modern materials in any rigid fashion. I remain unconvinced that the trickster is a figure that can or should be defined

---

134. It is, however, not my intention, nor am I interested in conjecturing in this book about the relationship between ancient Near Eastern divine deception and biblical portrayals of God as deceptive. My purpose here is solely to point out its presence in the ancient Near Eastern context of which ancient Israel was a part and thus to lend support to the idea of seeing divine deception in the Hebrew Bible. Investigating the relationship between the two bodies of literature—biblical and ancient Near Eastern—would be worthwhile in the future as the study of divine deception continues to mature.

135. Fontaine, "The Deceptive Goddess," 85, 95.

136. Ibid., 85, 87.

consistently across time, literature, and culture. Contemporary anthropological literature may shed some light on the biblical text, yet on the issue of divine tricksters there is nothing one can say about an Israelite awareness of or influence by the presence of trickster deities in other cultures. Where this discussion is helpful, however, pertains again to the importance of underscoring the existence and subsistence of the trickster-deity phenomenon.[137] Here, therefore, I will only note a few of the many examples of trickster deities in anthropological literature.

In Native American mythology, one encounters semidivine tricksters. The key figures are Hare, Spider, and Coyote. Paul Radin writes of the Winnebago Hare cycle and its cognates that the Trickster is simultaneously creator of the world and establisher of culture,[138] a dual nature leading Radin to muse about Trickster's relationship to deity:

> This, of course, raises an old question, namely, whether Trickster was originally a deity. Are we dealing here with a disintegration of his creative activities or with a merging of two entirely distinct figures, one a deity, the other a hero, represented either as human or animal? Has a hero here been elevated to the rank of a god, or was Trickster originally a deity with two sides to his nature, one constructive, one destructive, one spiritual, the other material? Or, again, does Trickster antedate the divine, the animal and the human?[139]

In response to this question, Radin posits that "Trickster's divinity is always secondary," yet several tribes still equate Trickster with the divine due to a view of Trickster's great antiquity.[140] Native American tricksters are at times explicitly connected with divinity as well. For example, an Oglala myth records Spider as saying, "I am a god and the son of a god. . . . I have done much good and should be treated as a god."[141]

---

137. My rationale here may sound a bit apologetic. What I desire to emphasize in this section is the viability of speaking of divine tricksters since their existence may initially be troubling to some readers. The attendant baggage accompanying literary and anthropological understandings of the trickster strike me as ultimately distracting and run the risk of pushing the topic too far afield. To reiterate, it seems to me (and increasingly to other scholars, as I will discuss below) that to compare, for instance, Native American tricksters with biblical tricksters ignores the issues of the vast chronological and cultural differences that separate the two. To argue for a comparison simply on the grounds that both may be representations of non-modern cultures again assumes far too much in the way of consistency across cultural boundaries, not to mention using the potentially unflattering label *non-modern*. Such a comparison also assumes that within a single culture the trickster figure is a monolithic entity, ignoring the possibility that tricksters may be quite different not only *across* cultures but also *within* the same culture.

138. Paul Radin, *The Trickster: A Study in American Indian Mythology* (New York: Philosophical Library, 1956) 124–25.

139. Ibid., 125.

140. Ibid., 164.

141. Ibid., 165.

Contemporary African mythology also witnesses trickster deities. The study by Robert Pelton stands as perhaps the most thorough on the topic. Pelton isolates his discussion within West Africa, focusing on Ananse (the Spider) of the Ashanti, Ogo-Yurugu of the Dogon, Legba of the Fon, and Eshu and Legba of the Yoruba.[142] John Pemberton looks specifically at the last of these deities, pointing out that Eshu has the power both to create and to destroy, very similar to the dual nature discussed above in regard to Native American semidivine tricksters.[143]

Toward a Theology of Deception

To return to the initial question—God's role in Jacob's deceptions—the previous survey of scholarship has made it clear that this issue has been neglected in the secondary literature. Scholars have recognized the presence of divine deception elsewhere in the Hebrew Bible, but no sustained treatment, beyond a few cursory references, has been advanced for the Jacob cycle, which is saturated with episodes of deception. The ancient Near Eastern and modern anthropological literature surveyed further attests to the viability of speaking of divine deception.

With this background in place, an investigation into divine deception in the Jacob cycle appears merited. Jacob's deceptions, as articulated above, are tethered to the moments of theophany that appear throughout the cycle. How might this connection between Jacob's activity and God's appearances contribute to the image of Yʜwʜ as a divine deceiver? Moreover, how does the ancestral promise (Gen 12:1–3) figure into this relationship? At the outset of this chapter, I introduced the thesis that God appears deeply involved in Jacob's deceptions, all with the intent of carrying forward the ancestral promise. The chapters that follow will make explicit what scholarship largely has left implicit: the association between promise, deception, and God. One may thus begin to see the makings of a *theology of deception*.

Assumptions and Methodology

With historical-critical methodologies still very much at the fore in pentateuchal studies, this investigation takes a different, synchronic route, emphasizing the final form of the book of Genesis as the primary locus of meaning and the appropriate base for theological inquiry. Although the biblical text as it exists in canonical form surely arose by means of a process of growth and development from different sources and traditions, one must also reckon with the fact that this same text has canonized these very tensions and inconsistencies. Their presence shows that they were considered meaningful and authoritative for a particular community.

---

142. R. D. Pelton, *The Trickster in West Africa: A Study of Mythic Irony and Sacred Delight* (Berkeley: University of California Press, 1980) 25–222.

143. John Pemberton, "The Yoruba Trickster God," *African Arts* 9 (1975) 22, 70.

This study eschews purely historical questions, not because they are unimportant, but because they are so abundant in relation to this material.[144]
Moreover, I am increasingly hesitant to see Old Testament theology as an
inherently historical, excavative discipline.[145] The works of Brevard Childs
and Walter Brueggemann, among others, have clearly shown this to be
the case. Moreover, Leo Perdue's seminal contribution *The Collapse of History: Reconstructing Old Testament Theology* chronicles a move away from
the hegemony of historical-critical methodologies in doing theology.[146] For
Perdue, we live in a world of plurality, and the task of doing Old Testament
theology is similarly a pluralistic exercise with great and worthwhile variety.[147] Part of the goal of Old Testament theology, says Perdue, is to articulate a theology that is relevant to contemporary life and faith, rather than
a theology permanently tethered to the history behind the text. History
retains a place in theological inquiry, yet it no longer exists as the only, or
even best, way to do Old Testament theology.

Perdue's emphasis on pluralism as a driving force of emphasis in Old
Testament theology is important for another reason. Not only does it highlight the explosion of approaches to the task of Old Testament theology, it
also says something about the nature of the Old Testament's theology. Old
Testament theology is not a monolithic entity; there are, rather, *theologies*
in the Bible.[148] In this book, I offer one such theology, a theology of deception in the Jacob cycle.

This book sets out to redress an imbalance between historical and literary approaches in Old Testament theology and Genesis scholarship, demonstrating that a close reading of the text with an eye toward its literary
artistry opens up new avenues of investigation that are worthy of theologi-

---

144. Walter Brueggemann (*Theology of the Old Testament: Testimony, Dispute, Advocacy*
[Minneapolis: Fortress, 1997] 118) takes a similar approach, claiming that one has very
few exegetical "tools" to uncover sound history. Brueggemann also writes that issues of
history "must be held in abeyance, pending the credibility and persuasiveness of Israel's
testimony, on which everything depends."

145. I am in agreement with Brevard Childs in *Old Testament Theology in a Canonical Context* (Philadelphia: Fortress, 1985) 4–5, where he identifies the most prevalent un-
solved problem as deciding whether one is doing Old Testament theology, a history of
Israel's religion, or both. Childs is correct, in my view, that the rightful object of theological reflection and work should be the received canonical text, replete with all its shaping,
and that this canonical text has not only preserved earlier historical traditions in ancient
Israel's life of faith but also reshaped them into a (cogent) whole (p. 11).

146. Leo Perdue, *The Collapse of History: Reconstructing Old Testament Theology* (OBT;
Minneapolis: Fortress, 1994).

147. Ibid., 5.

148. Erhard Gerstenberger (*Theologies in the Old Testament* [trans. John Bowden; Minneapolis: Fortress, 2002]) has shown this to be the case, though I do not believe that
the diverse theologies are limited to the different social settings in ancient Israel. Walter
Brueggemann has convincingly demonstrated the diversity of theologies in the Bible with
an attention to the differing (rhetorical) testimonies offered by the text.

cal mining. This book also advocates a return to theology proper, seeking literally a *"word about God."* Therefore, my investigation employs a synthesis of a close literary reading of the biblical text with theological aims. One must discern this meaning from the text that we have, not the text that we reconstruct or the text that we wish we had.

There are two mutually informing poles that will be operative in this study. First, rather than attempting to explain the numinous origins of the text or its formation, I will emphasize *what the text says.* Readers play a role in discerning a text's meaning, and this meaning arises in the dynamic relationship between text and reader. While no reading can be entirely disinterested, the text itself serves as a "control" for one's interpretation, and it is against the text that the authenticity of any interpretation must be judged. Walter Brueggemann gives adequate voice to the underpinnings of this aspect of my method:

> I shall insist, as consistently as I can, that the God of Old Testament theology as such lives in, with, and under the rhetorical enterprise of this text, and nowhere else and in no other way. This rhetorical enterprise operates with ontological assumptions, but these assumptions are open to dispute and revision in the ongoing rhetorical enterprise of Israel.[149]

God is not a static, predictable character but, rather, a character that emerges and takes shape from the reading process. Therefore, this book will offer a close reading of the text and glean from there what is said about God's character.[150] The process of reading engages the text and its characters in manifold ways, pressing the reader constantly to reevaluate and challenge earlier conclusions. God, therefore, through the narrative's portrayal of him as a character, is in a constant process of becoming.[151]

Second, my analysis emphasizes *how the text means.* Robert Alter's *Art of Biblical Narrative* is a seminal contribution on this point. Alter has demonstrated convincingly the veracity of a literary approach to the biblical text.

---

149. Brueggemann, *Theology of the Old Testament*, 66.

150. My reading is not colored by a priori ontological assumptions about God's character deriving from classical systematic theology. The primary operative assumption undergirding this study is that the God of the biblical text is the God with whom one must struggle. Humphreys (*The Character of God in the Book of Genesis*, 20) offers a helpful discussion of this posture of reading that illuminates the present study:

> I will seek to set aside from now both claims by historians of religion about the God(s) of ancient Israel and early Judaism and particular and fundamental claims about God from theologians and members of religious communities who assert an identity between God in Genesis and the God who commands their worship and allegiance. This too is, I recognize, a condition I can but approach, but again the effort will prove of interest.

151. Walter Brueggemann (*An Unsettling God: The Heart of the Hebrew Bible* [Minneapolis: Fortress, 2009] 2–5) argues that God in the Hebrew Bible is an unsettled, "flesh and bones" character who is personal and relational, two traits that are indelibly tied up with the biblical notion of covenant.

His work has also been generative for a great many other literary critics.[152] These works will contribute to and inform the subsequent chapters on matters of ambiguity/gaps, type scenes, narration and dialogue, story patterning, among other literary features germane to matters of meaning. This trajectory on how the text means is often absent in scholarly discussions on the Jacob cycle, yet it contributes a great deal to the exegetical task. Insights of this sort serve as a vital vector of meaning and will highlight new interpretive possibilities.

Adele Berlin in her *Poetics and Interpretation of Biblical Narrative* describes this dual hermeneutical posture in terms of poetics (how a text means) and interpretation (what a text means). The two exist, she maintains, in "a symbiotic relationship" with one another.[153] Poetics may inform interpretation, but interpretation may likewise inform poetics. Used independently of one another, they become "useless"; they cannot be practiced in isolation from one another.[154] She advocates a posture of approaching poetics that grounds itself in a close literary reading of the biblical text, with special attention paid to patterns, recurrent and unusual literary devices, and linguistic structures.[155] Emphasis for her lies not on the meaning of the various literary devices that one discerns but on their "function" in contributing to and elucidating textual meaning.[156] Berlin's methodological assumptions outlined here provide a helpful orientation to the task undertaken in the following chapters and are shared by this study.

Two additional points become important to this study, as an honest theological engagement with Israel's Scriptures. First, we must regard the Jacob cycle as highly theological. Von Rad has noted the complexity and difficulty in isolating "theological content" from the ancestral history, leading him to ask whether the entirety of the ancestral narratives was ever the object of theological interpretation.[157] The difficulty is amplified in the Jacob cycle, which von Rad describes as a "jungle of unedifying manifestations of human nature" in which God is often lost.[158] I have already shown, however, that the Jacob cycle is just as much a text about God as about Jacob. God's purposes and activity cannot be limited to the moments of theophany, which are quite revelatory in their own right and without

---

152. Robert Alter, *The Art of Biblical Narrative* (New York: Basic Books, 1981); Meir Sternberg, *The Poetics of Biblical Narrative: Ideological Literature and the Drama of Reading* (Bloomington: Indiana University Press, 1985); Shimon Bar-Efrat, *Narrative Art in the Bible* (JSOTSup 70; Sheffield: Almond, 1989); Adele Berlin, *Poetics and the Interpretation of Biblical Narrative* (Bible and Literature Series 9; Sheffield: Almond, 1983; repr. Winona Lake, IN: Eisenbrauns, 1994).

153. Ibid., 16.
154. Ibid., 16–17.
155. Ibid., 19.
156. Ibid.
157. Von Rad, *Old Testament Theology*, 1.165.
158. Ibid., 1.171.

fail disclose God's activity behind the scenes; however, they must also be discerned within the actions and interactions of the text's human characters. This point will become clearer as the study ensues. Second, an honest engagement cannot resort to apologetics or attempt to exclude problematic images such as a deceptive God from the discussion. A brief example helps to illustrate my point.

Eric Seibert's recent contribution, *Disturbing Divine Behavior*, contends that one must distinguish between the "textual God" and the "actual God."[159] He proposes a Christocentric hermeneutic to adjudicate between the two, arguing that Old Testament images of God conforming to the God revealed in Jesus—a God of nonviolence and love who is kind to the wicked and does not punish with disasters or physical infirmities—represent reliable images of the divine character, while the images that do not conform are to be rejected.[160] Seibert labels these dissident portraits "a distortion of God's true character" and "unworthy of God."[161] Readers of these problematic texts are encouraged to affirm without equivocation, "This is not God."[162]

Seibert's hermeneutic is unconvincing for many reasons, not least of which is that it empties these portraits of God of any theological profundity or significance, relegating them merely to the status of antiquated musings of ancient Israel. To be fair, Seibert does caution against an easy dismissal of texts with disturbing divine behavior, stating that one must strive to be a "discerning reader" who can "salvage" from the texts some basic theological tenets about God.[163] Unfortunately, because these offensive aspects of God have been deemed unreliable from Seibert's perspective, they are not worthy of being mined for any theological insight and thus do not figure in his theological analysis. They are rendered problematic and eliminated from theological consideration for this reason.[164] But the question persists: is it possible that disturbing divine behavior communicates something of theological import? Simply because Seibert holds that these texts are not

---

159. Eric A. Seibert, *Disturbing Divine Behavior: Troubling Old Testament Images of God* (Minneapolis: Fortress, 2009) 170–73.

160. Ibid., 185–87, 190–203.

161. Ibid., 216.

162. Ibid., 205, 210.

163. Ibid., 213.

164. I hesitate to label Seibert's reading neo-Marcionite, though to be fair this is a critique he faces head-on. Seibert (ibid., 211–12) avows that Marcion advocated a wholesale rejection of the Old Testament, while he himself has "proposed an interpretive approach that can help us evaluate the appropriateness of various portrayals of God in the Old Testament." However, Seibert's almost incessant use of the word *reject* as it relates to problematic portraits of God seems to push in another direction. I understand the distinction that he attempts to draw, though I continue to be unconvinced that this hermeneutic is the most honest or fruitful way of handling the matter. For a fuller articulation of Seibert's argument and my evaluation of it, see my review of *Disturbing Divine Behavior* published in *RBL* (2011).

reflective of the "actual God" (a point I am not convinced he proves) does not mean they do not carry any theological freight. Put simply, Seibert ignores any possibility that one may glean anything of theological value about God from disturbing divine behavior. To the contrary, I intend to show that a theological examination of a particular disturbing divine behavior, divine deception, reveals a great deal about God.[165]

The claim Seibert makes that "*some* Old Testament portrayals of God do not accurately reflect God's character" is further misleading.[166] It highlights the a priori assumption that one can exegetically discern who God is and who God is not. Borrowing from John Rogerson's most recent Old Testament theology, I maintain that Seibert's posture and method of reading

> impl[y] that there is only one genuine type of experience or knowledge of God. . . . It is a way of reading the Old Testament from the perspective of a type of orthodoxy that privileges certain strands of religious experience. This brings with it the danger that the theological witness of the Old Testament becomes restricted and diminished, because those who approach it in this way know in advance what it says, or ought to say, about God. The view taken in the present work is that the Old Testament speaks with many voices and that readers will do well to listen to them rather than decide in advance which are the most congenial.[167]

Undergirding Seibert's study are two weighty "assumptions": first, that Jesus most fully reveals God's moral character, and second, that God is a consistent character within the biblical text.[168] The first of these, as I have already hinted, runs the risk of supersessionism, while the second makes

---

165. A similar point is made by Gordon J. Wenham on the topic of Old Testament ethics. In his discussion of the implied author in biblical narrative, Wenham writes:

> When someone speaks or writes, he projects an image of himself and his attitudes that may differ considerably from what he is like in real life. . . . In dealing with biblical texts we are always dealing with the implied author not the real author, because all our knowledge of the author and his mind is derived from the texts themselves. We have no way of independently assessing whether the real Amos matched the Amos implied by the text of his prophecy. However *the inaccessibility of the real authors to readers of the Bible is no obstacle to discussing its ethics, for it is precisely the norms and values embodied in the texts that we are trying to elucidate.* (italics mine)

I suggest that Wenham's final sentence is most applicable here as a response to Seibert; it could just as well read "the inaccessibility of *the real God* to readers of the Bible is no obstacle to discussing its *theology*, for it is precisely the *theology* in the texts that we are trying to elucidate." See Gordon J. Wenham, *Story as Torah: Reading Old Testament Narrative Ethically* (Grand Rapids, MI: Baker Academic, 2004) 8–9.

166. Seibert, *Disturbing Divine Behavior*, 211 (italics his).

167. John W. Rogerson, *A Theology of the Old Testament: Cultural Memory, Communication, and Being Human* (Minneapolis: Fortress, 2010) 54. Rogerson is not referencing Seibert's work but, rather, a certain narrow way of reading Qoheleth; I feel that the quotation, however, is entirely applicable and boldly proclaims what I myself aim to do (and not to do) in this book.

168. Seibert, *Disturbing Divine Behavior*, 185–86.

a statement about God that cannot withstand even a facile reading of the Bible. The approach taken here, conversely, remains that the God of the text is the God readers must engage first and foremost. To jettison a particular image simply because it is unsavory or in tension with another more palatable image fails to take seriously the full and multifaceted witness of the biblical text. It is, as Collins has wisely admonished against, little more than lying for God.

One final caution is also especially pertinent at the outset of this investigation. In its original context, the Jacob cycle is *not* a narrative ultimately concerned with matters of ethics.[169] One should thus be cautious about importing contemporary sensibilities pertaining to ethics and morality back into these ancient texts, presuming that they must conform to one's own way of adjudicating what is and is not moral.[170] The ubiquity of deception in Genesis, the ancient Near East, and the Hebrew Bible reveals that it was a prevalent motif in that cultural milieu and was often not to be regarded negatively.[171] A number of commentators agree, among them

---

169. I do not intend to imply that these texts have nothing to contribute to discussions of this sort but only that there does not appear to be any moral commentary running throughout them. Gleaning ethical or moral truths from the Jacob cycle is not the goal of this book. For those interested in the issue of ethics in relation to Genesis, see Wenham, *Story as Torah*, esp. pp. 73–119. Here Wenham discusses ethics in relation to specific scenes in Genesis and identifies a number of character virtues that define the ethical person in the book of Genesis. My readings of particular texts in subsequent chapters will disagree with several of Wenham's conclusions, though he remains a helpful voice and conversation partner on this oft-ignored subject. His insistence also that Old Testament ethics is best subsumed under the rubric *imitatio Dei* is most revealing, given that I will look at Jacob as a trickster, just as God is also a trickster. On the topic of ethics and Genesis, see also Harry Lesser ("'It's Difficult to Understand': Dealing with Morally Difficult Passages in the Hebrew Bible," in *Jewish Ways of Reading the Bible* [ed. George J. Brooke; JSSSup 11; Oxford: Oxford University Press, 2000] 292–302) and most recently Richard S. Briggs (*The Virtuous Reader: Old Testament Narrative and Interpretive Virtue* [Studies in Theological Interpretation; Grand Rapids, MI: Baker Academic, 2010] 17–44, 193–212) for a discussion of the *ethical* dynamics of interaction between text and reader. While I disagree with the sentiment that a contemporary reader must deem these texts unethical, Lesser and Briggs bring up an aspect of the reading process that may prove helpful for some individuals.

170. Briggs (ibid., 203) rightly situates this difficulty with the *reader*, not with the text: "Furthermore, most biblical texts speak for some persons and against others, and often the social/political/ecclesial location of the reader is one key to whether a text is experienced as having a life-giving role or as profoundly challenging and unsettling."

171. Contra Sarna, *Genesis*, 397–98. Buttressing this point, Hartmut Gese ("Jakob, der Betruger," in *Meilenstein: Festgabe für Herbert Donner zum 16. Februar 1995* [ed. M. Weippert and S. Timm; Wiesbaden: Harrassowitz, 1995] 43) traces the narrative traditions of Jacob the deceiver as they have been received elsewhere in the canon. He cites Hos 12, Jer 9, and Mal 3 as containing no reference to Jacob's deception but only to his struggle for the right of the firstborn and blessing. Only in Isa 43:27, with its notion of all Israel standing in line behind a sinful ancestor, may one discern an implicit condemnation. Gese concludes that the already theologically loaded "Jacob as deceiver" has undergone a theological deepening (*theologischer Vertiefung*) in the prophetic corpus and the easy equation of "Jacob" with "deceiver" is itself alien to the rest of the Hebrew Bible. On this point, see also Childs,

Gunkel, who writes about the deception in Gen 27: "We are meant to be pleased about the cleverness of son and mother."[172] Similarly, O. H. Prouser argues: "Throughout biblical narrative, deception is considered a legitimate tool for less powerful people to use in order to succeed. In addition to not being punished for their actions, tricksters are often rewarded and applauded for their cleverness."[173] Deception was an ability that was often highly prized and even in the biblical text does not always receive a negative evaluation.[174] One must first analyze biblical divine deception on its own terms, with an eye toward its historical anchoring, and take seriously how the *narrative* reports it.

The Ancestral Promise in Genesis

Given that the ancestral promise is a key component in my overall argument in that it serves as the motivation for Yʜwʜ's role in Jacob's deceptions, it is necessary and helpful here to provide a brief overview of the way that one should understand the ancestral promise in Genesis.

The central theme and organizing principle throughout the ancestral narratives is the protection and passing on of the promise given to Abraham in Gen 12:1–3.[175] Here, Yʜwʜ delivers a threefold promise to Abraham: land, descendants, and blessing for all the nations of the earth through Abraham and his family. As the narrative progresses, one can easily discern the promise's trajectory: first it is given to Abraham in 12:1–3, then to Isaac in 26:2–5, and then to Jacob in 28:13–15.[176] Each time the promise is handed on to the next generation, the same tripartite formula—land,

---

Old Testament Theology in a Canonical Context, 212–21, where he maintains that the wider canon shows little concern for the immorality of the ancestors and instead tethers them to God's faithfulness to the promise.

172. Gunkel, *Genesis*, 310. See also John Skinner, *A Critical and Exegetical Commentary on Genesis* (ICC 1; Edinburgh: T. & T. Clark, 1930) 249; Bruce Vawter, *On Genesis: A New Reading* (New York: Doubleday, 1977) 181–82; Harry S. Pappas, "Deception as Patriarchal Self-Defense in a Foreign Land: A Form Critical Study of the Wife-Sister Stories in Genesis," *GOTR* 29 (1984) 35–50; Matthews and Mims, "Jacob the Trickster," 195.

173. O. H. Prouser, "The Truth about Women and Lying," *JSOT* 61 (1994) 16.

174. Williams (*Deception in Genesis*, 221) defines the events in Genesis to which he believes the narrator has ascribed a positive evaluation and those to which the narrator has given a negative evaluation. While I would quibble with some of his classifications, his point that biblical deception is not unequivocally negative stands. Wenham (*Story as Torah*, 1–2, 14) notes the complexity and difficulty inherent in identifying the ethical outlook of a given text; in some instances, the narrative offers no obvious moral judgments about a character's activities and how they should be viewed.

175. The promise is so pervasive that David J. A. Clines identifies its partial (non-)fulfillment as the theme uniting the Pentateuch into a cogent literary whole. See his *Theme of the Pentateuch* (JSOTSup 10; 2nd ed.; Sheffield: Sheffield Academic, 1997), esp. pp. 30–65.

176. George G. Nicol ("Story Patterning in Genesis," in *Text as Pretext: Essays in Honour of Robert Davidson* [ed. Robert P. Carroll; JSOTSup 138; Sheffield: JSOT Press, 1992] 219–22) understands the promise and its various repetitions as a mode of establishing textual continuity in Genesis.

descendants, blessing—is reiterated. It is also imperative that one recognize that, each time the promise is passed on, it is always at God's own behest and initiative.

With the patriarch Jacob, however, the usual pattern of one descendant alone receiving the promise breaks down. Prior to Jacob, as Christopher Heard aptly puts it, there has been a narrowing of the family tree in accord with God's purposes: Lot, Ishmael, and Esau respectively have become the "diselect," cut off from Yhwh's covenant with Abraham's family.[177] But now Yhwh grants Jacob not one child of the promise but, ultimately, 12 children of the promise, none of whom is "diselect." The significance of this shift is that God now begins to set the stage for the actualizing of the ancestral promise. From Jacob's children arise the entire people Israel. God's prior particularity with the ancestors alone begins to expand to include all nations. With Jacob's children, one observes in Gen 49:28 the democratization of the original blessing to Abraham.[178] Jacob, who becomes the namesake for the entire people Israel in Gen 32:28 (and 35:10!), passes on the promise of the blessing to all his children, who in turn will do the same until all the Israelites are bearers of the promise.

Two aspects of the ancestral promise are especially relevant to the topic at hand. First, the promise is in danger of being unfulfilled at nearly every turn of the narrative. Sarah's barrenness (11:30; 16:1), the wife-sister stories (12; 20; 26), which child is to serve as the appropriate heir (21; 25; 27), Rebekah and Rachel's barrenness (25:21; 30:1–2), Jacob's internment with Laban in Haran (29–31), the conflict between Joseph and his brothers leading to the family settling in Egypt (37–50), and a host of other events threaten the vitality of the promise. In each instance, however, God overcomes the threat, demonstrating his fealty to and unwavering concern for the promise's future. One should remain mindful that God's behavior in regard to the promise in some of these episodes is inexplicable, if not a bit unsettling. For example, in the wife-sister stories, both Abraham and Isaac deceive in the unsuccessful attempts to pass off their wives as sisters. Once the deception is uncovered, however, God intervenes in a way that seems to reward the deceptive behavior, inflicting plagues on Pharaoh in Gen 12 and, more strikingly, ensuring that Abraham leaves Gerar with great wealth at the expense of Abimelech in Gen 20. Similarly, Joseph's words at the close of Genesis (50:20) communicate the idea of retrospective providence, highlighting God's orchestrating of everything from Joseph's slavery to his family's settling in Egypt. Throughout Genesis, God is shown to be protecting the promise by any means necessary. It is within this context that one must interpret the God-Jacob relationship of promise.

---

177. Heard, *Dynamics of Diselection*, 184.
178. Josef Schreiner, "Segen für Völker in der Verheißung an die Väter," *BZ* 6 (1962) 4.

Second, the function of the promise, specifically the notion of "blessing" the other nations of the world in v. 3, highlights the cosmic implications of ancient Israel's task. Genesis 12:1–3 does not mark a new beginning of God's *desires* for creation; it marks a new *strategy* toward this end.[179] The concern for the entirety of creation evident in the Primeval History (Gen 1–11) remains at the fore in the divine initiative. David Petersen convincingly argues that the book of Genesis as a whole regards humanity in familial terms; as such, 12:3 shows that "one part of the human family can act for the benefit of others."[180] For Keith Grüneberg, the ancestral promise and its various iterations elsewhere in Genesis (22:18; 26:4; 28:14) climax with this recognition of being a blessing to the nations.[181]

In Gen 12:3, Yʜᴡʜ states, "[I]n you all families of the earth *will be blessed.*" The thrust of the Niphal נברכו, which I have translated 'be blessed', is central to the interpretive dynamics of this verse. Three possibilities exist. First, the Niphal may be reflexive ('bless themselves'), a perfectly good and common function of this stem. Second, the Niphal may carry a "middle" meaning ('gain/receive blessing'). Third, another frequent function of the stem, the Niphal may be passive ('be blessed').[182] These possible translations result in different ways of regarding Abraham in relation to the nations. The best option is what comports most accurately with the context of the entire promise in vv. 1–3. Grüneberg offers perhaps the most careful assessment of the contextual and grammatical issues involved, arguing compellingly that the reflexive sense misses the fact that this is a promise from God *to Abraham* and not to the nations, while the middle sense is without any linguistic corroboration.[183] A passive sense captures the fact that Yʜᴡʜ directs this word of promise *to Abraham*, who will be the instrument bringing blessing to all.[184] Grüneberg summarizes the relationship among the verses as follows:

> For the divine speech is a promise to Abraham, not a promise to the nations: Yʜᴡʜ asserts that Abraham will be blessed (vv2a–b), indeed signally blessed such that others will notice (vv2c–d), in fact so blessed that this will impact upon others' lives (v3). . . . Moreoover they are precisely promises, not a commission laid upon Abraham/Israel.[185]

---

179. Fretheim, *The Pentateuch*, 85.
180. David L. Petersen, "Genesis and Family Values," *JBL* 124 (2005) 16.
181. Keith N. Grüneberg, *Abraham, Blessing and the Nations: A Philological and Exegetical Study of Genesis 12:3 in Its Narrative Context* (BZAW 332; Berlin: de Gruyter, 2003) 84. See also Paul R. Williamson, *Abraham, Israel, and the Nations: The Patriarchal Promise and Its Covenantal Development in Genesis* (JSOTSup 315; Sheffield: Sheffield Academic Press, 2000).
182. For a more thorough analysis of these three grammatical possibilities, see Grüneberg, *Abraham, Blessing and the Nations*, 176–189.
183. Ibid., 178–180, see also pp. 65–66.
184. Ibid., 187.
185. Ibid., 244.

In a similar vein, R. W. L. Moberly has argued quite recently that the customary Christian appropriation of Gen 12:3 in support of universal salvation is wanting.[186] Recognizing the divine word as a promise to Abraham is essential for a proper understanding of the ancestral promise and its function in Genesis.

In emphasizing the ancestral promise as a divine word for Abraham, one must not lose sight of the universal implications in the deity's speech. But how can these two ideas—promise to Abraham with blessing for the nations—be held together? The answer is that the blessing in v. 3b is conditional. Immediately prior, Yнwн says, "I will bless those who bless you, and those who curse you I will curse." Patrick Miller has insightfully argued that the syntax of these verses informs their theology. The verb translated 'I will curse' (אאר) functions disjunctively in that it is not cohortative with a prefixed *waw* as are the other verbs in the sentence.[187] This grammatical disjunction succeeds in separating the intent to curse from the divine purpose in the world.[188] The curse instead operates as a mode of protection for Abraham and his family. It is a part of the blessing for Abraham and not indicative that Yнwн wills for Abraham to be an instrument of cursing just as he is an instrument of blessing.[189] Whether a given person or nation receives blessing or cursing is contingent upon whether they are a blessing or curse to Abraham's family.[190] Nations will receive in accordance with their treatment of Israel.

Grüneberg, Moberly, and Miller present an understanding of the ancestral promise with which this study is in favor: rather than reading the promise from the perspective of the people who receive blessing from Israel, one should imagine the promise *also* and *primarily* from the perspective of Abraham and his family. Read as such, the ancestral promise stands as a benefit to Abraham and his family, providing reassurance and hope for this particular people, whom Yнwн will bless and by whom others will be blessed.[191] Israel is not merely a prop through which Yнwн blesses the entire world; supporting the first point above, Israel itself is the object of divine blessing.

The ancestral promise is both cosmic and selective. God, as will be evident in the treatment in the chapters that follow, steadfastly accompanies and protects Jacob (Israel), the child of the promise, at every turn. At the

---

186. R. W. L. Moberly, *The Theology of the Book of Genesis* (Old Testament Theology; Cambridge: Cambridge University Press, 2009) 142–48.

187. Patrick D. Miller, Jr., "Syntax and Theology in Genesis XII 3a," *VT* 34 (1984) 473.

188. Ibid., 473–74.

189. Ibid., 474. Miller thus translates v. 3a as follows: "and that I may bless the ones blessing you—and should there be one who regards you with contempt I will curse him.

190. On this point, see my "Jacob, Laban, and a Divine Trickster: The Covenantal Framework of God's Deception in the Theology of the Jacob Cycle," *PRSt* 36 (2009) 13 n. 39; Grüneberg, *Abraham, Blessing and the Nations*, 171–85, 242–43.

191. Moberly, *The Theology of the Book of Genesis*, 148–50.

same time, Brueggemann rightly cautions against an elitist reading of Gen 12–36 that relegates Ishmael and Esau to the margins; here the special-ness of Israel is set alongside the people outside the bounds of the *ancestral* promise.[192] These characters, however, are afforded a certain level of narra-tive space in relation to the elected child. As symbolic of the nations Am-mon, Moab, and Edom, they are concurrently "incidental" to Israel's life of promise and an inescapable part of its destiny.[193] I have already shown in the discussion of the ancestral promise that Abraham's election is not to the detriment or exclusion of others unless they are an impediment to Is-rael. The either/or categories of elect and non-elect are thus superficial and inaccurate. It is better to speak, as does Joel Kaminsky, with the expanded categories of the elect, the non-elect, and the anti-elect.[194] People who are non-elect are not necessarily de facto anti-elect. At its most basic, the an-cestral promise is for the benefit of Abraham and his family, but it is not exclusionary of the rest of the created order as long as the individuals or nations do not become a stumbling block for Israel. In short, the universal-ity of Israel—here evident in the election of Abraham's family as bearers of the promise—lies exclusively in Jewish particularity.

Definitions

There exists a wealth of scholarly treatments on "the trickster" in an-thropological, folkloric, and historical literature. One may attribute the introduction of the term itself within scholarship to Daniel Brinton, who seems to have been the first to use it in the mid-nineteenth century in reference to North American Indian mythology.[195] Since Brinton, the term appears to have taken on a life of its own, being variously interpreted by scholars who have failed to wrestle with the trickster's inherent ambigu-ity.[196] Many attempts have been made at universal understandings of the trickster. The definition provided by Cristiano Grottanelli serves as a good example:

> Tricksters are breakers of rules, but, though they are often tragic in their own specific way, their breaking of rules is always comical. This funny

192. Brueggemann, *An Unsettling God*, 105.

193. Brueggemann (ibid., 106) notes the paradox: the nations are an "*impediment* to be eliminated, according to Yhwh's will" and "to be *blessed* and enhanced, according to Yhwh's mandate." On the topic of election and non-election from Christian and Jewish viewpoints, see most recently Joel N. Lohr (*Chosen and Unchosen: Conceptions of Election in the Pentateuch and Jewish-Christian Interpretation* [Siphrut: Literature and Theology of the Hebrew Scriptures 2; Winona Lake, IN: Eisenbrauns, 2009]), who argues that the unchosen still occupy a place in the economy of God's larger desires and intentions for the world.

194. Kaminsky, *Yet I Loved Jacob*, 111–36.

195. Daniel Brinton, *The Myths of the New World* (Philadelphia: McKay, 1868) 161–62. For a fine history of research on the term, see Pelton, *The Trickster in West Africa*, 5–10; or more recently Nicholas, *The Trickster Revisited*, 8–16, esp. pp. 13–15.

196. Pelton, *The Trickster in West Africa*, 7.

irregularity is the central quality of the trickster; and what makes the anomie comical is the trickster's lowliness. When he is an animal, the trickster is a crafty, rather than a powerful, beast . . . when a human being, he never ranks high, and his power lies in his witty brain or in some strange gift of nature. So a working definition of the trickster could be: 'a breaker of rules who is funny because he is lowly.'[197]

This definition presents the trickster as a wholly static figure from one culture to another. Such a view, however, is laden with problems.

Naomi Steinberg, in looking at various cross-cultural representations of the trickster in comparison with biblical tricksters, challenges the notion that the trickster is a monolithic entity. She argues that scholars have begun a transition away from noting the similarities among tricksters toward emphasizing what is unique about tricksters from diverse cultures.[198] As a result, these universal definitions are ultimately not only unhelpful but also misleading; the trickster figure is, fitting to its name, sundry and elusive.[199] One thus cannot assume that the trickster is portrayed in the same way in diverse cultures and texts. Likewise, William J. Hynes and William G. Doty raise this concern in their formative edited volume on the trickster.[200] In their introductory essay, "Introducing the Fascinating and Perplexing Trickster Figure," they write:

> The diversity and complexity of the appearances of the trickster figure raise doubt that it can be encompassed as a single phenomenon. Perhaps just such diversity and complexity help explain why three decades have lapsed since the first comprehensive portrait of the trickster appeared, in Paul Radin's *The Trickster* (1955). The number of studies of individual tricksters has grown, and the range of trickster phenomena is now such that many scholars argue against a generalizing, comparativist view.[201]

While Hynes and Doty go on to argue a sort of middle ground between the trickster as universal figure and the trickster as culturally specific (a reading that in my estimation still assumes too much cross-cultural continuity), their comments about the recent trend of trickster scholarship informs this work in a most important way. In this book, therefore, I will intentionally not focus on cross-cultural parallels with the biblical text. Rather, heeding Steinberg's admonition, I will base this investigation solely on the biblical

---

197. Cristiano Grottanelli, "Tricksters, Scapegoats, Champions, Saviors," *History of Religion* 23 (1983) 120.
198. Naomi Steinberg, "Israelite Tricksters, Their Analogues and Cross-Cultural Study," *Semeia* 42 (1988) 4.
199. Ibid., 4. 6, 10. Steinberg advocates "abandoning not only 'trickster' as a technical term but also broad questions of cross-cultural functions of this character" (p. 10).
200. See William J. Hynes and William G. Doty, eds., *Mythical Trickster Figures: Contours, Contexts, and Criticisms* (Tuscaloosa: University of Alabama Press, 1993).
201. Idem, "Introducing the Fascinating and Perplexing Trickster Figure," in ibid., 2.

text in order to produce a truly biblical—more specifically, Genesis—understanding of the divine trickster.

With this difficulty in mind, Susan Niditch offers a helpful introductory definition of the term *trickster*. Niditch's analysis of the term is informed by folkloric parallels but also, most importantly, by the biblical text. The breadth and depth of her study presents a sound definition from which I will work. She defines *trickster* as, at base, one who "brings about a change in a situation via trickery."[202] I have chosen to operate on this very basic— albeit well-attested—definition of the trickster as a way to begin to enter into the study of this thorny question. This definition in its utter simplicity also jettisons any claims at universal or absolute authority. Niditch's definition is broad enough for this prolegomenon and in its capacity to serve as a foundation upon which to build, yet specific enough (in conjunction with the definition of *trickery* or *deception* offered below) in that it dictates certain parameters for what constitutes the *trickster*. Subsequent studies may indeed reveal a specific listing of criteria for what is here identified as the divine trickster.

One may rightfully then wonder what is meant by *trickery* or *deception*. Given that it is a loaded word that carries for many contemporary readers a great deal of negative baggage, it is important also to define it here. *Trickery* or *deception* (which will be used synonymously throughout, as is often the scholarly convention) is what a trickster employs through any of various means of distorting, withholding, or manipulating information in order to serve or advance the trickster's own purposes and goals.[203] A vital component of this definition lies in the motive for the deception's being tied up with the trickster's ultimate goals. In this way, one can begin to see how

---

202. Niditch, *A Prelude to Biblical Folklore*, xv. Niditch further clarifies the trickster's character as that of "deceiver, creator, acculturator, unmasked liar, survivor" (p. 45), yet I hesitate—in line with Steinberg—to claim any sort of universality for this definition. Rather, it may be helpful to realize that, given the fact that Niditch's approach takes folklore into account, it is in a way quite similar methodologically to Gunkel's form criticism (which she notes), and one would thus be incorrect to aver that every aspect of the definition of a trickster must be manifest in every situation.

203. My definition is a streamlined version of what Williams (*Deception in Genesis*, 3) presents. Williams's definition reads: "Deception takes place when an agent intentionally distorts, withholds, or otherwise manipulates information reaching some person(s) in order to stimulate in the person(s) a belief that the agent does not believe in order to serve the agent's purposes." I have intentionally omitted the requirement that the trickster need not believe that what he or she is presenting is fact. This issue of what is and is not true reality is a complicated matter, especially in Gen 25–27 (for instance, is Jacob technically the firstborn by the very fact that he obtains the right of the firstborn in 25:29–34, and thus becomes the rightful recipient of the blessing in chap. 27?). It appears quite clear that Rebekah (and Jacob?) believe very deeply that God has ordained Jacob as the true firstborn and recipient of the blessing. Moreover, matters of belief run the risk of delving too deeply into a psychologizing of the biblical characters and often goes well beyond the bounds of what the biblical narrative makes known.

Y<small>HWH</small>'s role in Jacob's deceptions deals with the unfailing divine concern for the perpetuation of the ancestral promise.

A Brief Overview of the Book

This foray into divine deception in the Jacob cycle consists of five chapters. Chapter 1, this introduction, serves as an overall orientation to and necessary background for the central question of divine deception in the Jacob cycle and its related theological import. Chapter 2, "A Trickster Oracle: Reading Jacob and Esau between *Beten* and Bethel," treats Gen 25–28. Special emphasis will be placed on the fact that the divine oracle in 25:23—described as a "trickster oracle"—affects how one reads the chapters that follow, both bringing about and informing the subsequent scenes of deception (25:27–34; 27:1–45). This novel reading gives new import to the Bethel scene in Gen 28, seeing it as divine corroboration of the prior deceptions. In chap. 3, "Divine Deception and the Incipient Fulfillment of the Ancestral Promise," I devote attention to Jacob's prolonged stay with Laban in Gen 29–31. Here I address not only the incipient fulfillment of the ancestral promise evident in the birth of 12 children (29:31–30:24) and Laban's recognition that Y<small>HWH</small> has blessed him through Jacob's presence (30:27), but also the fact that this fulfillment is being carried out by means of deception. Emphasis is also placed on perhaps the most potent divine deception in the Jacob cycle in Gen 30–31 and its relation to the promise.

In chap. 4, "Replaying the Fool: Esau versus Y<small>HWH</small> and Jacob," I consider Gen 32–35, focusing on the fact that Jacob continues in his deceptive ways, even in the reconciliation scene with Esau. I read Jacob's encounter with his besmirched brother as a scene rife with deception, much akin to Jacob's first deception of Esau in Gen 25:27–34. Esau again plays the fool on a variety of levels: his acceptance of Jacob's ambiguous offer of the blessing (33:11; cf. 32:29) and his separation from Jacob by means of the latter's trickery (33:15–20). God again is deeply connected with these deceptions, both in the wrestling match with Jacob in Gen 32 and in the appearance in Gen 35, on the heels of a deadly act of deception. Chapter 5 serves as a conclusion to the entire work. Most of this section addresses the theological implications deriving from this reading and how one may reconcile the Hebrew Bible's dual witness to Y<small>HWH</small>'s trustworthiness and deception. I conclude with prospects for future study.

Chapter 2

A Trickster Oracle:
Reading Jacob and Esau between
Beten and Bethel (Genesis 25–28)

Introductory Remarks

The traditional interpretation of this opening block of Jacob and Esau stories sees the human actors in a less than flattering light. Jacob cons his brother Esau out of the right of the firstborn, and he and Rebekah cruelly deceive the aged, blind Isaac out of his paternal blessing. S. R. Driver offers the following moral commentary: "That the action of Rebekah and Jacob was utterly discreditable and indefensible is of course obvious."[1] This sort of reading is highly *anthrocentric*, focusing solely on the human characters and their engagements with one another.[2] The deceptions are human deceptions; the conflict is human conflict. These characters are self-motivated, self-interested, and above all disreputable, given their less than sterling motives and activities. Most striking perhaps is the implication that God has no involvement in and bears no responsibility for these unscrupulous acts. In chap. 1, I surveyed several scholars who hold similar views. Moreover, traditional interpretations seldom discuss the ancestral promise. Yhwh's oracle in Gen 25:23 receives little attention beyond forecasting what will happen. And, correspondingly, there is no mention of God beyond the utterance of this oracle.

More recently, commentators have begun to wonder at the tension that appears latent in the text: does deception fulfill the divine oracle in 25:23? Gordon Wenham has raised this question but does not answer it head on. He writes that these narratives do in fact say something about God, but it is God's unfailing mercy that receives notice and not how a history governed by God can unproblematically include deceptions as a method of fulfilling the divine plan.[3] Additionally, Wenham's statement comes in a very short paragraph at the end of his section on Gen 26:34–28:9. One searches

---

1. S. R. Driver, *The Book of Genesis* (Westminster Commentaries; London: Methuen, 1915) 255.

2. Gerhard von Rad (*Old Testament Theology* [2 vols.; trans. D. M. G. Stalker; New York: Harper & Row, 1962–65] 1, 171) describes these texts as "much less spiritual" than the earlier Abraham narratives.

3. Gordon J. Wenham, *Genesis 16–50* (WBC 2; Dallas: Word, 1994) 216.

48

almost in vain to find any mention of God elsewhere in this discussion. Despite asking the question, his commentary remains relegated to a focus on the human characters. The near dearth of space devoted to discussing God here is most salient.

Most recently, Yair Zakovitch has argued for the presence of two tensive forces at work in Gen 27 within the context of the larger Jacob cycle: the desire to justify Jacob and his behavior and the push to condemn Jacob and his activities.[4] Examples of methods to vindicate Jacob involve shifting responsibility and blame to either Rebekah or Isaac, discrediting Esau for his loathsome foreign wives and the spurning of his birthright, the blatant affirmation of Jacob's innocence (25:27 תם), and Rebekah's receipt of the oracle in 25:23, among others; conversely, Jacob is vilified by means of his falling prey to deceptions perpetrated by both Laban and his own sons, respectively (29:21–27; 37:31–33), which echo Jacob's own deceptive activities.[5] This central theological issue raised by the text, between Jacob the just and Jacob the cheat, opens up the possibility of appreciating another related tensive force that is truly theological in nature: the place of God in and among these deceptions.

These traditional interpretations ignore the potential for a *theocentric* reading of the opening chapters, indeed of the entire Jacob cycle. Upon further investigation, we find that Gen 25–28 addresses a much larger complex of ideas and themes that pervade Genesis: primarily, God's ancestral promise and God's vested interest in creation. God has broken into history yet again, choosing this particular family to serve as a blessing to all humanity.[6] Rebekah's troubling pregnancy coupled with the emergent conflict that comes to typify the chosen family's relationships serve as a threat to the vitality and viability of attaining this goal. The ancestral promise, therefore, retains a preeminent place in the story of Jacob and his family. Moreover, this first block of the narrative is bookended by theophanies that occur in Gen 25:23 and 28:10–22, respectively. In Gen 25:23, God offers his pronouncement on the fate of Rebekah and Isaac's still-unborn twins, and in Gen 28:10–22, this pronouncement comes to fruition with Jacob receiving—at God's behest—the ancestral promise. These two theophanies

---

4. Yair Zakovitch, "Inner-Biblical Interpretation," in *Reading Genesis: Ten Methods* (ed. R. Hendel; Cambridge: Cambridge University Press, 2010) 100.

5. Ibid., 102–16.

6. I am in agreement with Gerhard von Rad (*Genesis* [OTL; rev. ed.; trans. J. H. Marks; Philadelphia: Westminster, 1973] 153–55) that Gen 12:1–3 serves as the mitigation for the Tower of Babel scene in Gen 11, which seems to end on a note of judgment. I am less confident than von Rad, though, in ascribing the authorship of these three verses to J. This equivocation, however, is of little ultimate consequence, for in the final form of the text Gen 12:1–3 serves as a hinge connecting the primeval history and ancestral narratives. On the relationship between the two from the perspective of promise, see Carol M. Kaminski, *From Noah to Israel: Realization of the Primaeval Blessing after the Flood* (JSOTSup 413; London: T. & T. Clark, 2004), esp. pp. 92–123.

enclose and thus may inform one's reading of the intervening events. God is not a disinterested bystander or someone who withdraws and spasmodically appears when it is convenient for his characterization (that is, when there are no deceptions occurring) but is a figure deeply woven into the fabric of the story. The question then naturally presents itself: what characterization of God emerges when read in tandem with these scenes of deception? What if these very deceptions from which conventional readings of Gen 25–28 have apologetically sought to distance themselves not only fulfill but also are brought about by the divine purpose?

I contend that the divine oracle in Gen 25:23 announcing God's preference for Jacob over Esau serves as the hermeneutical key to comprehending the larger Jacob cycle. The traditional rendering of this oracle, however— the final line, specifically—as 'the older will serve the younger' presumes a greater level of lucid transparency than a close scrutiny of the Hebrew text will allow. Upon further analysis, one should instead render the line 'the greater will serve the lesser', attempting to preserve, though still not capturing entirely, the ambiguity evident in the Hebrew. Through the oracle's ambiguity on matters of syntax, meaning, and identity of the characters, most importantly the greater (רב) and lesser (צעיר), Yhwh withholds the vital information necessary to understand his desire that the firstborn, Esau, will not be preeminent but, rather, the secondborn, Jacob, will become the 'greater' (רב). At the narrative level, the oracle needs interpreting. This oracle, therefore, may be read as an example of Yhwh as trickster; accordingly, this initial divine word in Jacob's life may be described as a "trickster oracle."

The trickster oracle also results in subsequent deceptions. It impels the narrative's human actors to set in motion the deceptive means by which the divine wish comes to fruition. One sees this corollary in Jacob's shrewd manipulation of Esau so as to gain the right of the firstborn (25:27–34) and Jacob's deceptive obtaining of his father's blessing with Rebekah's (and God's) help (27:1–45). God is involved in Jacob and Rebekah's deceptions of Esau and Isaac from the very beginning. And it is only at Bethel (28:13–15) that the narrative makes it clear that Rebekah has interpreted the oracle correctly in favor of Jacob. In bringing about this change through deception, God ultimately advances the divine purpose—concern for the perpetuation of the ancestral promise (12:1–3)—which becomes manifest in the character and family of Jacob.

The reason this reading has been missed so often, I believe, lies in the failure to read the oracle in conjunction with the Bethel episode, Gen 28:13–15, more specifically. These two divine speeches, to Rebekah and at Bethel, respectively, form an inclusio around the first block of Jacob/Esau material, and Yhwh's giving of the ancestral promise to Jacob at Bethel can be read as corroborating the successful outcome of the preceding events in chaps. 25–27. God does not appear at Bethel and cast moral judgment on Jacob and Rebekah's shenanigans; God does not appear and castigate, rebuke, or reprimand Jacob. Rather, God confers the ancestral promise on this most wily, and deserving, of patriarchs! When one reads these opening narratives between these two poles—between *beten* ('womb') and Bethel— God's complicity in the deception comes to the fore, all with the divine intent to carry forward the ancestral promise. Bethel is the theological pivot of the Jacob cycle.

My analysis of Gen 25–28 in this chapter will commence in three parts. First, I will devote the bulk of this investigation to treating Gen 25:19–34, placing particular emphasis on the trickster oracle in 25:23, as a way of demonstrating the centrality of the oracle for the entire Jacob cycle and demonstrating how the oracle's ambiguity informs the deceptions that follow. Here I will also discuss the infamous birthright episode, Gen 25:27–34, with the intent of showing that its interpretation is informed by the trickster oracle. Second, this chapter will examine two specific aspects of Gen 27—the breakdown of the family and the presence of God in the deception—in hopes of highlighting both the effects of the trickster oracle and the emerging relationship between two tricksters, Jacob and Yhwh. And last, I will explore the connection between chaps. 27 and 28 as evidencing the divine corroboration with the foregoing deceptions.

A Trickster's Oracle (Genesis 25:19–34)

Vital to understanding any narrative is a thorough analysis of its beginning. It is here that the reader often encounters key ideas or themes that will help to orient and shape the subsequent reading process. The opening verses of the Jacob cycle are no different. Here the reader is introduced to the dual thrust of the narrative: an involved deity and the centrality of and concern for the perpetuation of the ancestral promise. The story of the birth of Jacob and his acquiring the right of the firstborn from Esau foreshadows from the outset what will be a life intimately bound up with God. Indeed, Gen 25:19–34 functions as the interpretive framework against which one must understand later episodes in Jacob's life. If the later deceptions are understood apart from these introductory verses, what results is an unremarkable Jacob who remains the problematic trickster with whom scholarship has struggled so long. However, understood within the context of this opening pericope, the remainder of the Jacob cycle becomes a narrative of strife and deception but also of promise and blessing at God's behest. The narrative contains two scenes.

Setting the Stage: God and the Ancestral Promise (Genesis 25:19–26)

This introductory scene prefigures the theological emphasis on divine promise that will pervade the Jacob cycle. In v. 19, the reader is introduced to the Isaac תולדת, yet almost immediately it becomes clear that what follows will not focus on Isaac.[7] The first occurrence of his name is followed by his being called 'son of Abraham' (בֶּן־אַבְרָהָם), which itself is followed by 'Abraham bore Isaac' (אַבְרָהָם הוֹלִיד אֶת־יִצְחָק). By mentioning Abraham's name twice in uninterrupted succession, the narrative points to the original recipient of the ancestral promise and thereby foreshadows the continuity with the promises to Abraham that will be so central to the story of Jacob. Similarly, this double mention of Abraham functions in a unique way in that Isaac's mother, Sarah, is not named; it is Abraham alone who is said to have borne Isaac.[8] Kenneth Mathews asserts correctly that this construction has the preceding Abraham narratives in mind and is thus concerned less with Isaac as a distinct character and more with Isaac as the individual through whom the promise is both fulfilled and allowed to continue (Gen 21:12).[9] Lieve Teugels also labels Isaac a passive character, especially in light of the active presentation of Rebekah, and sees Isaac's apparent purpose as being solely to transfer the promise to the subsequent generation.[10] So within the very first verse of the Jacob cycle, one can already see that the ancestral promise will play a pivotal role in what follows.

Recalling the Abraham story serves another purpose. The mention of Rebekah's barrenness (עֲקָרָה) hearkens back earlier to Sarah's barrenness in 11:30 and attests to God's desire that the promise continue. Obviously, with the barrenness of his wife, this promise to Abraham is seriously jeopardized. Only through God's direct intervention and opening of the womb does one become aware of God's fidelity to his promises and of the developing kinship between God, Abraham, and his descendants. Again in 25:21, the original promise to Abraham is in danger of not being realized. Isaac as the son of the promise turns to God, much like his father in Gen 15, in hopes that the promise will continue through him. If the line ends at Isaac, then the promise has been nullified; no "great nation" will arise in the genealogy of Abraham. Therefore, God's answering of Isaac's prayer is more than a response to Rebekah's barrenness. It is an assurance that the promise must continue and will continue in the lineage of one of the two sons.[11]

---

7. The *toledot* formula focuses on the next generation, or to put it another way, on the extended family of the patriarch mentioned. So, for example, while it is no surprise that Isaac's *toledot* focuses almost exclusively on his children, Jacob and Esau, the absence of an Abraham *toledot*, which would presumably center on Isaac, is notable.

8. See Gen 25:26, where Rebekah is said to bear the twins Jacob and Esau. This notice contributes to the marginalization of Isaac as a character from the outset.

9. Kenneth A. Mathews, *Genesis 11:27–50:26* (NAC 1B; Nashville: Broadman & Holman, 2005) 384.

10. Lieve Teugels, "A Matriarchal Cycle? The Portrayal of Isaac in Genesis in the Light of the Presentation of Rebekah," *Bijdragen, tijdschrift voor filosofie en theologie* 56 (1995) 61–72, esp. pp. 62–63, 68, 70.

11. Contra John Skinner (*A Critical and Exegetical Commentary on Genesis* [ICC 1; Edinburgh: T. & T. Clark, 1930] 358–59), who maintains that "no miraculous intervention is suggested and our only regret is that this glimpse of everyday family piety is so tantalizingly meagre." To suppose that Isaac's supplication to God achieves nothing miraculous,

These opening verses also succeed in introducing the deep divine concern for the ancestral promise that will typify the Jacob cycle. Verse 21 recounts Isaac's supplication on behalf of Rebekah's barrenness, and immediately the text reports that Yʜwʜ not only hears but responds to and remedies the situation. One mere verse contains barrenness, prayer, response, and conception! Fokkelman helpfully draws a comparison with the nearly unremitting tension of the promised child's birth in the Abraham narratives, citing that the Jacob cycle "spends as little time, narrative time," as possible on the toll that these 20 years (vv. 20, 26) would have exacted from Isaac.[12] That Yʜwʜ grants Isaac's prayer so quickly shows that barrenness is not to be the central issue in this generation.

Instead, it is Rebekah's pregnancy itself that is problematic. The twins 'crushed one another' (יתרצצו) within her (25:22). Compared with previous ancestral birth narratives, the keen reader is aware that something unique and special is occurring with the births of Jacob and Esau, aside from the fact that they will be the first twins born. For example, in 11:26 the birth of Abram is depicted almost in passing. He is merely one of three brothers born to Terah and does not assume a central role until the following chapter, where it is still puzzling why he has been chosen. In the case of Isaac, Ron Hendel astutely notices that "the birth story . . . proceeds at its own leisurely pace, interspersed with other stories and mixed with other themes."[13] By the time Isaac is born in 21:1–3, ten chapters have elapsed, yet there is nothing difficult or remarkable in the birth itself, aside from Yʜwʜ's giving Sarah a son of her own. The birth of Jacob and Esau, however, is different. Their intrauterine struggle presages the life of conflict into which they will enter and also into which their parents will be unwittingly thrust.[14] And similar to Isaac's prayer discussed above, the fact that Rebekah is the only woman in the Hebrew Bible to seek and *find* God with presumably little or no difficulty (the text records in succession that she sought Yʜwʜ, and Yʜwʜ answered) highlights all the more the closeness of this family to God and anticipates Yʜwʜ's activity in the history of the warring twins.

What the Jacob cycle affirms at the very outset, then, is the continued fidelity of Yʜwʜ to the ancestral promise and the expectation that Yʜwʜ will

---

let alone that it has no direct correspondence to the fact that Rebekah ends up pregnant, does not take into account the haste with which v. 21 is narrated.

12. J. P. Fokkelman (*Narrative Art in Genesis: Specimens of Stylistic and Structural Analysis* [Eugene, OR: Wipf & Stock, 1991] 87) only mentions Isaac, though one should not so easily forget or underestimate the impact that this period would also have on the mother of the children, Rebekah!

13. Ron Hendel, *The Epic of the Patriarch: The Jacob Cycle and the Narrative Traditions of Canaan and Israel* (HSM 42; Atlanta: Scholars Press, 1987) 41.

14. Susan Niditch (*A Prelude to Biblical Folklore: Underdogs and Tricksters* [Urbana: University of Illinois Press, 1987] 94–96) sees Jacob and Esau's "unusual birth" as part of the hero pattern (unusual birth, family conflict over status, journeying, marriage and success elsewhere, resolution). See pp. 71–79.

attend to the promise's vitality in the face of any threat. Terence Fretheim, discussing the promise in the traditionally defined "J" material in Genesis, gives potent voice to this reality:

> Time and time again the fate of the promise hangs in the balance, due either to the uncertain response of the Patriarchs themselves or to obstacles thrown up by outsiders. But the primary witness is always to [YHWH] himself and *the extreme lengths to which he will go to work out his promise within the historical process.*[15]

The sheer fact of God's intervention is not to be questioned; precisely *how* God will intervene, though, remains to be seen.

A Trickster Oracle and YHWH's Preference for a Trickster: Genesis 25:23 in Context

God's response in v. 23 shatters any notion that the promise will not be an object of contention in this generation. Cast in poetry, the oracle repeats the word 'two' (שני) twice—once in relation to "nations" and once "peoples"—evoking the well-established pattern in Genesis in which the promise is contested between two sons. The question then naturally becomes: which son does God want to carry the promise forward?

Unfortunately, the divine oracle itself is unreservedly ambiguous in regard to which son is the divine choice. Scholars have indeed discussed the nature of this oracle, though to my knowledge not in any sustained way. Fokkelman describes the oracle as "unambiguous."[16] Conversely, Johannes Taschner calls the oracle ambiguous (*zweideutig*), yet unfortunately, neither Fokkelman nor Taschner expounds on why or how this is the case.[17] Taschner is correct that the oracle is ambiguous, but he draws attention to different reasons. Its poetic movement does not tend toward further clarity but, conversely, ends in ambiguity. Brueggemann describes the oracle this way: "God does not explain or justify. God simply announces."[18] What God announces, however, does not lend itself easily to comprehension. Before turning to the oracle itself, we will find it helpful first to clarify what is meant by ambiguity, what dictates its presence, and how it contributes to literary meaning.

---

15. Terence E. Fretheim, "The Jacob Traditions: Theology and Hermeneutic," *Int* 26 (1972) 422. (italics mine).

16. Fokkelman, *Narrative Art in Genesis*, 89.

17. Johannes Taschner, *Verheissung und Erfüllung in der Jakoberzählung (Gen 25,19–33,17): Eine Analyse ihres Spannungsbogens* (Herders Biblische Studien 27; Freiburg: Herder, 2000) 79.

18. Walter Brueggemann, *Genesis* (Interpretation; Atlanta: John Knox, 1982) 215. I must note, however, that Brueggemann does not view the oracle as ambiguous in the same way that I do here. He is concerned, rather, with the bold fact that God does not find it necessary to clarify or legitimate his rationale for the subversion.

Narrative Reticence, Type Scenes, and Biblical Ambiguity

The most comprehensive treatment of ambiguity in the biblical text belongs to Meir Sternberg in his monumental volume *The Poetics of Biblical Narrative*. Sternberg's discussion is highly detailed, and I cannot hope to capture all its complexity here, though I will emphasize matters germane and informative to the present discussion.

Sternberg writes of "gaps," which he defines as "a lack of information about the world—an event, motive, causal link, character trait, plot structure, law of probability—contrived by a temporal displacement."[19] One may notice already a close resonance with the definition of deception offered in the previous chapter. Sternberg continues: "The storyteller's withholding of information opens gaps, gaps produce discontinuity, and discontinuity breeds ambiguity."[20] In the case of Gen 25:23, I will show that it is God who withholds this information. Vital to Sternberg's understanding of ambiguity is his recognition of both temporary and permanent gaps: temporary gaps are eventually resolved by the narrative, whereas permanent gaps are not.[21] As should become clear in the discussion that ensues, the ambiguity in the trickster oracle is temporary; the narrative maintains the tension but slowly unpacks the oracle, culminating in the ultimate clarification with a second divine utterance at Bethel in 28:13–15.

Sternberg's typology of gapping serves as a helpful foundation on which to build this inquiry, but his discussion is deficient in one particular aspect: his insistence that "temporal displacement" is required in order for a gap to be present. To clarify, Sternberg sweepingly and boldly avers that "all [gaps] result from a chronological twisting whereby the order of presentation does not conform to the order of occurrence."[22] Gapping thus becomes contingent upon the narrator's predilection for partitioning out narrative time and order for events. In cases where there may be no discernible order of events against which to judge later narrative developments but, rather, there is a simple utterance, as with the oracle in 25:23, Sternberg's definition creates unintended difficulties. Furthermore, it seems more convincing that ambiguity can arise as a literary tool employed by the biblical authors that functions to create and build suspense. To be fair, Sternberg does recognize a potential function of this sort, but it appears hardly to be in the foreground of his understanding and is still predicated on temporal displacement.[23] The first half of Sternberg's definition is of tremendous value in illuminating biblical ambiguity, especially in line with the view of

---

19. Meir Sternberg, *The Poetics of Biblical Narrative: Ideological Literature and the Drama of Reading* (Bloomington: Indiana University Press, 1985) 235.

20. Ibid., 236.

21. Ibid., 237–40.

22. Ibid., 235.

23. Ibid., 259.

deception articulated in chap. 1. It is Sternberg's contention about what creates a gap that is too rigid.

Robert Alter helps to fill this gap, pun intended. Alter approaches ambiguity from the perspective of a literary scholar, and he treats it in tandem with characterization. He describes biblical narrative as "selectively silent in a purposeful way," allowing the biblical authors a certain free range of play in how various characters are portrayed.[24] The narrator, says Alter, is omniscient, but as such is also free to share or withhold information for literary affect. God too is prone to such intentional character shaping. Alter writes: "[The narrator] may on occasion choose to privilege us with the knowledge of what God thinks of a particular character or action."[25] While Alter is here speaking of God's opinion as informing the characterization of another, one may similarly apply this statement to God, who is just as much a character in these texts as are Jacob, Esau, and Rebekah.[26] It appears as though the omniscient narrator is, from this perspective, wholly in control of even the divine word. The narrator presumably knows what God thinks or what God means; it is how the narrator opts to present this information that can contribute to ambiguity. Implicit in Alter's statement above is that the narrator may also choose *not* to privilege readers with God's thoughts about a given matter. Or, to extend this idea even further, God's speech can often *purposely* conceal rather than reveal. This chapter will demonstrate precisely this point in regard to the trickster oracle in 25:23.

In sum, Sternberg's definition of ambiguity/gaps as a lack of information provides a sound initial definition, but his overgeneralization that all ambiguity arises from temporal discontinuity is problematic. Rather, ambiguity possesses a literary-esthetic quality: it serves a particular purpose or narrative goal, which is captured much more fully in Alter's articulation. The analysis that follows brings both of these ideas together.

A final component contributing further to ambiguity is the biblical type scene. While Alter discusses ambiguity in a chapter entirely separate from his treatment of type scenes, the two are indeed quite complementary and mutually illuminating. Alter has persuasively argued that type scenes arise in the life of biblical heroes and, contrary to form criticism's focus on similarities in a given pattern, type scenes emphasize "what is done in each individual application of the schema to give it a sudden tilt of innovation or even to refashion it radically for the imaginative purposes at hand."[27] The type scene would create a certain expectation in readers (and hearers, given that Alter sees type scenes as requisite to oral composition) of the

---

24. Robert Alter, *The Art of Biblical Narrative* (New York: Basic Books, 1981) 115.
25. Ibid., 126.
26. See W. Lee Humphreys, *The Character of God in the Book of Genesis: A Narrative Appraisal* (Louisville: Westminster John Knox, 2001) 17, 20.
27. Alter, *The Art of Biblical Narrative*, 47, 52.

way that events would be described, and any deviation from or refashioning of this convention would be significant. How the scene is recorded thus becomes a vital vector for interpretation. An anticipated element may be entirely absent, or in the case of Gen 25:23, may be articulated differently from what one might expect based on other examples of the type scene. Herein lies meaning. Alter also notes that these divergences seem to be character specific; whether the narrative does or does not adhere to convention serves the needs of the relevant character.[28] It is interesting to reflect on this possibility in relation to my overarching argument: if Jacob is a trickster par excellence, would one not then expect the announcement of his birth perhaps to contain some similar element of trickery? Alter leaves this point tantalizingly undeveloped, yet if he is correct on this particular point, it serves only to substantiate the present study even further. In sum, ambiguity and type scenes can work in tandem, contributing to or resulting in ambiguity by virtue of the manner in which the narrative has opted to render a given episode.

Alter isolates a number of recurring type scenes, one of which is relevant to my purposes: "the annunciation . . . of the birth of the hero to his barren mother."[29] In Genesis, this announcement oftentimes serves to clarify which son will be the divinely chosen child of the promise. Accordingly, scholarship has seen the oracle in 25:23 as part of an overarching pattern in Genesis in which God favors the secondborn over the firstborn.[30] Alter resolutely writes: "The firstborn very often seem to be losers in Genesis by the very condition of their birth."[31] Indeed, one may easily compile an impressive list of instances showing God's favoritism of the younger child within Genesis: Abel, Isaac, Jacob, Rachel, and Joseph, to name but a few.[32] While I do not wish to challenge the idea that Gen 25:23 is part of this larger pattern, I do want to emphasize the uniqueness and innovation evident at the narrative level in this divine annunciation.

---

28. Ibid., 58.

29. Ibid., *The Art of Biblical Narrative*, 51.

30. Roger Syrén, *The Forsaken First-Born: A Study of a Recurrent Motif in the Patriarchal Narratives* (JSOTSup 133; Sheffield: JSOT Press, 1993) 9–13, 66–79; Victor Matthews and Frances Mims, "Jacob the Trickster and Heir of the Covenant: A Literary Interpretation," *PRSt* 12 (1985) 186, Mark G. Brett, *Genesis: Procreation and the Politics of Identity* (Old Testament Readings; London: Routledge, 2000) 83–84, 90–91; Sharon Pace Jeansonne, "Genesis 25:23: The Use of Poetry in the Rebekah Narratives," in *The Psalms and Other Studies on the Old Testament: Presented to Joseph I. Hunt* (ed. Jack C. Knight and Lawrence A. Sinclair; Nashotah: Nashotah House Seminary, 1990) 148; Thomas L. Thompson, "Conflict Themes in the Jacob Narratives," *Semeia* 15 (1979) 15.

31. Alter, *The Art of Biblical Narrative*, 6.

32. On Leah, see God's clear response in 29:31 and Jacob's retort to Rachel in 30:2 that it is God who has withheld children from her. Other examples exist, though the requirement of divine preference is not as ostensible in these, for instance in 48:13–20, where Jacob's blessing places the younger Ephraim before the older Manasseh.

Toward this end, it will be helpful to look closely at one specific example of this type scene at the outset in order to have a context in place with which to compare the ambiguous portrayal in Gen 25:23. The story of Isaac and Ishmael serves as an excellent, straightforward foil for comparison. In Gen 17:16, God announces that he will grant a son to Abraham through Sarah; it is important to note at this stage in the narrative that Ishmael has already been born (16:15–16). One therefore finds a similar problem in the story of Isaac and Ishmael and the story of Jacob and Esau: two children exist, both of whom arguably have an equal claim as heir to the promise. The difference, however, is that in 21:12–13 God unambiguously relays the message that Isaac, not Ishmael, is to be the child of the promise. The divine word is entirely lucid. God explicitly names Isaac as the one through whom Abraham's seed will continue, and God clearly refers to Ishmael as "the son of the maidservant." There is no equivocation or uncertainty regarding God's choice. The same cannot be said for the divine oracle in 25:23.

The differences in type scenes between Isaac's and Jacob's birth announcements become even more pronounced and significant if one recognizes the potential parallels that exist between the lives of these two characters. Turner points out a number of similarities: both narratives address the issue of barrenness (25:21; cf. 11:30; 16:1), two competing sons (25:22–23; cf. 17:18–19), and reference to two nations (25:22–23; cf. 16:12).[33] Elaborating on the connections even further, Turner notes that the deception of Isaac in Gen 27 is as decisive a scene in the overall narrative as is the Akedah in Gen 22.[34] And seemingly in line with Alter's view of biblical convention, Turner notes a key difference between the character's dialogue in the two scenes. In 22:7 the text says, ". . . his father, and he said, 'My father,' and he said, 'Here I am, *my father*,'" whereas in 27:18 one reads, ". . . his father, and he said, 'My father,' and he said, 'Here I am; *who are you, my son?*'" The lines are exactly the same except for the difference between indicative in Gen 22 and interrogative in Gen 27, which Turner claims serves to highlight all the more the prevalence of deception in the latter episode.[35] These parallels between the Isaac/Ishmael story and the Jacob/Esau narratives lend even further credence not only to the viability of reading them in relationship to one another but, more germane for

---

33. Laurence A. Turner, *Genesis* (2nd ed.; Readings; Sheffield: Sheffield Phoenix, 2009) 105.

34. Turner (ibid., 114–15) detects a number of parallels. In each scene, (1) a father and son are alone; (2) one of the two characters does not disclose the whole truth; (3) Isaac is victim; (4) the phrases "my son" and "here I am" occur frequently and within the same verse (22:7 and 27:2) only in these two chapters in Genesis; (5) the son is threatened; (6) Abraham 'went' (הלך) and 'took' (קח) the ram, just as Jacob 'went' (הלך) and 'took' (לקח) from the flocks; (7) the killing of an animal appears tied to something that appears inevitable: Isaac's death and Esau's blessing, neither of which occurs.

35. Ibid., 117.

the purpose at hand, to ascribing great import and meaning to the places where they differ.

In what follows, I address and read the oracle in 25:23 in the context of the book of Genesis. I pay special attention to the final line of the oracle for several reasons. First, this is not because the earlier lines are unimportant but because the oracle, in good Hebrew poetic fashion, is a fine example of synonymous parallelism. Therefore, a thorough discussion of the final line addresses a similar train of thought evident in earlier lines.[36] Second, scholars have most often made their interpretation of Jacob and Esau as mere eponyms for Israel and Edom contingent on the initial lines of the oracle. While the oracle in 25:23 very likely does speak of a political or national entity by using words such as 'nations' (גוים) and 'peoples' (לאמים)—a point that the subsequent renaming of the brothers as "Edom" (25:30; cf. 36:1) and "Israel" (32:29 and 35:10), respectively, corroborates—the propensity of scholars to reduce these dynamic texts solely to political allegory for the interactions between the two nations is unfounded. Turner provides a helpful and adequate statement that informs this study: "I shall argue that these key passages are not to be read *exclusively* as relating to the political relationship between Israel and Edom, as though they had no reference to the fortunes of the main protagonists in the plot of the Jacob story."[37] Third, even a cursory reading of the narrative reveals that the mention of "nations" and "peoples" lacks any accompanying clarity from God about who will comprise them, let alone how they relate to Rebekah's immediate question about her still-unborn child(ren). And fourth, it is the final line of the oracle that has proven most prone to misunderstanding and mistranslation.

Here, in line with the aforementioned definition of ambiguity and understanding of the convention of biblical type scenes, my analysis will emphasize the innovation and ambiguity with which the narrative portrays the divine oracle in three areas: diction and meaning, matters of syntax, and contextual difficulties.

Diction and Meaning

The key interpretive phrase and the object of greatest contention in the oracle is the final line. In extant scholarship, the typical translation has been: 'the older will serve the younger' (ורב יעבד צעיר). In fact, this translation seems to have achieved a sort of unspoken orthodoxy. Chris Heard lists no less than 16 scholars who prefer this sort of translation, in addition to several notable English translations of the Bible that also hold to this

---

36. See Fokkelman (*Narrative Art in Genesis*, 89), who describes the oracle as incrementally growing in four steps, with each subsequent line going further than the one prior.

37. Laurence A. Turner, *Announcements of Plot in Genesis* (JSOTSup 96; Sheffield: JSOT Press, 1990) 116 (italics original).

reading, among them the ASV, KJV, NIV, NJB, and NRSV.[38] The hegemony of this reading rests on the assumption, as was previously noted, that here one sees yet another instance in Genesis of divine preference for the "younger" over the "older." What is lacking is a careful and nuanced analysis of how this divine word differs from the convention. In an attempt to capture better the ambiguity, I suggest the rendering 'the greater will serve the lesser', though even this translation cannot attend to all the ambiguity latent in the Hebrew. To my knowledge, only two scholars have advanced this translation. The earlier, R. A. Kraft, translates the line similarly in his brief text-critical notes on Gen 25:23.[39] Unfortunately, Kraft offers nothing in the way of explanation for his translation or its implications. More recently, Laurence Turner correctly recognizes that the Hebrew words properly denoting 'older' and 'younger' do not in fact occur here; instead the text records "the more general" terms 'greater' and 'lesser'.[40] Based on context, however, Turner concludes that the reader is to equate greater/lesser with older/younger, essentially giving way to the traditional translation.[41] In his more recent commentary, Turner seems to have changed his position, now translating the line 'the elder shall serve the younger'.[42] Humphreys's translation 'and greater shall serve younger' is a hybrid, though it still assumes age and birth order to be the central and unambiguous elements under discussion.[43] As will become clear in what follows, the traditional rendering assumes the use of stereotypical language that is by no means present in Gen 25:23.

Within Genesis, the narrative uses גד(ו)ל to label a given child the 'older'. In 10:21, Shem is called the 'older' (הגדול) brother of Japheth, 29:16 calls Leah the 'older' (הגדלה) daughter of Laban, and 44:12 notes that Joseph begins his search for the hidden cup in the sack of the 'oldest' (גדול) of Jacob's sons.[44] Even within the Jacob/Esau narratives themselves, the text uses גדל three times in regard to Esau as the 'older' son (27:1, 15, 42).[45] Conversely, רב occurs nowhere in Genesis or the entire Hebrew Bible, for that matter, as a designation for 'older'—a fact that greatly calls into question the assump-

---

38. R. Christopher Heard, *Dynamics of Diselection: Ambiguity in Genesis 12–36 and Ethnic Boundaries in Post-exilic Judah* (Semeia Studies; Atlanta: Society of Biblical Literature, 2001) 98–99.

39. R. A. Kraft, "A Note on the Oracle of Rebecca (Gen xxv. 23)," *JTS* 13 (1962) 318.

40. Turner, *Announcements of Plot*, 119, 121. He renders the oracle's final line as I do: "the greater will serve the lesser."

41. Turner, ibid., 121.

42. Ibid., 106.

43. Humphreys, *The Character of God in the Book of Genesis*, 157.

44. BDB lists 'elder/eldest' as a viable meaning for גדול in the texts that I enumerate here, and also in Ezek 16:46. See also *HALOT* 1.177.

45. That גדל in chap. 27 may mean 'great(er)' seems unwarranted given that in two of the three instances (vv. 15 and 42) 'her son' (בנה) precedes גדל; as the narrative makes clear (and as I will show below), if Rebekah were to regard either of her children as 'great', she would surely choose Jacob, not Esau.

tion that it means 'older' here.[46] It does, however, appear frequently in Genesis with the sense of 'great'.[47] Two of these occurrences are associated with Jacob: once in Isaac's blessing of Jacob in 27:28, and once in Jacob's blessing of Joseph's sons in 48:16.

The final word in 25:23, צעיר ('lesser'), creates further ambiguity. One might instead expect קטן ('small, insignificant'), which the narrative uses of Jacob in 27:15, 42, two of the same verses that use גדל in reference to Esau's age. In 29:16, this word pair occurs similarly in the feminine, גדלה and קטנה, in reference to Leah and Rachel's birth order. This word pair, then, appears to address issues of *age*, with קטן designating the 'younger' and גדל the 'older'. To substantiate this point further, the Joseph cycle (Gen 37–50) contains several uses of קטן for the younger as opposed to צעיר.[48]

Compunding this ambiguity is the fact that within Genesis צעיר occurs with 'firstborn' (בכר) on all but two other occasions (19:35, 38), where its

---

46. BDB 913 lists the plural רבים in Job 32:9 as the only other example, as does *HALOT* 2.1172, likely because of its parallelism with זקנים 'old/elderly ones'. To my eye, this instance is equivocal, and רבים here could satisfy the parallelism just as well if it meant 'great ones'. The ASV, JPS, and KJV all attest to this latter translation. And *HALOT* appears also to express some hesitancy on seeing age in relation to the plural in Job 32:9, suggesting an emendation that would add ימים ('years') to produce the translation 'elder, great in years'. *HALOT* 2.1172 includes Gen 25:23 with the meaning 'great' under the heading "references where this meaning is quite clear." *HALOT* suggests 'larger (older)' as a meaning for רב and "smaller (younger)" as a meaning for צעיר, thus assuming as do many others that this reference is an unambiguous indicator of age. The fact the word for 'years' is not present in Gen 25:23 and is not suggested by *HALOT* makes this an uneasy assumption to make. It is interesting to note, however, that in each of the examples offered by *HALOT* (except for Gen 25:23) where the meaning is said to be "quite clear," *HALOT* translates the word as the entry suggests, 'great'; the next section under this same entry, however, provides a much shorter list of "fewer unambiguous examples," implying the possibility for ambiguity earlier in the list. The fact that *HALOT* expresses some equivocation about the meaning of the word as an overt indicator of age in Job 32:9 coupled with exhibiting some liberty in translating Gen 25:23 as *connoting* (not meaning) older and younger highlights the ambiguity of this pairing all the more. See also Taschner (*Verheissung und Erfüllung*, 25), who claims that רב is seldom used in the Hebrew Bible in reference to the firstborn, leading to the possibility that Jacob is the "greater" from the outset.

47. See Gen 6:5; 7:11; 13:6; 16:10; 26:14; 27:28; 36:7; 48:16.

48. See Gen 42:13, 15, 20, 32, 34; 43:29; 44:2, 12, 20, 23, 26 (2x). One may object to this comparison, given the dissimilarity scholarship has often seen between the two cycles. Recent scholars, however, have begun reading the two stories as more integrated, still paying attention to their differences, but keeping a keen eye also on how they are similar. On this point, see Carleen Mandolfo, "'You Meant Evil against Me': Dialogic Truth and the Character of Jacob in Joseph's Story," *JSOT* 28 (2004) 449–65; Peter D. Miscall, "The Jacob and Joseph Stories as Analogies," *JSOT* 6 (1978) 28–40; Niditch, *Underdogs and Tricksters*, 70–125. See also David Carr (*Reading the Fractures of Genesis: Historical and Literary Approaches* [Louisville: Westminster John Knox, 1996]), who argues for two versions of a joint Jacob-Joseph narrative—one from the North and the other from the South—in circulation during the first of a five-stage evolution of the book of Genesis into its final canonical form. One should also remain mindful that Jacob continues as a character—a very active one in several scenes—well into the Joseph cycle.

occurrence alongside בכר is presupposed.[49] In Gen 19:31, 34, this word pair appears in reference to Lot's daughters, while in 29:26 the pair is used by Laban in reference to his daughters. Similarly, in 43:33 the words describe the seating arrangement of Jacob's children when they come before Joseph, and in 48:14 an aged Jacob blesses the younger (צעיר) Ephraim over the firstborn (בכר) Manasseh. This word pair, therefore, serves as another way to communicate matters pertaining to age.

That the final line of Gen 25:23 does not employ this more traditional and expected word pair, בכר and צעיר, is thus all the more striking. Were בכר used, there would be no ambiguity that Esau was the child under consideration, but replacing בכר with רב removes the clarity. The reader's expectation is interrupted. Speiser points to what he deems an exact parallel for the word pair רב and צעיר in v. 23 in Akkadian family law with the meaning 'older' and 'younger'.[50] Turner, however, correctly cautions against any certainty "that terms based on common Semitic roots necessarily carry identical connotations in different cultures."[51] Given that the text records רב and צעיר, the contrast with what one would expect based on other instances of the type scene (בכר and צעיר) enhances the ambiguity of the oracle's final line.

Based on this analysis, one can make several initial observations. The final line of Gen 25:23 makes a statement about the divine perspective regarding the status of the twins in an ambiguous way. The conventional indicators for age in Genesis, גדל and קטן, do not appear, and the use of רב and צעיר creates dissonance regarding whether issues of age are even operative concerns here. My more ambiguous translation of 'greater' and 'lesser', respectively, raises the question whether this pairing may invoke questions of status rather than, or perhaps alongside, expected issues of age, thus contributing all the more to the ambiguity. What seems clear, however, is that God's speech employs two terms that are much more vague in nature than one would expect based on examples found elsewhere in Genesis. Who is to be the "greater" and who the "lesser"? God has provided no names, no precision.[52] Moreover, God's (intentional?) reticence to call either child

---

49. According to Deut 21:17, the firstborn son was granted a double portion of all his father's possessions. On the biblical law of the firstborn, see especially Jon D. Levenson, *The Death and Resurrection of the Beloved Son: The Transformation of Child Sacrifice in Judaism and Christianity* (New Haven, CT: Yale University Press, 1993) 55–60. See also Kevin Walton, *Thou Traveller Unknown: The Presence and Absence of God in the Jacob Narrative* (Carlisle: Paternoster, 2003) 21–24; Skinner, *Genesis*, 362; Claus Westermann, *Genesis 12–36: A Continental Commentary* (trans. John J. Scullion; Minneapolis: Fortress, 1995) 418; and Taschner, *Verheissung und Erfüllung*, 32, for a helpful synopsis of the right of the firstborn in the Hebrew Bible.

50. E. A. Speiser, *Genesis: Introduction, Translation, and Notes* (AB 1; New York: Doubleday, 1964) 95.

51. Turner, *Announcements of Plot*, 121.

52. Frank Anthony Spina, "The 'Face of God': Esau in Canonical Context," in *The Quest for Context and Meaning: Studies in Biblical Intertextuality in Honor of James A. Sanders*

"firstborn" is patent in the narrative; only Jacob and Esau ever use the title of themselves.[53] In line with the understanding of biblical type scenes discussed above, the absence of the expected term בכר contributes something to how the text means. By substituting רב, the narrative makes a statement, removing any certainty about the proper character antecedents for these modifiers. Were בכר employed, there would be no equivocation that Jacob was indeed the lesser, the צעיר; but as the text stands, God has interrupted the convention by introducing ambiguity through the use of a word pair that is unconventional in Genesis.

Matters of Syntax

God's oracle is not only lexically ambiguous but also syntactically ambiguous. The rules governing Hebrew syntax allow for two entirely opposite readings. Within the oracle itself, one finds the word order following the pattern subject-verb-object which, while natural in English, is unnatural in Hebrew. According to Gesenius (GKC §142), Hebrew verbal syntax can occur with five differing word orders; however, in each of the potential syntactical arrangements that he outlines, none replicates the order found in 25:23. A Hebrew sentence may be constructed according to the following syntax: (a) verb-subject-object; (b) object-verb-subject; (c) verb-object-subject; (d) subject-object-verb; (e) object-subject-verb.[54] The only ordering that Gesenius offers with a verb between two nouns is object-verb-subject, which would require the final line of the oracle to be translated 'the lesser will serve the greater'. Gesenius also notes, however, that the subject may precede the verb for emphasis. A construction of this sort, he maintains, describes a *"state"* or *"circumstance."*[55] If רב is indeed the subject of the sentence, Gesenius seems to imply that this ordering names a certain condition or, given a possibility raised in the lexical discussion in the previous section, perhaps a *status*. Could the Hebrew grammar itself contribute to an understanding of the two titles, רב and צעיר, as connoting the status of the twins in some ambiguous way? Grammatically, this line is an anomaly, diverging from conventional Hebrew word order; its unique syntax contributes to its ambiguity.

The difficulty is unfortunately not as easily resolved on closer scrutiny of the text. Absent את to distinguish between subject and object,

---

(ed. Craig A. Evans and Shemaryahu Talmon; Leiden: Brill, 1997) 6; Westermann, *Genesis 12–36*, 413.

53. Taschner (*Verheissung und Erfüllung*, 48) characterizes this silence as the narrator's way of passing judgment on both Jacob and Esau by distancing himself from any responsibility in naming the characters too clearly. Fokkelmann (*Narrative Art in Genesis*, 107) argues to the contrary that the narrator sees the right of the firstborn as a non-issue; Gen 25:23 guarantees that Jacob is "destined" to be firstborn.

54. *Gesenius' Hebrew Grammar* (ed. E. Kautzsch; trans. A. E. Cowley; 2nd ed. Oxford: Clarendon, 1910) §142.

55. Ibid.

both רב and צעיר are unmarked for case.[56] One may thus render the line either 'the greater will serve the lesser' or 'the lesser will serve the greater'. Heard attempts to capture in English the ambiguity of the Hebrew with his translation 'the older the younger will serve'.[57] Joel Kaminsky, while noting the value in recognizing the ambiguity, responds as follows:

> [the proposal] does not work well with the larger pattern found in Israelite society or in the Bible. The oracle makes much more sense if it is announcing that the normal societal expectation that favored the elder child was being challenged. Inasmuch as what has often been called the 'underdog motif' is pervasive throughout Genesis's stories of brotherly struggle, it would be strange to find an oracle announcing the preeminence of an elder child.[58]

Kaminsky's point that a pattern underlying much of Genesis seems to highlight the necessity of reading the oracle as a vital component of this very pattern makes sense. The difficulty with his view, however, is threefold. First, as has been shown above, it is not at all clear that רב and צעיר connote age in a way that is customary in Genesis. Second, although it may be clear to the reader who knows the story well that Jacob will ultimately come out on top, in the narrative of the oracle itself and in the lives of its characters (Rebekah, specifically, as the sole recipient of the oracle) the result is by no means unequivocal. In fact, God's withholding of information in the oracle creates the necessity for Rebekah to interpret for herself which child will be the רב and which the צעיר. As will become clear below, this interpretation leads to Rebekah and Jacob's deception of Isaac in chap. 27. Assuming the posture of a first-time reader, we see that at this stage in the narrative the reader knows as little as Rebekah does. And third, the fact that a given text "makes much more sense" when viewed from one perspective does not necessitate the understanding that this perspective is de facto correct. This point is especially potent when one is dealing with patterns, or type scenes, as I have called them. To reiterate, what is necessary is a recognition of how the narration of this scene deviates from convention, not a smoothing out or erasure of difficulties in the interest of clarity. Taking Alter's position, the a priori subsuming of the oracle under a larger pattern for the sake of convenience and "making sense" is problematic. What is most important is how a given manifestation of the pattern *differs* from one's expectation; therein lies the key to unlocking meaning, even if this meaning is ambiguous.

---

56. Heard, *Dynamics of Diselection*, 99.
57. Ibid. On this point, see also Richard E. Friedman, *The Disappearance of God: A Divine Mystery* (Boston: Little, Brown, 1995) 112.
58. Joel S. Kaminsky, *Yet I Loved Jacob: Reclaiming the Biblical Concept of Election* (Nashville: Abingdon, 2007) 44.

The oracle gains another layer of ambiguity, then, by virtue of its unclear syntax. Who is to serve whom? Does the greater serve the lesser, or the lesser serve the greater? Adding to the problem is that, even if one feels competent to resolve the syntactical ambiguity, the lexical ambiguity persists. Given the nature of Hebrew poetic parallelism, this final line is most convincingly translated in the same order in which the Hebrew occurs: the greater will serve the lesser. In each of the preceding lines, what appears to be the subject comes first in the sentence. One must remain mindful, however, of the syntactical possibility for both readings. Additionally, one should be cautious about attempting to smooth out the tangled syntax too readily. In the process, meaning may be lost.

Contextual Difficulties

A final potential point of interest is the way in which the oracle does not cohere entirely with the remainder of the Jacob cycle. The account of the twins' birth that follows *immediately* after the oracle does not provide any further precision in identifying who is the רב and who the צעיר. Verse 25 describes Esau as the 'first' (הראשׁון) to emerge from the womb, but nothing in the narrative hints at or requires הראשׁון to have רב as its antecedent. Esau's description at birth further contributes to the ambiguity. Commentators generally accept the fact that he is born 'red' (אדמוני) and covered in a mantle of 'hair' (שׂער) as being an attempt to cast him as a type of wild, uncivilized man, much akin to Enkidu in the *Gilgamesh Epic.*[59] However, some commentators conversely read the description in tandem with the only other biblical occurrence of אדמוני, which is in 1 Sam 16:12, where it appears as part of a description of David's handsomeness.[60]

The result, then, is that Esau's characterization at this point is also ambiguous; the narrative does not make it clear whether his appearance is to be commended or ridiculed. Adele Berlin argues that biblical narrative seldom offers character descriptions pertaining to appearance or dress, yet when these details are provided it is a matter of great significance, typically for plot advancement.[61] Thus, only as the narrative continues do these ostensibly innocuous details lend themselves to a negative portrayal of Esau. His 'red' (אדמוני) appearance anticipates the bowl of 'red stuff' (אדם) that he will wolf down at the cost of his birthright, and his hairiness (שׂער)

---

59. Westermann, *Genesis 12–36*, 414; Alter, *The Art of Biblical Narrative*, 43; Speiser, *Genesis*, 196; Wenham, *Genesis 16–50*, 176; Hendel, *The Epic of the Patriarch*, 117; Nahum M. Sarna, *The JPS Torah Commentary: Genesis* (Philadelphia: Jewish Publication Society, 1989) 180

60. Heard, *Dynamics of Diselection*, 101; Westermann, *Genesis 12–36*, 414; Mathews, *Genesis 11:27–50:26*, 388.

61. Adele Berlin, *Poetics and Interpretation of Biblical Narrative* (Bible and Literature Series 9; Sheffield: Almond, 1993; repr. Winona Lake, IN: Eisenbrauns, 1994) 34. See also Shimon Bar-Efrat, *Narrative Art in the Bible* (JSOTSup 70; Sheffield: Almond, 1989) 48.

presages Jacob's disguise in chap. 27.[62] For Berlin, the character description may also shed light on the type of person the character is; Esau provides a fine example because readers will come to see that his physical description matches his brutish, shortsighted demeanor.[63]

One may also discern, however, a narrative cue about how things will progress at this early stage in the story. Esau's hairiness (שֵׂעָר) produces a striking homophony with the final word in the oracle, 'lesser' (צָעִיר). This sort of wordplay highlights the literary artistry of the passage and shows an early equation at the narrative level of the hirsute Esau with the lesser in the trickster oracle.[64]

The situation is similar with regard to Jacob's birth. His grasping onto Esau's heel gives no indication whether this activity will qualify him to be the רַב or the צָעִיר. Not until 27:36, after Jacob and Rebekah's successful co-deception (with God) of Isaac, when Esau reinterprets Jacob's name to mean 'deceiver' (עֲקַב) does one realize that Jacob is a deceiver from the very outset.[65] Taschner understands Jacob's activity at birth as signifying an initial movement toward fulfillment of the oracle.[66] Hamilton astutely notices that Esau is named for his appearance at birth whereas Jacob is named for his actions.[67] Although some presume that this notice serves as a sure indicator of God's preference for the active Jacob, ambiguity still reigns; Jacob may be the active child, but he is also the secondborn twin, a fact he cannot escape. Will Yhwh's preference for the younger son continue? Moreover, the oracle still gives no transparency regarding Yhwh's true desires. Already in the seemingly innocuous naming of Jacob, a life of deception guided by God is foreshadowed.[68]

At the narrative level, the second block of Jacob/Esau narratives (Gen 32–33) also underscores the oracle's ambiguity. Turner contends that what typifies the Jacob cycle is the "nonfulfillment" of the oracle—along with Isaac's blessings of his two sons (27:27b–29, 39b–40)—in various nuances.[69]

---

62. For a detailed and thorough treatment of how this opening scene of the Jacob cycle looks forward to what will occur, see Michael Fishbane, "Composition and Structure in the Jacob Cycle (Gen. 25:19–35:22)," *JJS* 26 (1975) 22–23.

63. Berlin, *Poetics and Interpretation*, 36, 39. Contra Bar-Efrat (*Narrative Art in the Bible*, 48), who writes that character descriptions have no relation to a character's personality.

64. Contra Victor Hamilton (*The Book of Genesis: Chapters 18–50* [NICOT; Grand Rapids, MI: Eerdmans, 1995] 177), who sees this wordplay as evidence of the irony that the "younger" Jacob will prevail over the man called Seir.

65. Simone Paganini, "Wir haben Wasser gefunden: Beobachtungen zur Erzählanalyse von Gen 25,19–26,36," *ZAW* 117 (2005) 30.

66. Taschner, *Verheissung und Erfüllung*, 25.

67. Hamilton, *Genesis 18–50*, 178.

68. One should be mindful of the three different etymologies ascribed to Jacob's name. In 25:26, he is the 'heel', and in 27:36, Esau interprets his name to mean 'deceiver'. Another etymology that is seldom commented on is that Jacob is a shortened form of Jacob-El, meaning 'may God protect'. See my "Jacob, Laban, and a Divine Trickster," 3 n. 1.

69. Turner, *Announcements of Plot*, 119. Conversely, Albert de Pury (*Promesse Divine et Légende Cultuelle dans le Cycle de Jacob: Genèse 28 et les traditions patriarcales* [2 vols.; Études

One cannot and should not trust the oracle, argues Turner, as a realistic indicator of the plot that will ensue.[70] Primary among Turner's examples is that Esau never serves (עבד) Jacob; quite the contrary, for in the reconciliation scene Jacob constantly refers to himself as Esau's 'servant' (עבדך) and addresses Esau as 'my lord' (אדני). One of the main problems with Turner's thesis is that, while he here translates the oracle correctly as 'the greater will serve the lesser', he still reads the oracle as though it refers solely to age, making Esau the 'greater' even at the very end of the Jacob cycle. Given that Esau disappears from the narrative at the end of chap. 27 and only makes two brief cameo appearances after that in a narrative that certainly centers on Jacob, it would be odd for Esau still to be the 'greater' after all that Jacob has endured. Turner's notice of a discontinuity between what the oracle apparently proclaims and what results is important, yet it is not so much that the oracle cannot be trusted in comparison with what truly happens but more that the oracle is indistinct when uttered and thus does not define clearly its actors or what is to happen. Additionally, I will show in chap. 4 below that Jacob exploits the oracle, using the points that Turner raises for his own benefit as he deceives his brother, Esau, yet again.

Summary

In light of the above presentation on matters of diction and meaning, syntax, and context, God's oracular speech appears to be ambiguous lexically, syntactically, and contextually, resulting in an obfuscation of the divine prerogative. Moreover, it is not clear that God even addresses the question that Rebekah poses.[71] God instead speaks of the future realities that will typify the lives of each child. But what is the payoff in God's word remaining so convoluted and unclear when first spoken? Or, to ask a question very few have asked of the oracle: what does 25:23 reveal not only about the lives of Jacob and Esau but also, and perhaps more importantly, *about God*?

Given that ambiguity pervades the oracle, one may view the divine word as the word of a divine trickster. God is unnecessarily evasive in response to Rebekah's legitimate question. Rather than offering her an unambiguous word of reassurance and clarity as was evident in the Ishmael/Isaac narrative (21:12–13; cf. 17–18), God speaks in oracular poetry, casting the divine word as one that conceals rather than reveals. Assuming Rebekah's facility with Hebrew to be quite good, the oracle still retains a numinous quality about it at all levels, and Rebekah's understanding of the oracle as forecasting Jacob as the divinely chosen son is by no means the only possible reading. Rebekah's question is ultimately met with a non-answer[72] and thus

Bibliques; Paris: Gabalda, 1975] 103) sees what follows as the realization of the promise ("realization de la bénédiction").

70. Turner, *Announcements of Plot*, 181.

71. See Humphreys, *The Character of God in the Book of Genesis*, 157.

72. See God's response to Job in Job 38–40, where, similarly, I believe that God gives a non-answer.

only creates more questions that Rebekah must address on her own, which arguably lead to her strong sense of duty in Gen 27.

This evasive quality of God's speech also fits well with the definition of deception provided in chap. 1 above. God clearly withholds the relevant information that Rebekah requests or, at the very least, needs in order to live. Divine reticence, divine ambiguity ultimately become divine trickery. But for what purpose? What does this obfuscation accomplish in the story of Jacob? No other divine annunciation in Genesis is even remotely as ambiguous as 25:23. These opening verses of the Jacob cycle introduce readers to a God who cares deeply about the success of the ancestral promise but also to a God who at times engages in trickery for the purposes of that promise.[73] God's speech, therefore, seems to mirror God's presence.[74] God will not be bound by convention and type scenes. Indeed, Brueggemann seems to move in this direction, albeit for different reasons and with different emphases. He writes:

> This oracle expresses a scandalous decision on the part of God. . . . The oracle discloses something crucial about God. It affirms that by the power of his promise, God is free to work his will in the face of every human convention and every definition of propriety. Jacob is ordained as a man of conflict because the God who wrought him is a God in conflict as well.[75]

Brueggemann's statement is particularly apt at this point in the narrative because it draws attention not only to God as a veritable trickster but also to the one who was to be the greater, the divine choice to be the child of the promise, Jacob, who is equally as "scandalous" as the God of the promise. And it is to the human characters that the narrative now turns, yet always with an eye to the trickster oracle and trickster God.

First Signs of a Trickster: Extorting the Right of the Firstborn (Genesis 25:27–34)

Two notices open this second scene and are pivotal in comprehending and interpreting what follows: the "nature" of each child, and each parent's corresponding preference for one child over the other. The narrative describes Esau in v. 27 as 'a man knowing game, a man of the field' (אִישׁ

---

73. Taschner (*Verheissung und Erfüllung*, 29) holds that 25:21–28 is an intentional construct based on the entirety of the Jacob cycle and mindfully placed here as an introduction to the whole.

74. Robert L. Cohn ("Narrative Structure and Canonical Perspective in Genesis," *JSOT* 25 [1983] 9) sees God's presence in the Jacob cycle to be "more numinous . . . more eerie, more exceptional" than in the Abraham cycle. I disagree with Cohn that these qualities typifying divine appearance in the Jacob cycle require one to ascribe greater responsibility to human characters in the events that ensue. But Cohn's statement is helpful in seeing a potential connection between God's manner of appearing and manner of speaking in the Jacob cycle.

75. Brueggemann, *Genesis*, 216.

ידע ציד איש שדה). The reason the narrative gives for Isaac's love of Esau is, literally, because 'he [Isaac] had game in his mouth' (כי־ציד בפיו). It is striking and worth noting that father and son share a love of cuisine, a love that will partly result in each one's undoing. Esau will fall victim to Jacob's simple bowl of lentils in 25:29–34, and Isaac wrongly believes that he is eating wild game in 27:1–45 when in reality it is domesticated goats from the family's flocks. Both men's palates and appetites become a means that the tricksters exploit in realizing God's purposes.

Jacob, on the other hand, is said to be an איש תם, an outwardly simple phrase that has given rise to countless scholarly attempts to construe a meaning that resonates with the way that the narrative will depict Jacob as a character. The usual translation is either 'mild man' or 'quiet man'.[76] Spina reads the designation as an ironic statement in that Jacob is "simultaneously morally bankrupt and morally upright."[77] Ellen Davis puzzlingly understands the phrase to indicate that Jacob "is well-adapted to the *mores*, if not the morals, of society," yet she notes that, "if indeed *tam* denotes ethical integrity, then Jacob is not an obvious candidate for that accolade."[78] Brueggemann views the term through the appropriate lens of covenant, maintaining that it describes one who unites "neighborliness" with "the rigorous discipline of presence with God."[79] Fokkelman translates the phrase as "bent on one purpose," which represents one of the better attempts to make sense of the phrase in the context of perpetual deception.[80] Yair Zakovitch understands the phrase within the larger context of the narrative's desire to justify Jacob and his actions, taking the term literally as connoting the fact that Jacob is not a liar.[81] And Alter sees the phrase as being intentionally jarring, requiring that the reader wrestle with its meaning and implications as the Jacob cycle unfolds.[82]

In reference to humans, the word תם appears in Gen 6:9 and 17:1 as a descriptor for Noah and Abraham respectively, yet again there is no reason to assume morality to be the operative issue. Interestingly, within the entire Hebrew Bible only Jacob and Job (1:8; 2:3) are described as איש תם. Yet within the Hebrew Bible, the word תמ(ים) also occurs frequently in Leviticus

---

76. Sarna, *Genesis*, 180; Wenham, *Genesis 16–50*, 177; Mathews, *Genesis 11:27–50:26*, 391; Westermann, *Genesis 12–36*, 411; Hendel, *The Epic of the Patriarch*, 112; Skinner, *Genesis*, 361; Speiser, *Genesis*, 195.

77. Spina, "Esau in Canonical Context," 8.

78. Ellen F. Davis, "Job and Jacob: The Integrity of Faith," in *Reading between Texts: Intertextuality and the Hebrew Bible* (ed. D. N. Fewell; Louisville: Westminster John Knox, 1992) 211.

79. Walter Brueggemann, *An Unsettling God: The Heart of the Hebrew Bible* (Minneapolis: Fortress, 2009) 34–35. Brueggemann understands the term as describing what is integral to Israel's obedience to its dialogical partner, God.

80. Fokkelman, *Narrative Art in Genesis*, 91.

81. Zakovitch, "Inner-Biblical Interpretation," 108.

82. Alter, *The Art of Biblical Narrative*, 42–46.

in reference to an unblemished animal that is worthy of being sacrificed to YHWH.[83] The assumption, then, that this word *must* elicit moral uprightness is unfounded. The concern is not whether the animal is a moral exemplar but whether it is appropriate for sacrifice to YHWH. Similarly with Noah, Abraham, and Job, the pertinent qualifier seems to be less the character's moral convictions than describing whether he is sound enough to be pleasing to YHWH.[84] With Jacob, one must remain mindful that the narrative never explicitly censures him for the way he goes about matters.[85] One is enjoined also to recall from chap. 1 the discussion of morality in relation to these texts; the relationship historically is, if anything, tenuous. Given the evidence, this description of Jacob likely says something about his status in relationship to God. Something about Jacob makes him worthy and pleasing for YHWH. However, I have also shown that Jacob is a trickster from the beginning by virtue of his heel-grabbing birth and by virtue of the fact that it is a trickster God who chooses him.

Thus, the epithet must take Jacob's deceptive character into account. Perhaps mirroring this inherent complexity in defining Jacob's character conclusively, the narrative tersely states that Rebekah loved Jacob. Unlike the reasons given for Isaac's love for Esau, no reason is given for Rebekah's love of Jacob, a fact that may testify to the unconditional quality of her love in contrast to Isaac's conditional love of Esau.[86] Interpreters will sometimes take Jacob's being an איש תם to mean that he is a domesticated man, and thus Rebekah as the domesticated housewife would naturally have an affinity for him. This view is laden with several difficulties, not least of which is that the narrative presents Rebekah as much more than a simple housewife. In fact, in 27:1–17 it is she who is active and purposeful in ensuring Jacob's obtaining of the blessing. Sharon Pace Jeansonne hence argues that Rebekah's love for Jacob is not governed by any similar characteristics that the two may share but by Rebekah's own sense of the oracle in 25:23 that Jacob will be the "greater."[87] Tammi Schneider suggests that the motivation for Rebekah's risky behavior in assuming a curse should the plan fail may in

---

83. See Lev 1:3, 10; 3:1, 6; 4:3, 23; 5:15, 18, 25; 22:19, 21; 23:12; also Num 6:14. For this definition, see *Theological Wordbook of the Old Testament* (ed. R. L. Harris and G. L. Archer Jr.; 2 vols., Chicago: Moody, 1980) 2522e, where the word is described as "the divine standard for [humanity's] attainment."

84. Moral uprightness appears problematic as an explanation for yet another reason. Abraham is by no means blameless, as the wife-sister stories in Gen 12 and 20 show. Similarly, Abraham's ambivalence toward Hagar does not cast him in a positive light. And Noah's family again quickly slides into sin as the postdiluvian world repopulates.

85. C. D. Evans, "The Patriarch Jacob: An Innocent Man," *BRev* 2 (1986) 32–37; Hamilton, *Genesis 18–50*, 186.

86. Zakovitch, "Inner-Biblical Interpretation," 104–5.

87. Sharon Pace Jeansonne, *The Women of Genesis: From Sarah to Potiphar's Wife* (Minneapolis: Fortress, 1990) 63.

fact say more about her commitment to God than her devotion to Jacob.[88]
One may wonder, however, whether Jacob cuts his deceptive teeth also by
being in the presence of his mother, who the reader sees is clearly capable
of hatching a near-foolproof plan. Viewed from this perspective of the utter
discontinuity of the twins, however, God's oracle is already beginning to
work itself out in the lives of this family.

The first postuterine interaction between the two brothers revolves
around the right of the firstborn, and it is here that for the first time one
begins to see glimpses that the cunning Jacob may indeed be the רב. In
these verses (29–34), the narrative depicts Esau's character as diametrically
the opposite of Jacob's character. While Esau is shortsighted and overly
dramatic, Jacob is cold, calculating, and "businesslike."[89]

The difference between the two characters is manifested most in the
way each communicates with the other. Alter calls this literary technique
"contrastive dialogue."[90] Esau comes in from the field famished and weak,
claiming he is about to die (vv. 29, 32). It is difficult to assume that Esau is
actually near death as the result of a simple hunting expedition, most notably due to the description in v. 27 that he is an adept hunter. Esau implores
Jacob to let him 'gulp down from the red—this red!' The verb used here is
the Hiphil הלעיטני (from לעט), the only time that this verb ever occurs in the
Hebrew Bible. Heard points out that the word does appear in postbiblical
Hebrew as a description of the eating practices of animals, yet he contends
that this attestation should not inform its usage here in Genesis so that it
does not impose on the reader a negative evaluation of Esau's character.[91]
Similarly, Joseph Prouser understands Esau's request as much more carefully crafted and polite, opting for the following translation: 'Please may
I have just a taste of that lovely red soup, weary as I am?'[92] It seems odd,
however, that the narrative does not use the standard word for 'eat', אכל,
but instead uses this hapax, which seems to intend a sort of eating that is
different from the eating of most humans.[93] In context, the specific choice
of לעט makes great sense, given its animalistic associations, which fit with

---

88. Tammi J. Schneider, *Mothers of Promise: Women in the Book of Genesis* (Grand Rapids, MI: Baker Academic, 2008) 61.

89. Alter, *The Art of Biblical Narrative*, 45.

90. Ibid., 72.

91. Heard, *Dynamics of Diselection*, 103–4.

92. Joseph H. Prouser, "Seeing Red: On Translating Esau's Request for Soup," *Conservative Judaism* 56 (2004) 18. I do not find Prouser's semantic analysis convincing, and he
makes unfounded leaps at several places to "gussy up" the translation. For example, he
argues that Esau's double use of the word for 'red' (אדם) may just as likely mean 'dark red
stew', which is fine; he then takes poetic license and states in the very next sentence that
'lovely red soup' may be more accurate!

93. Alter (*The Art of Biblical Narrative*, 44) translates the verb 'let me cram my maw'.
He further notes the possibility that the Hiphil form be read as carrying the sense of a plea
for Jacob physically to feed Esau (*Genesis: Translation and Commentary* [New York: Norton,
1996] 129). For more on this verb, see Taschner, *Verheissung und Erfüllung*, 33.

Esau's life as an outdoorsman, where he surely would have interactions with animals and their eating habits. Esau may also ironically have used food as bait, much like Jacob does here to entrap his dim-witted brother. Just as Esau the skilled hunter would await an opportunity to attack his prey, perhaps when it was eating, so too the conniving Jacob seizes his opportunity when Esau is about to eat. What is more, Esau appears unable to conjure up even the name of the dish that Jacob is preparing, testifying to his boorish demeanor, merely calling it twice by its color: 'red' (אדם).

God is not outside these events. Not only does the narrative present the trickster oracle as both tricking and impelling further trickery, it provides textual hints at a divine hand at work. Continuing to emphasize the characters' speech, we see that Esau's exasperated and difficult-to-translate words in v. 32 (הנה אנכי הולך למות ולמה־זה לי בכרה) mirror a similar and equally difficult-to-translate expression used by his mother, Rebekah, in v. 22 (אם־כן למה זה אנכי). In both cases, their statements speak to a situation of peril that they perceive themselves to have entered. The difference, however, is that Rebekah's words are met with a word from God, leading to her favoritism of Jacob and actions on his behalf in Gen 27. Esau's words, however, are met with nothing, no divine response or clarification. God's silence at Esau's cry of distress hints even further that the divine trickster has sided with the trickster Jacob. In fact, Esau is the only character in this narrative never to receive a word from God.[94] The narrative unmistakably portrays Esau not only as unfit to carry the promise forward but also as unfit to hear a divine word.

In contrast to Esau, Jacob speaks with both a plan and a purpose. Even though the narrative does not say so explicitly, it remains difficult and odd to assume that Rebekah would not have made the oracle—and her interpretation of it—known to Jacob. Only against this backdrop do vv. 29–34 make sense as the partial fulfillment of the trickster oracle, and only in this way does Rebekah's risky advocacy of Jacob in chap. 27 make sense. Jacob's words are methodical, his sentences terse and to the point. Otherwise he is ominously silent. Between the two occasions on which he addresses Esau here, he speaks a mere eight words, but these are all that he needs to succeed in acquiring the right of the firstborn from his brother. Additionally, the narrative begins to push Esau out. One can see the transferral of roles taking place here by the presence of Jacob's name alongside the absence of Esau's in the narrative. Esau is merely the assumed subject of the verbs ישבע and ימכר (v. 33) as well as a string of four successive verbs (v. 34). Verse 34 begins with Jacob's name (יעקב) and emphasizes Jacob by straying from the usual verb-subject-object of Hebrew syntax. This structure, however, parallels the final line of the oracle in v. 23, where רב emphatically opens the verse. The scene closes with Esau's despising (בזה) not בכרהו

---

94. Turner, *Genesis*, 123–24.

'*his* birthright' but now the other בכרה 'birthright'; the shift from the possessive to the definite here helps articulate the fact that the transaction is complete. All that remains on the stage is Jacob, possessor of the right of the firstborn.

A heretofore unrecognized comparison may be drawn between Jacob's speech in this section and Yʜwʜ's speech in 25:23. Both Jacob and Yʜwʜ are tantalizingly and deceptively silent regarding the reality of each respective situation. For God the trickster, the details of who is/will be the רב and who the צעיר are withheld, just as Jacob withholds from Esau the details regarding the true contents of the red pottage (נזיד). Not until the final verse in the scene (v. 34), after Jacob has already acquired the right of the firstborn, does the narrative reveal that the pottage on which Esau stakes his life and birthright is a simple dish of lentils (עדשים).[95] Many commentators have been reticent to label this episode as a deception, yet I cannot escape reading Jacob's demeanor and calculating silence as evidence of the trickster at work.[96] Indeed, Esau himself regards this episode as one of deception in 27:36! Furthermore, Hugh White points to a fascinating pun centered on the verb יזד ('cooking') used in v. 29 to allude to deception. The Hiphil form here occurs nowhere else in Biblical Hebrew with this meaning; it does occur, however, with the meaning 'to act presumptuously, or with willful forethought' in Exod 21:14; Deut 1:43; and 18:20.[97] A contemporary, parallel English colloquialism is "to cook up," meaning "to scheme."[98] This episode is therefore not a matter of mere happenstance; Jacob has planned for this moment and has a plan already devised. By means of this clever wordplay, the deceptive undertones of the scene become much more potent. Jacob has not only cooked up a stew, he has also cooked up a plan that will deceive Esau into giving him the right of the firstborn. The scene has been set for the next act of deception in Gen 27.

Fulfilling the Trickster Oracle (Genesis 27:1–45)

Scholars have dealt well with the complexity and intricacies that must accompany any discussion of Gen 27. Here I will not recapitulate the entire breadth of research on this seminal scene but instead discuss in more detail two specific areas on which the trickster oracle seems to have a bearing: the

---

95. Taschner, *Verheissung und Erfüllung*, 34. Paganini ("Wir haben Wasser gefunden," 29) makes a similar point that Esau sold his right of the firstborn without knowing what he was getting for it.

96. Von Rad, *Genesis*, 266; Brueggemann, *Genesis*, 230. Conversely, see Niditch (*Underdogs and Tricksters*, 101), who deems this episode one of "extortion by a clever con artist" with the purpose of "provid[ing] an initial and incomplete working out of the trickster pattern fully articulated in chapter 27."

97. Hugh C. White, *Narration and Discourse in the Book of Genesis* (Cambridge: Cambridge University Press, 1991) 211.

98. Ibid.

oracle's introduction of strife and conflict into the family relationship and God's place in the deception of Isaac. Regarding the conflict, Brueggemann rightly notes, "[I]t is clear that the oracle of 25:23 governs even here."[99] Thus, I will pay special attention not only to the oracle but also, by extension, to the way that God figures into this episode rife with deception.

The Trickster Oracle and Family Dissonance

I have already shown that the oracle introduces dissonance into the family as early as 25:27–34. This very dissonance swells to irreparable proportions in Gen 27. The separation and conflict that Yhwh spoke of in the prenatal oracle carry over to and involve the parents in deeply intimate ways. The family is ostensibly split in two, with Rebekah and Jacob on one side and Esau and Isaac on the other. But with the trickster oracle in play, God becomes an actor behind the scenes as well, ensuring that his purposes, whatever they may be, come to fruition.

That the family dynamic has already experienced considerable rupture is evidenced from the very beginning of the chapter. Isaac summons Esau so that he may bless him before his death; no attempt or mention is made that Jacob will also receive a blessing (which is surprising in itself, given that Isaac is in the end able to bless both Jacob and Esau, vv. 28–29, 39–40).[100] Wenham sees in Isaac's ostensible desire to bless *only* Esau and *not* Jacob a breach with convention (type scene) in that elsewhere in Genesis—specifically Gen 49; 50:24–25—all male family members expected to receive some type of blessing from a dying relative.[101] This deviation from convention highlights the family rupture all the more. Going further, Craig Smith offers a provocative reading that Isaac in fact falls quite short as a patriarch according to Yhwh's standards by his failure to pass on the full ancestral promise in Gen 27:26–29, coupled with his passivity in allowing Esau to marry such odious Hittite women.[102] The payoff in Smith's reading is that the fault for disjunction in the family lay solely with Isaac and his inability to function as a proper patriarch should. Smith's study, however, suffers from several difficulties, not least of which is the fact that Isaac does commend Jacob to receive the full ancestral promise in 28:1–5, a section that Smith consigns to the status of "additional material concerning Isaac and his activities as a patriarch."[103] Additionally, the Genesis narrative makes it quite clear that Yhwh alone, not a human patriarch, bestows the ancestral

---

99. Brueggemann, *Genesis*, 226.

100. See Claus Westermann (*Blessing in the Bible and the Life of the Church* [trans. Keith Crim; OBT; Philadelphia: Fortress, 1978] 1–62) for a thorough discussion of blessing in the Hebrew Bible. See especially pp. 54–56 on Gen 27.

101. Wenham, *Genesis 16–50*, 205, 215.

102. Craig A. Smith, "Reinstating Isaac: The Centrality of Abraham's Son in the 'Jacob-Esau' Narrative of Genesis 27," *BTB* 31 (2001) 130–34.

103. Ibid., 133.

promise on its rightful recipient (12:1–3; 26:2–5; 28:13–15). Brueggemann summarizes the matter nicely:

> The father gives the blessing he wants to give. But he gives it to the son whom he does not want to have it. *Surely there is more working against Isaac than the cunning of Rebekah. There is also the power of God at work for Jacob.* From the beginning, Isaac cannot resist it.[104]

Isaac is not in control of the situation; God, however, is very much in control.

Another indicator of the brokenness of the family lies in the fact that Rebekah must eavesdrop to obtain this information. This blessing is not to be a festive family affair. Rather, she has long thought Jacob to be the רב, and now she has the opportunity to act on this thought. Rebekah is a whirlwind of activity, instructing Jacob precisely through near-verbatim repetitions of Isaac's words to Esau. To be sure, Jacob's assent to Rebekah's plans further evinces a rift in the family. Westermann correctly notices that Jacob does not object to the plan but only to its "feasibility."[105] He is more than ready to go along with her plan and only questions *how* they will, not *whether* they should pull off the trick. Rebekah is not the sole trickster; Jacob has already shown his savvy in the birthright episode. Among Jacob's main concerns now is that his own smoothness will reveal him as a 'trickster' (מתעתע, v. 12) to his father.[106] Rebekah prepares the deception, but the successful completion of the task is left to Jacob.

Again, the narrative portrays Jacob in a way that is consonant with the divine trickster oracle in 25:23. Jacob, having just come to his father, nearly reveals himself by being a bit too garrulous (vv. 19, 20); perhaps suspecting his slipup, he shortens his response to merely one word when asked whether he is Esau or not: אני. In this way, Jacob again—just as in 25:27–34—remains deceptively silent about the details of his situation. Similarly, the divine speech in 25:23 withholds pertinent information from Rebekah albeit, conversely, in more verbose speech. The narrative further connects the two scenes through the realization that Rebekah and Jacob are, in fact, acting deceptively based on their own understanding of the trickster oracle.

The most concrete evidence of a family divide attributed to the oracle is the way that the chapter continually refers to each child in relation to each parent. At the outset, the narrative reports that Isaac summons 'his older son' (בנו הגדל), an inoffensive enough point until v. 5, when the narrative further reports that Rebekah overhears Isaac speaking to 'his son' (בנו). It is

---

104. Brueggemann, *Genesis*, 231–232. (italics mine)

105. Westermann, *Genesis 12–36*, 438. On this point, see also Fokkelman, *Narrative Art in Genesis*, 103; and Spina, "Esau in Canonical Context," 9.

106. Spina (Ibid., 10) notes the "double entendre" present in Jacob's smoothness, which the narrative underscores all the more in Jacob's own recognition of himself as a trickster (v. 12). See also Hendel, *The Epic of the Patriarch*, 128–29.

striking that the narrative does not call Esau "her son" or even "their son." This pattern continues when in v. 6 Rebekah addresses '*her* son Jacob' (יעקב בנה) and refers to Esau only as '*your* brother' (אחיך). This differentiation persists throughout the entire chapter. Jacob is called 'her son' (בנה) four times (vv. 6, 15, 17, 42) *by the narrator*, and Rebekah always calls Jacob 'my son" (בני, vv. 8, 13, 43). Isaac also calls Jacob "my son," but only because he believes Esau is in front of him (vv. 18, 20, 21 (2x), 24, 25, 26, 27).[107] The absolute irony in Isaac's near incessant use of "my son" for the disguised Jacob makes the distinction in the family that much more undeniable. Indeed, the oracle results not only in the separation of the twins, as promised, but also in an ever-widening divide of the entire family unit.[108]

God in the Deception of Isaac

Some scholars have sought to soften the fact that a divine purpose attains fulfillment by deception, and thus in the following analysis I mention two of these scholars briefly. Joseph Rackman challenges the validity and feasibility of a genuine blessing gained by deception. In an attempt to make sense of the text, Rackman avers that it was Isaac's intention all along to bless Jacob rather than Esau.[109] As evidence, he adduces the fact that the blessing given to Jacob disguised as Esau is concerned with material things, while in 28:3–4, when Isaac knows that Jacob is in front of him, he passes on the ancestral blessing.[110] But Rackman's textual analysis is nothing short of psychologizing with regard to the biblical characters.[111] Likewise, Mignon Jacobs wonders whether Isaac actually knows that Jacob is in front of him, in a way testing to see what lengths Jacob will go to in order to garner the blessing.[112] Certainly some psychologizing may be endemic to the art of biblical interpretation, yet one must remain grounded in and reliant on the text as the arbiter of what can and cannot be legitimated. Both Rackman and Jacobs frame their arguments as possibilities; they appear to do little in the way of addressing the probability of their readings. Moreover, each of these readings succumbs to a number of problems. First, the portrayal of Isaac offered by Rackman and Jacobs is inconsistent with the

---

107. Jeansonne, "The Use of Poetry," 149; idem, *The Women of Genesis*, 66; Niditch, *Underdogs and Tricksters*, 86.

108. See Fokkelman (*Narrative Art in Genesis*, 100–112) for a discussion of the breakdown of the family dynamic in this chapter from a strictly literary-esthetic perspective.

109. Joseph Rackman, "Was Isaac Deceived?" *Judaism* 43 (1993) 38.

110. Ibid.

111. Rackman (ibid., 40–41) suggests that Rebekah went about her deceptive plan because she failed to understand that the blessings could be separated. He further speculates regarding Isaac's mental health following the events of Gen 22; Isaac did not want to have to make the same choice between sons that his father had done.

112. Mignon Jacobs, *Gender, Power, and Persuasion: The Genesis Narratives and Contemporary Portraits* (Grand Rapids, MI: Baker Academic, 2007) 115–18.

biblical portrayal.[113] Isaac's great trembling in 27:33 attests to his absolute surprise in being tricked. If Isaac is in fact himself acting deceptively here, simply putting on a convincing show, he is doing so quite out of character, and quite compellingly! Second, Isaac's continued testing by means of all of his senses to discover who is truly in front of him, not to mention his persistent hesitancy in actually delivering the blessing, makes little sense if Isaac meant all along to bless Jacob. And third, again it is God alone who passes on the ancestral blessing; all Isaac does in 28:3–4 is commend Jacob to God. The line of argumentation advanced by Rackman and Jacobs does not appear convincing or viable based on a close scrutiny of the text.

While God does not appear as an explicit character in chap. 27, one should not conclude that silence bespeaks absence. Niditch writes of Gen 27 that "God is in the wings as helper and determinator."[114] And given that the oracle in 25:23 governs the entire Jacob cycle, one cannot help but see God as operative behind the scenes by means of that very oracle. Brueggemann, therefore, correctly underscores the highly theological nature of Gen 27. For him, the text is ultimately about God's desires; Rebekah's role, while no doubt active, is one that she herself does not choose but that God imposes and makes necessary with the oracle. He writes:

> Given the oracle of 25:23 and its undoubted continuing importance for the Jacob tradition, we may dare to conclude that the real issue here is not primarily about Isaac and Esau, nor about Rebekah and Jacob. It is, rather, about the *power of the blessing in the service of God's purpose of inversion.* . . . For this narrator, Rebekah plays a role she does not know about and did not choose. . . . We know only from 25:19–34 about the larger mystery at work here. . . . The bargaining for the birthright (25:29–34) and the scheme for the blessing (27:1–45) *implement the oracle* in ways unrecognized by every participant. God has evoked the conflict. The conflict causes pain or shame to every player. But God does not shrink from the conflict, *for a holy purpose is underway.*[115]

While Brueggemann is correct in noticing the purposes of God, he is incorrect in implying that Rebekah and Jacob appear merely as unwitting pawns in a divine game of chess. Rebekah especially acts with great volition. Simply because Rebekah and Jacob do not achieve success on their own does not mean they have not made the choice to act in this way. Indeed, given the ambiguity of the trickster oracle, they are likely unaware of the true divine intention and are only trying to bring about one possible under-

---

113. J. Cheryl Exum and J. William Whedbee ("Isaac, Samson, and Saul: Reflections on the Comic and Tragic Visions," in *Beyond Form Criticism: Essays in Old Testament Literary Criticism* [ed. Paul R. House; Sources for Biblical and Theological Study 2; Winona Lake, IN: Eisenbrauns, 1992] 277–86) contend that Isaac is a pathetically comic figure. See esp. pp. 284–85 on Gen 27.

114. Niditch, *Underdogs and Tricksters*, 100.

115. Brueggemann, *Genesis*, 235 (italics mine).

standing of it. Their sense of purpose is strong. They also probably assume that God is at work, as the following treatment will show; what remains shrouded from them is whether God is working for them or against them. God plays a part, to be sure, and a vital part at that, but it is a part that will not come to the fore until Bethel.

Genesis 27 does, however, adduce God in three instances that buttress his underlying role. The first reference is in v. 7, where Rebekah repeats to Jacob nearly verbatim what she overhears between Isaac and Esau. She cleverly adds that Isaac wishes to bless Esau 'before YHWH' (לפני יהוה). Scholars have struggled with how to handle this addition. Both Dillman and Skinner understand the phrase to connote a blessing in YHWH's presence.[116] For Wenham, it serves to convince Jacob that now is the moment to act.[117] Speiser and Sarna go one step further, maintaining that it means "with [YHWH's] approval."[118] While this supplement is clearly a lie—Isaac says no such thing—the line evokes the oracle based on which Rebekah understands Jacob to be preeminent. It is by means of this blessing given by God (vv. 28–29) that Rebekah probably perceives that Jacob will become the רב. And, as will become clear at Bethel, YHWH does approve!

The second time that YHWH appears is on the lips of Jacob. In v. 20, he responds to Isaac's query about the speed with which he was able to find the wild game by stating, "because YHWH your God caused it to happen (הקרה) for me." Commentators have long excoriated Jacob here for perverting the divine name and employing it in a blatant deception. Hamilton calls this the "low point" of the narrative.[119] Mignon Jacobs argues that Jacob implicates God in the deception in order to ensure his success, which "demonstrates a reckless abandon in achieving his goal."[120] Friedmann Golka says that Jacob's answer reverberates with theological insolence (*theologischen Unverschämtheit*).[121] Mathews accuses Jacob of blasphemy.[122] However, among the earliest interpreters of this text—the authors of the Jewish midrashim—one finds quite a different understanding. In one text, the divine is indeed at work on Jacob's behalf, just as the patriarch says. One midrash says:

> When Esau was hunting and tying [his catch], the angel was untying and setting it free . . . and why? In order to prolong the hours until Jacob will

---

116. August Dillman, *Genesis Critically and Exegetically Expounded* (vol. 2; Edinburgh: T. & T. Clark, 1897) 214; Skinner, *Genesis*, 370.

117. Wenham, *Genesis 16–50*, 206.

118. Speiser, *Genesis*, 209; Sarna, *Genesis*, 190.

119. Hamilton, *Genesis 18–50*, 220.

120. Jacobs, *Gender, Power, and Persuasion*, 113.

121. Friedmann Golka, "Bechorah und Berachah: Erstgeburtsrecht und Segen," in *Recht und Ethos im Alten Testament: Gestalt und Wirkung: Festschrift für Horst Seebass zum 65. Geburtstag* (ed. S. Beyerle, G. Mayer, and H. Strauss; Neukirchen-Vluyn; Neukirchener Verlag, 1999) 140.

122. Mathews, *Genesis 11:27–50:26*, 430.

go and do [what he needs] and goes in to his father and his father will eat and Jacob will take the blessing. (*Tanhuma Buber, Toledot* 10)[123]

The midrash fills in the gaps of the story (as midrash does) with an explication of the text that seemingly takes Jacob's words to his father at face value. The divine not only ensures Jacob's success; God also orchestrates Esau's failure.

What, then, if the midrash is correct? What if Jacob is, in a way, speaking the truth here? Several textual indicators point in this direction. Turner muses over the question, noting that Jacob's words use the same idiom employed in the speech of Abraham's servant in 24:12 when sent to fetch Isaac a wife; has God truly orchestrated success in both ventures?[124] Yes, though the narrative does not define precisely how this is the case. Schneider raises another informative parallel with Abraham and Sarah that underscores divine justification for the deception. Rebekah's reference to a "curse" in 27:12 followed by her instruction that Jacob "listen to my voice; go and take for me" (27:13) recalls Sarah's feelings when Hagar conceives a child for Abraham.[125] In Gen 21:12, God appears and instructs Abraham to "listen to [Sarah's] voice," revealing that Isaac is the child of the promise, not Ishmael. This textual echo, argues Schneider, "reinforces the legitimacy of Rebekah's actions through Sarah's earlier actions justified by the Deity."[126] Hamilton likewise argues that the use of קרה here and in 24:12 dictates that these events are not mere coincidence but, rather, are governed by divine providence.[127] Despite not appearing on stage, God is mysteriously at work in the deception of Isaac.

Two additional examples from early Jewish literature divulge an understanding that God participates on Jacob's behalf in the deception of Isaac. *Genesis Rabbah* 65:19 records an instance of divine assistance in strengthening Jacob's resolve to carry out the deception of his father and literally supporting him in this venture:

> When [Isaac] told Jacob, "Come closer that I may feel you, my son" (Gen 27:21), Jacob urinated onto his calves, and his heart became as soft as wax, and God assigned to him two angels, one on his right and one on his left, in order to hold him up by his elbows.[128]

---

123. Quoted in Zakovitch, "Inner-Biblical Interpretation," 118.
124. Turner, *Genesis*, 118.
125. Schneider, *Mothers of Promise*, 51.
126. Ibid., 52.
127. Hamilton, *Genesis 18–50*, 218.
128. Quoted in Zakovitch, "Inner-Biblical Interpretation," 118. Another translation of *Gen. Rab.* 65:19 reads, "Isaac said to Jacob, 'Come closer that I may feel you, my son,' but perspiration poured over his legs." Translational differences aside, both renderings capture the essence of the point I wish to make: the rabbis seemingly had no qualms about integrating God deeply into the fabric of Jacob's deception of his father.

In *Jub.* 26:18, one reads, "[Isaac] discerned him not, because it was a dispensation from heaven to remove his power of perception."[129] These examples evince the fact that it was not incongruous in early Jewish thought and interpretation to equate God with deception.[130]

The third and final mention of God in Gen 27 appears in Isaac's blessing of a disguised Jacob. Verse 28 begins "may God give you . . . ," which accentuates that Jacob's blessing actually comes from God.[131] What is most vital to recognize, however, is that once the deception is uncovered Isaac affirms and upholds Jacob's blessed status (v. 33). Esau too receives a blessing (vv. 39–40) that is remarkably similar to Jacob's. Two glaring differences stand out. First, Esau's blessing reverses the first two lines of Jacob's blessing, leading many scholars incorrectly to regard it as a curse or anti-blessing.[132] Second, and most importantly, God appears nowhere in the blessing of Esau. Taken in tandem, this second fact is not a denigration of Esau for the future but is simply a concern to show that *the ancestral promise* will go to Jacob, not Esau. And this is precisely what happens as the text continues.

Divine Corroboration at Bethel:
Genesis 28 and Deception

The plan does not work out as tidily as the tricksters might have hoped. While Jacob receives the blessing, the deception puts his life in mortal danger as Rebekah learns of Esau's plot to murder his brother (vv. 41–42). Rebekah thus hatches another deception, with Isaac as the deceived, this time withholding Esau's machinations as the impetus for her desire to send Jacob away and instead couching the rationale for doing so in their shared desire that Jacob find a proper wife (vv. 43–46). What emerges from this further deception, however, is quite remarkable. Chapter 28 begins with 'and Isaac called to Jacob' (ויקרא יצחק אל־יעקב), which hearks back to the beginning of chap. 27, where Isaac 'called to Esau' (ויקרא את־עשׂו). A change has

---

129. Quoted in Zakovitch, ibid.

130. Zakovitch (ibid.) contends that these texts are ultimately concerned with "clear-[ing] Jacob's name of accusations of deceit." While this may be the case, what is actually achieved in these (re-)interpretations is an implicating of God in the deception. That early Jewish literature appears to have little issue with tethering God to deception—even if in the attempt to exonerate Jacob—reveals that the idea of a divine trickster may in fact *not* be foreign, not only to early Judaism, but also to an understanding of the texts of the Jacob cycle.

131. Fokkelman, *Narrative Art in Genesis*, 110; Taschner, *Verheissung und Erfüllung*, 45.

132. Fokkelman, *Narrative Art in Genesis*, 104; von Rad, *Genesis*, 279; Syrén, *The Forsaken First-Born*, 99; Gunkel, *Genesis*, 306; Skinner, *Genesis*, 378. The crux of this interpretation revolves around the construal of מן in each blessing, according to these scholars. Is it partitive or privative? I argue instead, as is evident above, that the key interpretive issue is not how one translates the particle מן but that any mention of God is entirely absent from Esau's blessing. One cannot call it a curse, for in Gen 33 Esau most certainly appears to have a great deal of wealth.

surely taken place! Moreover, without any blatant reason given, Isaac again blesses Jacob, this time commending Jacob to God as the viable recipient of the ancestral promise (28:3–4). One must remain mindful that Isaac does not confer the promise itself on Jacob; he requests that Yʜwʜ do it.[133] Presumably Yʜwʜ could withhold the promise from Jacob, showing distaste for the unpalatable way that Jacob obtained the birthright and blessing. On the run, Jacob's life is now laden with questions, not answers. Perhaps he fears how God will respond to such duplicity. How striking and revelatory it is, then, that *Yʜwʜ does give* Jacob the ancestral promise in 28:13–15, on the very heels of a family-shattering act of deception!

The proximity of Isaac's blessing in 28:3–4 and Yʜwʜ's granting Jacob the ancestral promise in 28:13–15 tethers chaps. 27 and 28 together.[134] When read in this way, God's appearance to Jacob in the dream theophany at Bethel acts as a confirmation of all that has come before. De Pury astutely reads the Bethel scene as a confirmation of not just the promise but the promise gained by fraud.[135]

The Genesis narrative itself also communicates this same sort of divine authentication and corroboration of the events in chaps. 25 and 27. Diana Lipton's *Revisions of the Night* is a careful and judicious study of the various dreams in the ancestral narratives. Lipton isolates six recurrent themes in each of these dream scenes, one theme of which is most pertinent to my purposes here. She writes: "Each dream recasts recent events to reveal divine involvement in what had previously appeared as an exclusively human affair."[136] One can already see the relevance of Lipton's thesis for the present study. Proponents of removing God from the narrative scene in these episodes have not yet adequately attended to the function of Bethel in the overall experience of Jacob's life. Truly, Lipton asserts that, if God does not approve, then readers are hard-pressed to explain Jacob's extraordinary

---

133. On this point, see especially Terence E. Fretheim, "Which Blessing Does Isaac Give Jacob?" in *Jews, Christians, and the Theology of the Hebrew Scriptures* (ed. Alice Ogden Bellis and Joel S. Kaminsky; SBLSymS 8; Atlanta: Society of Biblical Literature, 2000) 289–90.

134. Susan Ackerman ("The Deception of Isaac, Jacob's Dream at Bethel, and Incubation on an Animal Skin," in *Priesthood and Cult in Ancient Israel* [ed. Gary A. Anderson and Saul M. Olyan; JSOTSup 125; Sheffield: Sheffield Academic Press, 1991] 119) further sees Gen 27 and 28 as "two acts in one play." Genesis 27 results in the necessity for Jacob to flee, which ultimately brings him to Bethel, where he receives the ancestral promise.

135. De Pury, *Promesse Divine*, 101. He writes: "Après avoir obtenu la bénédiction paternelle par la fraude (Gen 27), bénédiction qui, il est vrai, lui avait été confirmée par Dieu à Béthel (28:13–15)."

136. Diana Lipton, *Revisions of the Night: Politics and Promise in the Patriarchal Dreams of Genesis* (JSOTSup 288; Sheffield: Sheffield Academic Press, 1999) 33. The five other unifying themes are as follows: (1) the dream occurs at a time of anxiety or danger; (2) descendants and threat to one's progeny are in sight; (3) the dream signifies the dreamer's change in status; (4) the dream treats in some way the relationship between Israelites and non-Israelites; (5) exile from the land is a motif.

vision of a staircase with God perched atop it.[137] Going further, if God does not approve, why does he grant the ancestral promise to Jacob? God has shown in 25:23 that he feels free to act as he prefers; why would now be any different?

Lipton uncovers several ways in which the Bethel narrative communicates Yhwh's approval of Jacob, his activity, and the results. God's first words explicitly to Jacob in v. 13, "I am Yhwh, God of *Abraham your father,* and God of Isaac," show a "divine displeasure" with Isaac's preference for Esau by identifying Jacob as Abraham's son.[138] Hamilton on the other hand deems this introductory phrase an example of Yhwh's "indirect censure" of Jacob in that Yhwh identifies himself as the "God of Isaac," or put another way, the God of the father you deceived.[139] Hamilton's assertion is unconvincing. First, Hamilton is incorrect that Yhwh reveals himself as "God of his [Jacob's] grandfather and the God of his father."[140] Isaac is nowhere here called Jacob's father; Abraham receives this accolade. "Abraham *your father"* is far too jarring and significant a phrase, especially based on my discussion of the beginning of the Jacob cycle, and the phrase "God of Isaac" is said almost in passing. It is also a wonder that if God intends to reprimand Jacob the chosen mode of punishment is not divine rebuke but a litany of unconditional promises!

One may also see this return to focusing on Abraham as hearking back to the emphasis placed on Abraham in the opening verses of the Isaac *toledot* (25:19–22). There I discussed how the themes of barrenness, promise, and the fatherhood of Abraham connected the two narratives together and relegated Isaac to the margins. Remember also that it is Rebekah, not Isaac, who receives the trickster oracle. Reading Abraham's paternity of Jacob in 28:13 as a judgment on Isaac allows for a reading of the marginalization of Isaac and focus on Abraham's paternity of Isaac in 25:19–20 as an early sign of God's discontentment with this most passive of patriarchs. One may also read this return to Abraham as another sign of assurance that the promise rightly belongs to Jacob.

Two additional rationales underscore God's ratification of Jacob and the blessing. First, for Lipton several parallels exist in the wording of part of God's promise to Jacob in 28:14 and God's affirming of the land promise to Abraham in 13:14–15. The fact that these connections skip over Isaac further reinforces Yhwh's annoyance at Isaac's initial preference for blessing Esau.[141] Second, Bethel (Gen 28) is typologically related to Babel (Gen 11); both share elements of a structure stretching between heaven and earth,

---

137. Ibid., 68.
138. Ibid., 69–70.
139. Hamilton, *Genesis 18–50,* 241.
140. Ibid.
141. Lipton, *Revisions of the Night,* 70.

divine presence, scattering, and the etiological naming of a place.[142] In the story of Babel, humanity is scattered for acting outside the bounds of divine approval, and God comes down to observe a structure that the people have built; in the story of Bethel, Jacob's vision mentions scattering in a positive light, as the fulfillment of the ancestral promise, and God shows a structure to Jacob that is actually able to reach the heavens.[143] The compound effect of these narrative cues demonstrates that God views Jacob and his duplicitous actions positively.

A final question remains to be asked, however: what is one to make of Jacob's response to God in 28:20–22? The ancestral promise bestowed on Jacob in 28:13–15 is clearly unconditional: land, descendants, and blessing, not to mention the two additional elements of presence and protection granted in v. 15. Several commentators argue that Jacob responds by placing stipulations on his acceptance of Yhwh as his God. Humphreys maintains that Jacob alleviates any responsibility placed on him by the promise and rephrases it so that Yhwh bears sole responsibility for ensuring that the particulars of the promise come to fruition.[144] Jeffrey Geoghegan presses the issue further, arguing that Jacob's duplicitous words to his father, "Yhwh, *your God*," in 27:20 show that Jacob is glad to avail himself of God to advance his own purposes, but he has no other interest outside his own self-interest.[145] According to this line of interpretation, Jacob's "if-then" statement sets conditions on a relationship that has yet to be forged. According to Geoghegan, Jacob requests three things: protection, provision, and peaceful return, and the rest of the cycle works toward the fulfillment of each of these items.[146] The liability latent in this reading is that Yhwh accepts Jacob, deceptions and all, but Jacob may not accept Yhwh, an argument that seems out of place given all that Jacob has experienced prior to his chancing upon Bethel.[147]

Adequate and convincing reasons exist to challenge this aforementioned reading of Jacob's vow. Primary among these is the fact that one cannot properly comprehend Jacob's vow apart from the promise in vv. 13–15. The three "stipulations" that Jacob supposedly advances according to Geoghegan in fact correspond almost precisely to the expanded promise in v. 15. Table 2.1 summarizes these affinities.

---

142. Ibid., 103.

143. Ibid. On this point, see also Hamilton, *Genesis 18–50*, 240.

144. Humphreys, *The Character of God in the Book of Genesis*, 172.

145. Jeffrey C. Geoghegan, "Jacob's Bargain with God (Gen 28:20–22) and Its Implications for the Documentary Hypothesis," in *Milk and Honey: Essays on Ancient Israel and the Bible in Appreciation of the Judaic Studies Program at the University of California, San Diego* (ed. Sarah Malena and David Miano; Winona Lake, IN: Eisenbrauns, 2007) 25.

146. Ibid., 27.

147. Lipton (*Revisions of the Night*, 76) writes, "Jacob is hardly likely to have responded to the confirmation that God will accept him by implying that he may not accept God."

Table 2.1. Jacob's Vow and the Ancestral Promise

Jacob's Vow	Ancestral Promise
[20]If Yʜwʜ God will be with me and protect me on this way that I am going,	[15]And behold, I am with you, and I will protect you everywhere you go.
and give me bread to eat and a garment to wear,	
[21]and I return in peace to the house of my father,	And I will bring you back to this land, for I will not forsake you until I have done what I say to you.
Yʜwʜ will be God to me.	

The only part of Jacob's vow that lacks a direct counterpart in the promise is the request for food and clothing, but basic necessities could easily fall under the purview of God's abiding protection. What sense can one make of Jacob's vow in light of this analysis?

Jacob's vow expresses the divine promise in terms that seek to clarify its particulars, not to challenge the feasibility of this new relationship. For Lipton, Jacob repeats and paraphrases the ancestral promise "to clarify precisely how it will be fulfilled."[148] His requests for protection, safe passage and return, as well as food and clothing are quite sensible for a man who has just fled and left everything behind.[149] Moreover, John Van Seters holds that in Gen 28:10–22 the expected pattern of supplication followed by promise sees a reversal, but this reversal makes perfect sense given that Jacob was unable to pray to a God he did not yet know.[150] This early ignorance on Jacob's part helps level a challenge to the view that Jacob places conditions on his acceptance of God. In 27:20, Jacob has already used the divine name in a statement that rings much truer than one may think at first glance. Van Seters avers that Jacob's use of "your God" in reference to Yʜwʜ in 27:20 conforms well to Yʜwʜ's self-revelation in 28:13: "I am the God of Abraham your father, and God of Isaac." In the vow, then, Jacob continues the line, affirming that Yʜwʜ will now be his God.[151]

One may still, however, see in Jacob's acceptance of the ancestral promise resonances of the trickster at work. Jacob's words may also be laden with ambiguity, shrouding the whole truth. Indeed, where the protasis ends and the apodosis begins is quite unclear. This ambiguity suggests that Jacob

---

148. Ibid., 77. Lipton also translates the oracle differently from many, marking the transition from protasis to apodosis at the beginning of v. 22 ("then this stone . . .") rather than in the middle of v. 21 (p. 75).

149. Walton (*Thou Traveller Unknown*, 53) sees Jacob as practical, asking only for "bare essentials."

150. John Van Seters, "Divine Encounter at Bethel (Gen 28.10–22) in Recent Literary-Critical Study of Genesis," *ZAW* 110 (1998) 508.

151. Ibid., 509.

has ensured that he has some maneuverability should Y<small>HWH</small> not uphold his end of the bargain. One should not make the leap to assuming that, if Jacob's words may still be those of a trickster, then he does not accept the divine offer. For now, Jacob accepts, but the ambiguous and numinous speech of the trickster allows Jacob a potential "out" from this new relationship should he need it.[152]

Placed in this context, Bethel serves a dual purpose. It presses the Jacob cycle forward as a story about God's presence with and protection of Jacob. It also shows God's acceptance of and role in the previous deceptions of Esau and Isaac by means of God's choice of Jacob. In the trickster oracle, Y<small>HWH</small> ambiguously announces that "the greater will serve the lesser." Jacob and Rebekah work toward fulfilling a particular understanding of the oracle that regards Jacob as the רב, and through several deceptions Jacob achieves the right of the firstborn and the paternal blessing, entitling him also to the ancestral promise. At Bethel, God reveals that Rebekah has interpreted correctly. Jacob the trickster is the divine choice to carry the promise forward.

Conclusion:
A Trickster Oracle and Y<small>HWH</small>'s Preference for a Trickster

In the foregoing analysis, I read Gen 25:23, Y<small>HWH</small>'s oracle to Rebekah, as an example of a trickster oracle. First, I argued that the opening verses of the Jacob cycle underscore both the importance of the ancestral promise and the highly theological nature of the cycle. Second, focus on the oracle itself in 25:23 demonstrated that one cannot read it under the a priori assumption that it coheres with other narratives of inversion in Genesis. Rather, in light of Alter's understanding of the biblical type scene, what is seminal in understanding the oracle is how it differs from the convention of annunciation of birth elsewhere in Genesis. What emerges from this examination is a recognition of the oracle's ambiguity which, in line with the definition of "deception" as the withholding or manipulating of information, supports reading the oracle as a trickster oracle. Through it, God shows himself to be a trickster by means of the oracle's blatant ambiguity in matters of diction and meaning, syntax, and context. Additionally, God's very reticence to name the "greater" and the "lesser" impels the narrative's human characters—Rebekah and Jacob—to bring about their own interpretation of the divine will, which they succeed in doing by means of several deceptions.

---

152. Unfortunately, space precludes a more sustained treatment of this possibility, yet the constant debate within scholarship over how one should understand Jacob in this instance may well attest to the viability of reading Jacob's acceptance of the promise not as imposing conditions upon God but as leaving room to renegotiate, should the terms need to change.

With this point in mind, two scenes of deception—Jacob's extorting the right of the firstborn from Esau (Gen 25:27–34) and the deception of Isaac that leads to the theft of the blessing as well (Gen 27:1–45)—were interpreted in light of the oracle. One discerns that God's purposes are operative throughout, and the trickster oracle has had a lasting effect on this family. This function of the oracle, in all its vagueness, as an introduction of sorts to the entire Jacob cycle thus intimately involves God in the various deceptions and, ultimately, God is deemed complicit. I have argued, however, that the "mitigating factor" (if one can call it such a thing) during all this deception appears in the second theophany in the cycle, in which Jacob receives the ancestral promise solely at Yhwh's behest. Yhwh's bestowal of the ancestral promise on the trickster Jacob succeeds in affirming the deceptive measures employed to get to this point and upholds Jacob as the rightful recipient of the promise. And it is the perpetuation of this very promise, at times by deceptive measures, that is the principal concern of Yhwh in Genesis.

In the end, the oracle does not appear ever to have been concerned with Jacob's *becoming* the greater. Instead, he *is* the greater from the very outset, a status substantiated through his cunning and shrewd characterization as opposed to the dim-witted and overly dramatic Esau. Why then, has God chosen this sort of individual as bearer of the ancestral promise, and why is it he who becomes Israel? The interpretation offered here provides a plausible response: God the trickster selects Jacob because it is he, not Esau, who is a trickster from the very beginning.

Chapter 3

Divine Deception and Incipient Fulfillment of the Ancestral Promise (Genesis 29–31)

Introductory Remarks

Commentators often regard Jacob's sojourn in Haran as an extended period of trial and toil in his life. Episodes such as Laban's deception of Jacob, Jacob's obtaining a wife he does not love (Leah), and Laban's incessant manipulations to ensure a prolonging of Jacob's services serve as the prism through which these negative experiences are refracted. For instance, Victor Hamilton describes Jacob's stay with Laban as a period "filled with heartaches" and one that is "far from ideal."[1] Nahum Sarna argues that Jacob's kissing of Rachel (29:11) and Laban's kissing of Jacob (29:13) echo Isaac's kissing of a disguised Jacob in 27:26–27, communicating that what follows serves as "retributive justice" for Jacob's wrongdoing.[2] And Gordon Wenham maintains that the onslaught of tribulation and misfortune that follows Jacob's deception of Isaac and Esau indicates that the implied author does not commend this activity.[3] Yet in emphasizing the prevalence of Jacob's negative experiences in Haran, one quickly loses sight of the concomitant theme of fulfillment that begins to emerge by and through the narrative's many deceptions.

A new chapter in the unfolding of the ancestral promise appears in Gen 29–31. Until now, Jacob has done all that he can simply to obtain the promise, deceiving both his father and his brother in the process. Now, with the promise unequivocally his, one's attention turns to matters of fulfillment. The narrative, however, presents other attendant difficulties that have the capacity to impede any fulfillment of the promise. As a result of his deceptions, Jacob has been forced to flee what was once the security of his family and home in order to escape Esau's murderous machinations. He leaves behind a broken family, to whom he has hardly been a *blessing*.

---

1. Victor P. Hamilton, *The Book of Genesis: Chapters 18–50* (NICOT; Grand Rapids, MI: Eerdmans, 1995) 252.

2. Nahum M. Sarna, *The JPS Torah Commentary: Genesis* (Philadelphia: Jewish Publication Society, 1989) 203.

3. Gordon J. Wenham, *Story as Torah: Reading Old Testament Narrative Ethically* (Grand Rapids, MI: Baker Academic, 2004) 77.

Jacob has left not only his family but also the *land* that Yʜwʜ promised to Abraham in Gen 12:1. And last, while Jacob has set off in pursuit of an appropriate wife, no guarantee exists that Jacob will be met with acceptance in Laban's household, especially in light of the unceremonious way that Jacob has left his own family. A threat therefore exists to the prospect of a *great nation* as well. What's more, the journey to Laban's family is part of what appears to be a most uncertain future. One wonders when the fulfillment will take place for Jacob, the man on the run. Notices such as these lead Turner to conclude that within the entire Jacob cycle no advancement of the ancestral promise beyond the advancement to nationhood exists.[4] I will challenge Turner's claim in this chapter.

One should remain mindful, however, that Jacob is not alone. At Bethel, God has bestowed on him the ancestral promise along with the additional promises of presence and protection. Humphreys, thus, rightly reminds the reader that, despite the situation in which Jacob leaves his family, God makes it abundantly clear that the divine preference is for Jacob; indeed, God joins Jacob in his exile.[5] The question then becomes not only *when* fulfillment will occur but also *how* it will occur. I have already shown in chap. 2 that the trickster oracle in 25:23 both employs and brings about further deceptions in the pursuit of its fulfillment. Now, with the promise in place, will deception recede, or will it continue as a medium of fulfillment?

Throughout Gen 29–31, one discerns movement toward and, in some respects, the incipient fulfillment of the three particulars of the ancestral promise: progeny, blessing, and land. Scholars have readily noted the first of these, with increasingly less attention to the second and third. Moreover, what remains absent in any treatment of Gen 29–31 is the relationship that fulfillment shares with the multiple deceptions that occur. Indeed, little seems to have changed; just as the trickster oracle attains fulfillment by means of deception, so also the ancestral promise advances amid and through various deceptions.

A recurrent theme from chap. 2 also reemerges: the providence of a divine trickster. While again Yʜwʜ is remarkably silent for much of Jacob's internment with Laban, the text provides several narrative cues that God continues to be at work. First, as Michael Fishbane and Walter Brueggemann, among others, have noted, the trickster oracle continues to inform one's reading of the Jacob cycle.[6] Second, theophany and deception again occur in literary proximity to one another. Bethel thus possesses a double

---

4. Laurence A. Turner, *Announcements of Plot in Genesis* (JSOTSup 96; Sheffield: JSOT Press, 1990) 140.

5. W. Lee Humphreys, *The Character of God in the Book of Genesis: A Narrative Appraisal* (Louisville: Westminster John Knox, 2001) 169.

6. Michael A. Fishbane, "Composition and Structure in the Jacob Cycle (Gen. 25:19–35:22)," *JJS* 26 (1975) 21; Walter Brueggemann, *Genesis* (Interpretation; Atlanta: John Knox, 1982) 257.

function—both authenticating the deceptive events of Gen 25 and 27 and setting the stage for the deceptive interactions between Jacob and Laban. Even more salient is one instance in which theophany and deception actually coincide in Gen 30–31. This episode will receive sustained treatment in what follows. Third, reminiscent of Gen 27, the narrative mentions Yʜᴡʜ in several instances, which highlight divine involvement in the unfolding story of these characters.

In this chapter, I will explore this connection between divine deception and movement toward fulfillment of the ancestral promise in four specific areas. First, the narrative of Jacob's arrival in Haran (29:1–14a) will be shown to introduce the ancestral promise and concerns for its fulfillment. Relatedly, I will examine Laban's subsequent deception of Jacob by giving him Leah before giving him Rachel (29:14b–30) for the way that it provides the circumstances under which fulfillment may begin to take place. This act of trickery will be seen to serve as an orientation to the larger complex of Jacob/Laban stories in Gen 29–31, quite similar to the trickster oracle in 25:23, which was treated in detail in the previous chapter, in that it sets the stage for subsequent deceptions and fulfillments. Second, the extended narrative recording the births of Jacob's children will underscore Yʜᴡʜ's commitment to and use of deception as a means of fulfilling the ancestral promise of a "great nation" (12:2). Third, the promise of blessing in Gen 12:2b–3 reaches a qualified fulfillment in Laban's recognition that Jacob has blessed him (30:27). I will read this statement against the backdrop of the prevailing deceptions and highlight how they contribute to and yet also temper fulfillment. And fourth, I will devote a great deal of attention to analyzing perhaps the most potent instance of divine deception in the Jacob cycle, the numinous breeding-of-the-flocks episode in Gen 30:37–43 and Jacob's subsequent clarification of the scene in 31:1–16. This analysis will have a twin focus on what this activity reveals about God and how it helps advance the promise of land.

The Trickster Tricked and Yʜᴡʜ's Role (Genesis 29:1–30)

In chap. 2, I discussed how the opening verses of the Jacob cycle introduced an emphasis on Abraham and Yʜᴡʜ's concern for the ancestral promise. Here, at the outset of this second block of material narrating the life of Jacob, a similar focus appears, except that in this instance it hearks back specifically to the ancestral promise granted to Jacob at Bethel in Gen 28:13–15. The promise will again be central in the stories that follow, but it will be central in a different way. Whereas Gen 25:19–20 was seen to conjure up past images of Yʜᴡʜ's desires for the promise, in Gen 29–31 the promise becomes a present reality, the outworking of which begins to take center stage. The focus does not rest solely on the promise itself but also on the startling ways in which it begins to reach fulfillment.

Bethel and the Providence of a Divine Trickster (Genesis 29:1–14a)

Jacob continues his journey from Bethel, arriving at an unnamed place. It is unclear initially why Jacob has opted to stop at this particular location. Does he merely see it as another junction on a much longer trip, or does he believe he has arrived at his destination? The latter possibility is tenuous in light of Jacob's question to the shepherds gathered at the well, asking where he is. In considering the response to this question, we must realize that the text does not provide a name for the place, calling it only 'the land of the sons of the east' (ארצה בני־קדם). Commentators often take this vague descriptor to be an indicator of alienation or judgment.[7] For instance, Mathews adduces a number of texts (Gen 2:8; 3:24; 4:14; 11:2) in support of his claim that the word 'east' (קדם) in Genesis carries a double meaning, serving as a directional marker as well as connoting rejection.[8] Mathews's assertion falters, however, on several fronts.

First, the word קדם does not in fact occur in 4:14, but it does in 4:16 in reference to Yнwн's settling Cain in the land of Nod, "east of Eden." Certainly one may see judgment as operative here, given Cain's heinous crime. However, one should not undermine the fact that, not only has Yнwн settled Cain in the east, Yнwн has also shown Cain mercy by placing a protective mark on him. Second, close scrutiny of these texts shows in some cases that Mathews reads them in questionable ways. Genesis 2:8 only declares that God places a garden in the eastern part of Eden, where God also puts the man. This scene is depicting the initial beauty and bounty of creation rather than judgment for an offense that has not yet happened. Likewise, 3:24 only states that Yнwн places the cherubim and flaming sword at the "east of Eden" to protect the Tree of Life; nothing is said about where Yнwн drives the man.[9] In 11:2, the people come '*from* the east' (מקדם) and settle in Shinar, only then beginning to cause trouble; Jacob, conversely, is traveling *to* the east.

At other places in Genesis, the word "east" occurs in connection with blessing and promise. In 10:30, Noah's descendants become so great that they spread to the hill country of the east, which may be read as a fulfill-

---

7. See Martin Ravndal Hauge ("The Struggles of the Blessed in Estrangement I," *ST* 29 [1975] 15), who holds that the designation "east" stands as a place toward which the loser of a conflict is exiled. Jacob, however, coming off Gen 25–28 is hardly the loser; he will also leave Laban after a number of years as the winner of a conflict, again with God's assistance.

8. Kenneth A. Mathews, *Genesis 11:27–50:26* (NAC 1B; Nashville: Broadman & Holman, 2005) 461. See also Hamilton (*Genesis 18–50*, 252) for a similar, though abbreviated list. Hamilton proposes that *movement toward* the east occurs in reference to judgment (4:16), vanity (11:2; 13:11), or alienation (25:6).

9. The location of the Tree of Life in Gen 3:24 as situated in the eastern part of the garden of Eden also informs the occurrence of "east" in 2:8. Here, Yнwн places the man, not in a situation of judgment, but in the exact same place as the Tree of Life.

ment of YHWH's postdiluvian command to "be fruitful and multiply and fill the earth" (9:1). In 12:8, the word appears twice, referencing Abraham's obedient response to YHWH's call in 12:1–3 and his journey toward the hill country *"east* of Bethel." The mention of Bethel here provides an even deeper connection to the promise in 29:1. In 25:6, Abraham does indeed send his children by concubines "eastward, to the land of the east," but the text says he does so only to separate them from the child of the promise, Isaac. One need not, therefore, read this scene in a wholly negative manner. After all, Abraham does give these children gifts before sending them away. This separation, therefore, may just as well function to protect the rightful heir to the promise from any potential threats (albeit putting his "extended family" in jeopardy, treating them as expendable). Last, Gen 13:11 narrates the separation of Abraham and Lot, the latter of whom chooses the whole land of the east. This scene, however, creates a threat to the promise; Lot could have chosen the promised land of Canaan. Cementing the connection to the ancestral promise, in 13:14 YHWH instructs Abraham to look in all directions, to the north, *east*, south, and west, again affirming that the entire land would belong to Abraham. The parallel with Bethel of four compass points and the final appearance of "east" in 28:14 is most striking.

From this perspective, the designation "land of the sons of the east" stands as an indicator that the ancestral promise is moving toward fulfillment. At Bethel, YHWH had promised Jacob that he would "spread out to the west and *to the east* (קדמה) and to the north and to the south" (28:14), recalling the repeated promise to Abraham in Gen 13:14. That Jacob now arrives in an area described by one of these compass points serves as a cue to the attentive reader to expect what follows to bear some relation and import to the ancestral promise that Jacob has just received from YHWH.

In fact, Jacob does not learn he has reached his destination until v. 4, when one of the shepherds tending his flock responds that Jacob is in Haran. The mention of Haran again evokes Abraham; Haran was his ancestral home prior to YHWH's calling (12:4, 5). One should not, however, see here a sort of reversal of the promise, as though it were moving even further away from fulfillment, given that Jacob has returned to the place of its original utterance. Quite the contrary, for Haran is precisely where Rebekah had instructed him to go to find a suitable wife (27:43). Jacob is exactly where he is meant to be, and more importantly, as will become clear, exactly where God intends him.

The mention of Haran also recalls Gen 24, the story of Abraham's sending his servant to Haran to acquire a suitable wife for his son Isaac. Robert Alter describes this scene of betrothal at a well as another compelling instance of a biblical type scene.[10] One may recall from chap. 2 that a type

---

10. Robert Alter, *The Art of Biblical Narrative* (New York: Basic Books, 1981) 51. Hamilton (*Genesis 18–50*, 254–55), enumerates the various parts of the scene: (1) character

scene is a conventional or stock way of articulating a particular scene, including certain elements that an audience would expect, yet adapting—or even eliminating—some aspects in order to give the story its own particular nuance and meaning. If one compares these two examples of a type scene, in Gen 24 and 29, several significant differences emerge that may inform one's reading of chap. 29.[11] First, unlike Abraham's servant, who arrived with an impressive arsenal of animals and riches (24:10, 22, 30, 53), Jacob arrives destitute. Turner sees Jacob's status here as resulting from Jacob's previous misdeeds, evidencing the fact that Jacob now "lacks everything his stolen blessing had supposedly conferred on him."[12] Further, Turner argues that, while Abraham's servant has humbly beseeched God for guidance along the way (24:12–14), Jacob conversely has arrogantly sworn an oath at Bethel.[13] In chap. 1, I argued that this negative reading of Jacob's vow is wanting. One also should not forget, as Turner seems to have done, that, while Jacob does not come equipped with the same accoutrements as Abraham's servant did, he will in the end acquire them with God's assistance during his stay with Laban. Sharon Pace Jeansonne argues that already one may discern a foreshadowing of Jacob's future prosperity in the repeated mention of Laban's flocks accompanying Rachel to the well (vv. 6, 9, 10).[14] Jacob may not come with impressive wealth, but he also does not come entirely empty-handed; he comes both with the ancestral promise and with God.

Second, and perhaps most germane to the present discussion, whereas Abraham and his servant incessantly credit God with the success of the mission (24:7, 12, 27, 40, 42, 48), God appears nowhere in Gen 29. Esther Fuchs sees an overarching trajectory spanning the three betrothal type scenes—Gen 24; 29:1–15; and Exod 2:5–11—showing an increasing de-emphasis on the soon-to-be wife, concomitant with an increasing emphasis on the soon-to-be husband.[15] For Fuchs, repetition and attention to detail show that Gen 24 is "divinely sanctioned," while in Gen 29, it is Jacob who is bursting with activity.[16] Jacob sees Rachel, rolls the stone away on his

---

journeys to a far-off land; (2) character arrives at a well; (3) female(s) comes to draw water; (4) male draws water for the female, or vice versa; (5) female goes home and relates the encounter to father or brother; (6) male is brought to the female's house; (7) marriage.

11. For a full account of the differences and how they may contribute to both characterization and foreshadowing, see Alter, *The Art of Biblical Narrative*, 52–56.

12. Laurence A. Turner, *Genesis* (Readings; 2nd ed.; Sheffield: Sheffield Phoenix, 2009) 126.

13. Ibid., 126.

14. Sharon Pace Jeansonne, *The Women of Genesis: From Sarah to Potiphar's Wife* (Minneapolis: Fortress, 1990) 71.

15. Esther Fuchs, "Structure, Ideology and Politics in the Biblical Betrothal Type-Scene," in *A Feminist Companion to Genesis* (ed. Athalya Brenner; Sheffield: Sheffield Academic, 1993) 273.

16. Ibid., 274, 276.

own, kisses Rachel, and then weeps. Latent in Fuchs's analysis is that while God is active in Gen 24 it is Jacob who is active in Gen 29. Jacob's activity, however, is quite telling of a divine hand at work in a way that Fuchs has not noted. Humphreys points out that in both instances of the type scene in Genesis the characters arrive without issue and almost immediately at the exact well where they will find those for whom they are looking.[17] Humphreys correctly claims that, when Gen 29 is read alongside Gen 24 and Yʜᴡʜ's promise in Gen 28, one may discern God at work. In what follows, we will focus more intently on the stone and its connection to divine presence. Jacob's kissing of Rachel serves as a sign that he has completed his journey on which Yʜᴡʜ has promised presence and protection. Similarly, Hamilton sees Jacob's uncharacteristic crying as a recognition of this same fact.[18]

Susanne Gillmayr-Bucher stresses the import of Yʜᴡʜ's guidance as a prerequisite for success in Gen 24, but also the way in which the two scenes may inform one another.[19] In Gen 29, Jacob becomes a sort of "stand-in" for Abraham's servant.[20] This does not, of course, automatically place the words of Abraham's servant on the lips of Jacob, but it does cause one to wonder how the latter scene employs the convention in its own unique way.

Despite Jacob's lack of repeatedly professing a divine hand at work, one need look only to Jacob's parting words at Bethel in response to a divine word of promise to find the necessary evidence that God is with Jacob.[21] Indeed, another difference between Gen 24 and 29 is conspicuous if one views Bethel in conjunction with Jacob's arrival at Haran. Abraham's servant only speaks *about God*, though God never utters a word in Gen 24. Jacob, however, not only receives an unsolicited divine word in 28:10–22, he actually speaks *with God*. One may also postulate that the fact that God does not respond to Jacob's vow (28:20–22) with words but instead shows his assent with successful action, leading Jacob safely to his destination (28:15; cf. 29:4–6), highlights all the more the fact that God is behind what is occurring. Unlike Gen 24 and the Abraham cycle of stories, where God

---

17. Humphreys, *The Character of God in the Book of Genesis*, 174.

18. Hamilton, *Genesis 18–50*, 256.

19. Susanne Gillmayr-Bucher, "Genesis 24: Ein Mosaik aus Texten," in *Studies in the Book of Genesis: Literature, Redaction and History* (ed. A. Wénin; Leuven: Leuven University Press, 2001) 527. See also her "Begegnungen am Brunnen," *BN* 75 (1994) 48–66.

20. Idem, "Genesis 24," 529–30.

21. Gerhard von Rad (*Genesis* [rev. ed.; trans. J. H. Marks; OTL; Philadelphia: Westminster, 1973] 289) points out that the next example of this type scene in Exod 2:15–21, when Moses obtains a wife in the land of Midian. Here again, there is no word from or mention of God; this will come immediately after the scene, in Exod 3, when Moses sees and hears the burning bush. One therefore may understand that absence or presence of the divine word does not appear to be the issue at all in this type scene but, rather, when the divine speech comes, what it reveals and how it is articulated.

is a much more overt character, Gen 29 expresses the scene in a way that I have already shown is fitting with God's character in the Jacob cycle: often silent but never absent.[22] The question is not so much whether God is at work in either instance but how he is at work. Jacob's arrival at the well, like that of his grandfather's servant, is hardly fortuitous.

Other signs are further evocative of the ancestral promise and function to connect Jacob's arrival in Haran with the promise given at Bethel. Perhaps the most prominent is the large stone covering the well (29:2, 3 [2x], 10). This seemingly innocuous stone actually appears quite significant given that it is mentioned four separate times in the span of a few verses. Alter astutely recognizes that this stone and the prominence afforded to it deviate from the conventional betrothal type scene, further attesting to its importance.[23] What, then, is its significance?

Jacob's life is intimately bound up with stones. At Bethel, he uses a stone as a pillow and on awakening erects a *massebah* to commemorate his dream theophany. He will again use stones when he and Laban enter into their covenant agreement (31:46–54) and when he returns to Bethel and builds an altar (35:7) and a *massebah* (35:14) there. In terms of the overall flow of the narrative thus far, the only two places where Jacob has encountered a stone are at Bethel and now at the well. The stone covering the well, then, functions to connect this scene with the previous scene at Bethel. But what does this connection reveal? Sarna sees the prevalence given to the stone at the well as a "reminder" that the same God who promised to protect Jacob is the God who now imbues the patriarch "with superhuman strength."[24] Mathews avers that the stone shows that God has stood by his promise and is indeed present with Jacob.[25] Pressing the connection even more, Alter underscores the metaphorical function of stones as contributing to Jacob's characterization as a man "contending with the hard unyielding nature of things."[26] Fokkelman provides a helpful summation:

> Lastly, at a more profound level the explanation for Jacob's strength is, as we saw, Providence. The balance and harmony of this arrival and recognition have been achieved by virtue of the blessing. God is indeed with him, leads him to the circle of relatives and inside it he meets the woman

22. Robert L. Cohn ("Narrative Structure and Canonical Perspective in Genesis," *JSOT* 25 [1983] 8–9) describes this difference in God's character between the Abraham and Jacob cycle of stories. I disagree, however, with Cohn's assessment that a "lowering of the divine profile is matched by a correspondingly higher level of human responsibility for the course of events" in the Jacob cycle. Even Cohn ultimately admits that the blessing and promise come from God despite deception.

23. Alter, *The Art of Biblical Narrative*, 55.

24. Sarna, *Genesis*, 202.

25. Mathews, *Genesis 11:27–50:26*, 462.

26. Alter, *The Art of Biblical Narrative*, 55.

who is to be his bride. Whenever Jacob acknowledges this and when he feels he is under God's special protection, he makes it clear with stones.[27]

But one can say more. The stone not only is redolent with images of the promise but also, through its recalling of Bethel, testifies to an impending fulfillment. Stones are not a recurring part of the betrothal type scene, and the mentions of the stone draw the reader's attention away from the expected arrival of a wife to this seemingly unimportant object. Given the unique appearance of the word (אבן) in this type scene in Gen 29 and the narrative's insistence that one notice it by appealing to it four times recall the last stone in Jacob's life, which served as a marker of the land of the promise, Bethel. While Jacob used a stone at Bethel to commemorate receiving the ancestral promise, he now interacts with a stone at the place where the promise has almost immediately led him. It is not insignificant that he does so at the moment he first sees Rachel (v. 10).

Stephen Sherwood emphasizes another relevant aspect of the stone: the way in which it presages Laban's first deception of Jacob in 29:21–30. In v. 2, the stone is said to be 'large' or 'great' (גדלה), the exact same word used in v. 16 to distinguish the 'younger' (קטנה) Rachel from the 'older' (גדלה) Leah.[28] Both the stone and Leah serve as obstacles that Jacob must overcome in order to earn Rachel's heart and hand. The imagery it connotes, therefore, is much more "complicated" than one may assume at first read.[29] Already in the opening scene of Jacob's time with Laban, the text introduces the reader to a symbol, the stone, that reverberates with connections not only to the ancestral promise but also to deception.

One final element of the story both concretizes the providential nature of events thus far and foreshadows the next scene of deception. The text accentuates Jacob's arrival at the proper destination by means of repeated familial terminology. In v. 10, the phrase 'Laban, brother of his mother' (לבן אחי אמו) occurs three separate times. Sternberg sees in this recurrence an example of "how a redundant family attribution implies motive."[30] That is to say, the text tightens the relational bond between Jacob and Laban through a threefold appeal to Rebekah who, readers remember, loved Jacob most (25:28). This repetition, furthermore, echoes Rebekah's instruction in 27:43 that Jacob go to 'Laban, my brother' (לבן אחי), showing that Jacob has arrived at the proper place.

---

27. J. P. Fokkelman, *Narrative Art in Genesis: Specimens of Stylistic and Structural Analysis* (Eugene, OR: Wipf & Stock, 1991) 125.

28. Stephen K. Sherwood, *Had God Not Been on My Side: An Examination of the Narrative Technique of the Story of Jacob and Laban, Genesis 29:1–32:2* (Europäische Hochschulschriften Reihe 23: Theologie 400; Frankfurt a/M: Peter Lang, 1990) 37.

29. Ibid., 57.

30. Meir Sternberg, *The Poetics of Biblical Narrative: Ideological Literature and the Drama of Reading* (Bloomington: Indiana University Press, 1985) 538 n. 15.

Laban's response to Jacob is equally telling. Upon running to meet Jacob, embracing and kissing him, and hearing everything that has happened,[31] Laban responds to Jacob by saying, "Surely you are my bone and my flesh!" Fokkelman's view that אַךְ here is best translated 'oh well', showing Laban's disappointment that Jacob does not come bearing great riches as did Abraham's servant, is problematic in that it is dissonant with the surrounding context.[32] No mention is made of Jacob's poverty, and Laban has without doubt greeted Jacob in a most magnanimous way.[33] Instead, Brueggemann offers a compelling case that this phrase serves as a "covenant formula" that binds the two together in a relationship of mutual loyalty yet unequal status.[34] This covenant formula does not preclude recognition of a genetic relationship between the two, though as the narrative progresses, these issues quickly fade away.[35] Brueggemann's notice that a covenant marks the beginning and ending of the Jacob/Laban relationship opens up the possibility that Laban's consequent deceptions of Jacob breach one covenant in working toward the fulfillment of another, the ancestral promise. Finally, Hamilton points out that Laban employs only four Hebrew words here, a remarkably terse response to "all these things" that Jacob may have made known.[36] The reader may recall from chap. 2 above my discussion of the brevity of Jacob's speech in the deceptions of Esau (25:27–34) and Isaac (27:1–45) as an indicator of the trickster at work. Might Laban's succinctness here in addressing Jacob signal to the reader that he too is a trickster, and might it foreshadow the fact that deception will soon follow? In the next scene, this is precisely the case.

These opening verses of the Jacob/Laban narratives, therefore, call attention to the ancestral promise and condition readers to maintain a keen eye on how Yʜᴡʜ will begin to bring about its fulfillment. Already, in guiding Jacob safely to Haran, Yʜᴡʜ has acted in accordance with the promise

---

31. The phrase 'all these things' (כל־הדברים האלה) is, as one may expect of the trickster Jacob, ambiguous. Sarna (*Genesis*, 203) proffers that Jacob tells Laban about his parents' sending him to find a suitable wife, along with his "misadventures" along the way. Mathews (*Genesis 11:27–50:26*) instead believes Jacob to be much more selective, relating only what had taken place at the well, which perhaps makes sense, given what follows; if Laban has heard of Jacob's herculean strength in single-handedly moving the stone, he may know that he has a prospective worker facing him.

32. Fokkelman, *Narrative Art in Genesis*, 126.

33. I do not mean to suggest that Laban's haste in running to meet Jacob does not arise from his hope that Jacob, like Abraham's servant, comes bearing riches. The narrative, however, seems unconcerned to report such details, stating in rapid succession that Laban ran, greeted, embraced, kissed, and took Jacob into his home.

34. Walter Brueggemann ("Of the Same Flesh and Bone (Gn 2,23a)," *CBQ* 32 [1970] 537–38) examines the multiple occurrences of this phrase in the Hebrew Bible and sees in it a sort of covenant formula that presents the partners in unequal positions of power. Here specifically Laban retains power and Jacob a secondary role.

35. Ibid., 537.

36. Hamilton, *Genesis 18–50*, 256.

at Bethel that he would be present with, guide, and protect Jacob (28:15). Little reason exists at the narrative level for Yhwh to abandon Jacob now. One thus expects to continue to see that divine activity is dictating and guiding events toward fulfillment. What remain unclear, and ultimately surprising, are the ways in which this fulfillment comes about.

Laban's Deception of Jacob and the Ancestral Promise (Genesis 29:14b–30)

With the ancestral promise again serving as the operative interpretive context, Laban's deception of Jacob creates the necessary circumstances that ultimately begin to lead toward the promise's fulfillment. Again God does not appear overtly on stage as a character, yet the previous analysis shows that he has accompanied and continues to accompany Jacob in accordance with the promise uttered at Bethel. One may, therefore, wonder at the possibility that Yhwh is not only behind Jacob's deceptions of others but also behind others' deceptions of Jacob.

The narrative is redolent with ambiguity and wordplays that demonstrate the activity of the trickster at work. The second instance of Laban's speaking to Jacob in v. 15 appears, at first glance, quite straightforward: 'Are you not my brother; will you serve me for nothing?' (הכי־אחי אתה ועבדתני חנם). Further scrutiny, however, shows that the thrust of this line is not as clear-cut. Daube and Yaron have posited a quite different understanding of this verse. They contend that the first clause is better translated as a rhetorical question, 'Are you my brother?' which then follows with the second question, 'Will you serve me for nothing?'[37] This type of question, they advance, suggests a negative response: Indeed, you are not my brother![38]

Based on this view, Laban is here demonstrating his abjuration of any familial ties with Jacob, perhaps, given Brueggemann's understanding of Laban's earlier "my bone and my flesh," opting to lean now entirely on the unequal covenant relationship over which Laban has hegemony. Translating the clause in the traditional manner, 'Are you not my brother?' would require הלא rather than הכי.[39] Hamilton presents an equally convincing alternative: 'Because you are my brother . . .', which may fit better with Laban's initial exuberant response to Jacob (vv. 13–14).[40] Interestingly, one finds the only other occurrence of הכי in Genesis in 27:36, prefacing Esau's cry of distress at learning of Jacob's deception. Recalling the previous chapter and its emphasis on the connection between ambiguity and trickery,

---

37. David Daube and Reuven Yaron, "Jacob's Reception by Laban," *JSS* 1 (1956) 61–62.

38. Ibid., 62.

39. Ibid., 61. R. Christopher Heard (*Dynamics of Diselection: Ambiguity in Genesis 12–36 and Ethnic Boundaries in Post-exilic Judah* [Semeia Studies; Atlanta: Society of Biblical Literature, 2001] 149–50) challenges Daube and Yaron's interpretation but similarly concludes that their reading draws attention to the ambiguity latent in Laban's speech.

40. Hamilton, *Genesis 18–50*, 258.

here one may see the ambiguity evident in Laban's speech as indicative of the suggestion that the trickster is plotting a future deception. The ensuing narrative makes this point explicit by introducing a number of cues that evoke Jacob's deception of Esau in the reader's mind.

The ambiguity continues, setting the stage for another deception. After Laban presses Jacob to name his own wage, the narrator introduces the reader to the fact that Laban actually has two daughters. Leah is named the 'older' (הגדלה) and Rachel the 'younger' (הקטנה), wording that clearly evokes Jacob and Rebekah's deception of Esau and Isaac. Another connection with an earlier deception comes to the fore; the text says, "Jacob loved Rachel" (v. 18), which recalls Rebekah's love for Jacob (25:28). Jacob unambiguously names his price, solidifying his choice of Rachel by identifying her as the "younger" (v. 18). Laban, however, does not respond with the same transparency. Instead he says, "Better that I give *her* (אתה) to you than that I give *her* (אתה) to another man" (v. 19). Conspicuously, Laban fails to use Rachel's name, instead saying twice that he will give "her" to Jacob. Granting Laban the benefit of the doubt, perhaps Wenham's musing is correct, that Laban "was keeping his options open" but hoped to marry off Leah before the end of Jacob's seven years of service.[41] More convincing, however, is that Laban's speech is ambiguous regarding which daughter he plans on giving Jacob in exchange for his work.[42] Jeansonne furthermore notes that Laban in no way provides his assent to Jacob's offer of seven years, instead plainly saying, "Stay with me," and connoting an "indefinite period of time," foreshadowing what will become a quite lengthy stay for Jacob.[43]

These first seven years are for Jacob only "like a few days (כימים אחדים) because of his love for her [Rachel]" (v. 20). Ironically, Rebekah uses this same phrase when she suggests that Jacob stay only 'a few days' (ימים אחדים) with Laban (27:44). Turner perceptively notices that the second set of seven years does not receive the same mitigating comment (29:30b).[44] Now experiencing a deception himself, Jacob serves Laban for the wife he desires.

The deception itself is replete with echoes of the earlier deception of Isaac in Gen 27, a fact that has not been lost on scholars. Turner offers a thorough summary:

> Just as back home there had been the elder (Esau), and the younger (Jacob), so here we have the elder (Leah), and the younger (Rachel). Leah and Esau are each the elder child, both in danger of being marginalized.
>
> . . . Jacob's deception had been to disguise the younger as the older; Laban reverses this, substituting the older for the younger. The connection with Jacob's previous schemes is made blatantly obvious by Laban's response to Jacob's protest, 'This is not done in our country—giving the

---

41. Gordon J. Wenham, *Genesis 16–50* (WBC 2; Dallas: Word, 1994) 235.
42. Hamilton, *Genesis 18–50*, 259.
43. Jeansonne, *The Women of Genesis*, 72.
44. Turner, *Genesis*, 128.

younger before the firstborn' (29:26). . . . The reader can certainly see how Laban's ploy subtly replicates Jacob's earlier act. Leah's eyes are described as *rak*, which could mean that they were either weak (cf. 33:13), or lovely (cf. 18:7). However, since a contrast between the sisters is implied in 29:17, the negative connotation seems more likely. The reader will recall that Isaac's eyes were 'dim' (*khh*, 27:1). Previously the victim had poor eyesight, here it is the co-conspirator. Like his father, Jacob is also in the dark, unable to see. . . . Measure for measure: as Jacob had deceived Isaac with kid dressed as venison, so now he is deceived by mutton dressed as lamb. The turning of the tables on Jacob the trickster is amplified by Laban's choice of words. Jacob had tricked the firstborn out of his birthright (*bᵉkōrâ*, 27:31–34); Laban has now tricked him into receiving the firstborn (*bᵉkîrâ*, 29:26).[45]

The similarities are too strong to insist that they arise by accident. Alter writes that comparable scenes are often used to provide comment on one another in the biblical text.[46] What comment does this connection make?

Many scholars believe that Laban's deception of Jacob exists as a sort of punishment for Jacob's earlier deception of his father.[47] In a sort of poetic reversal, Jacob falls prey to the wiles of his own previous scheming. This view presents several difficulties. Wenham suggests that one indicator that a character's behavior is virtuous is that the behavior is part of a recurring pattern in the text.[48] The fact that Laban dupes Jacob by substituting the older for the younger, just as Jacob did with his father and brother, indicates that the behavior is not commendable. The problem with this reading is that Gen 29:21–30 is not the final narrative comment on Gen 27. As I mentioned in chap. 1, the themes of blindness, blessing, and birthright will again appear in Gen 48:13–20, when the blind Jacob crosses his arms and puts his right hand on the head of the 'younger' (הקטן) Ephraim, proclaiming that he will be 'greater' (יגדל) than the 'firstborn' (הבכר) Manasseh. The recurrence of these words, along with an emphasis on peoplehood (עם) and the similarities between Jacob's and Isaac's blindness provide a more fitting final, positive word on Gen 27 than Laban's deception of Jacob does. It is also significant that Jacob resists Joseph's attempt at correction, responding

---

45. Ibid. For other commentators who note (in varying degrees) the connections with Jacob's earlier deceptions, see Hermann Gunkel, *Genesis* (trans. Mark E. Biddle; Macon, GA: Mercer University Press, 1997) 319; E.A. Speiser, *Genesis: Introduction, Translation, and Notes* (AB 1; New York: Doubleday, 1964) 227; Wenham, *Genesis 16–50*, 236–38; Brueggemann, *Genesis*, 253; Hamilton, *Genesis 18–50*, 262; Yair Zakovitch, "Inner-Biblical Interpretation," in *Reading Genesis: Ten Methods* (ed. R. Hendel; Cambridge: Cambridge University Press, 2010) 113.

46. Alter, *The Art of Biblical Narrative*, 7.

47. See Mark G. Brett, *Genesis: Procreation and the Politics of Identity* (Old Testament Readings; London: Routledge, 2000) 89, 92; Sarna, *Genesis*, 205, 397–98; Turner, *Genesis*, 129; Wenham, *Genesis 16–50*, 236–37; Robert Alter, *Genesis: Translation and Commentary* (New York: Norton, 1996) 155, among others.

48. Wenham, *Story as Torah*, 88.

solemnly with "I know, my son, I know" (48:19) and then proceeding with the blessing. Unlike his father, Isaac, Jacob will not fall prey to his blindness; he will bless the grandson he intends and, in doing so, continue to act as a trickster.

Second, if Laban's deception serves as a punishment for Jacob, it then serves also as an implicit judgment on the trickster oracle in Gen 25:23 that set that deception in motion. Recall from chap. 2 also the analysis of the way in which Yhwh participates in Gen 27. Should one desire to see Jacob being censured here, one must also extend this censure to Yhwh.

A third objection gives way to an important theological sentiment that the remainder of this chapter will explore: the matter of fulfillment. Genesis 27 *fulfills* the trickster oracle. Bethel corroborates this deceptive fulfillment. Alter's notice that similar narratives comment on one another raises the question of what necessitates reading Gen 29:21–30 in a wholly negative light? By recalling Jacob's (and Yhwh's) deception of Isaac, the narrative points not to a concern for punishment but, rather, as was argued to be the case in Gen 27, to a concern for fulfillment. I have already emphasized this very context in the opening verses of chap. 29.

Genesis 29:21–30 and Gen 27 are tied closely together in a way that is absent from Turner's summary above. Genesis 27 presents Yhwh as mysteriously involved in the deception as the agent of Jacob's successful and stealthy "hunt" (v. 20) as well as being the agent of blessing through Isaac (vv. 7, 28). In Gen 29, Yhwh appears equally obscured yet at work with Jacob and Laban; vv. 1–14 make this point all the more plausible. But how does Laban succeed in making his switch undetected? J. A. Diamond cites an idea as old as Josephus (*Ant.* 1.19.6), that Jacob becomes inebriated at the 'drinking feast' (מִשְׁתֶּה) that Laban throws and thus is unable to tell the two sisters apart.[49]

Even if Laban's success were to be chalked up to Jacob's alleged drunkenness, however, the narrative gives no indication that alcohol is the primary beverage of choice, nor does it say that Jacob partakes to excess or even that he is intoxicated. The narrative remains silent on these matters, creating an aura of mystery surrounding the deception of Jacob. The question of precisely how Laban achieves success in ensuring that Jacob does not detect the switch lends support to the enigma of the scene and allows for the possibility that Yhwh is as mysteriously engaged now as he was in Gen 27. Von Rad holds a similar view, arguing for a "darker mystery" concealed in Laban's deception, with far-reaching implications for Israelite history: had Jacob not married Leah, then Reuben, Levi, and Judah would not have been born and, consequently, neither would Moses or David.[50] Petersen

---

49. J. A. Diamond, "The Deception of Jacob: A New Perspective on an Ancient Solution to the Problem," *VT* 34 (1984) 211–13.

50. Von Rad, *Genesis*, 291.

notes that "sororal polygny"—two sisters sharing a single husband—is well-attested in anthropological literature as a way of maximizing the prospects for an heir to safeguard the family's property.[51] In a related vein, Wenham holds that the divine purpose functions through the deception in that it provides the means by which the promise of progeny will begin to reach fulfillment.[52] Therefore, not only the trick but the marriage arrangement that results from it accentuates the importance of advancing the promise of progeny.

One may demur, however, and suggest that Yhwh stands on the side of Jacob, not against him. To be sure, the ancestral promise that Jacob receives at Bethel says as much. Does not, then, Yhwh's failure to prevent Laban's deception pose a challenge to Yhwh's fidelity to Jacob and to the ancestral promise? Perhaps, but only if one wants to ignore fulfillment as a key to understanding Gen 29:21–30. Brueggemann suggests that this scene does not level a challenge against Yhwh's ability or willingness to keep the promise, but it does require patience on Jacob's part, for promise-keeping may be postponed.[53] While Brueggemann is right that Yhwh remains steadfast to Jacob and the promise, he does not mention the ways in which Laban's deception advances the promise. Directly after this scene, Yhwh will return to the narrative to begin working toward the promise of progeny in orchestrating the multiple births of Jacob's wives. Here Yhwh seems free to work inversion *against* Jacob, given the divine preference shown for the unloved Leah, posing an initial challenge to the assumption that Yhwh fails to protect Jacob from Laban's plot.

The common denominator in all these instances is the ancestral promise. Yhwh supports Jacob, as the ensuing narrative will make clear, but Yhwh's primary focus is on the outworking of the promise; once again, Yhwh is not beyond availing himself of deception in the interest of moving toward fulfillment.

Laban's deception of Jacob by giving him Leah before Rachel creates the circumstances allowing for a preliminary movement toward fulfillment of the ancestral promise. Jacob now has recourse to multiple wives, who will for the first time bear multiple *children* of the promise (29:31–30:24). The requirement that Jacob work another seven years for Rachel protracts his stay, allowing for Laban both to experience and to recognize Yhwh's *blessing* by means of Jacob's presence (30:27–30). The promise of *land* becomes a bit more difficult to parse, but three factors indirectly contribute to the fulfillment of the land promise. First, only after reaping great benefits during his time with Laban does Jacob acquire what is necessary in allowing him to return to the land and, more importantly, to face Esau. Second, Jacob's

---

51. David L. Petersen, "Genesis and Family Values," *JBL* 124 (2005) 17.
52. Wenham, *Genesis 16–50*, 238.
53. Brueggemann, *Genesis*, 253.

residing with Laban for an additional seven years provides even more narrative time for Esau's anger to abate and thus to make Jacob's safe return to the land more certain. The fact that Rebekah has yet to send word to Jacob (cf. 27:44–45) supports this point all the more. Third, Laban's deception will be met with another deception, in which this time he will play the victim (Gen 30:25–31:54); Jacob and Yhwh will be the perpetrators. It is within this context rife with deception, under these circumstances, that fulfillment of the ancestral promise begins to take shape.

Children, the Ancestral Promise, and Deception (Genesis 29:31–30:24)

Among the most fundamental tenets of God's promise to Abraham is the assurance that he will be the father of many descendants, a promise occurring at least three times within the span of a few short chapters (12:2; 15:5; 17:2). The importance of this aspect of the promise in the life of Jacob receives structural legitimation from Fishbane, who situates this narrative depicting an onslaught of childbirth at the center of the Jacob cycle.[54] Thus far, however, all one could surmise from the narrative was not the great numbers of descendants claiming Abraham as their father but, rather, according to Christopher Heard, a divine winnowing of several branches of the elect's family tree—removing Lot, Ishmael, and Esau from covenantal consideration.[55] With Jacob's children, however, Yhwh again returns to the narrative scene as a character with an agenda: fulfilling the promise of progeny.

In 29:31–30:24, it is God alone who hears and answers Rachel's and Leah's respective concerns, granting not just one child of the promise but ultimately 12 children of the promise. That God becomes the principal actor here is clear from the narrative: Jacob receives no notice in the 4 conceptions of Leah in 29:31–35, though one should not question his paternity of the children.[56] He also does not participate in any way in naming the children.[57] The disappearance of Jacob's name in these verses serves to highlight all the more the fact that God bears primary responsibility for the births. It is God's initiative and no other that brings about these children, a theological point deeply embedded in the narrative through the tethering of several of the names to a direct action of or response to God. Table 3.1 attempts to synthesize this information.

---

54. Fishbane, "Composition and Structure in the Jacob Cycle," 31–32. See the helpful graphic representation of his structure on his p. 20.
55. Heard, *Dynamics of Diselection*, 184.
56. Hamilton, *Genesis 18–50*, 266.
57. Ibid., 268.

Table 3.1. God in the Names of Jacob's Children

Verses	Wife	Child's Name	Etiology
29:32	Leah	Reuben (ראובן)	Yhwh *has seen* (ראה) my affliction
29:33	Leah	Simeon (שמעון)	Yhwh *heard* (שמע)
29:34	Leah	Levi (לוי)	My husband will *attach himself* to me (ילוה)
29:35	Leah	Judah (יהודה)	I will *praise* Yhwh (אודה את־יהוה)
30:5–6	Bilhah	Dan (דן)	God has *vindicated* me (דנני)
30:7–8	Bilhah	Naphtali (נפתלי)	I *struggled* (נפתולי) with God, I *struggled* (נפתלתי) with my sister
30:10–11	Zilpah	Gad (גד)	*Luck* (גד) has come
30:12–13	Zilpah	Asher (אשר)	In *happiness* (באשרי)
30:17–18	Leah	Issachar (יששכר)	God has given my *reward* (שכרי)
30:19–20	Leah	Zebulun (זבלון)	God has given me a good gift, this time my husband will *exult* me (יזבלני)
30:21	Leah	Dinah (דינה)	———
30:22–24	Rachel	Joseph (יוסף)	God has *taken away* (אסף) . . . May Yhwh *add* (יסף)

The confluence between each child's name and God is evident. Of the 12 children named here, 8 contain some tie with the deity.[58] All except Dinah become an eponymous ancestor for the later Israelite tribes.[59] All, therefore, have a role in fulfilling the promise. In fact, the first and last births, of Reuben and Joseph, contain names highlighting Yhwh's action. One should not, however, conclude that this structure de-emphasizes the intermittent children, as does Thomas Meurer.[60] Meurer contends that the middle children come primarily from the maidservants; thus, not from the initiative of Yhwh but from the strategies and stratagems of Leah and Rachel alone. Coats also isolates the central theme as conflict, noting that the promise

---

58. Technically, the proportion is even higher if one removes Dinah from contention. Hers is the most terse of narrations, and her name receives no explanation like her brothers' names. Similarly, she does not become the eponymous ancestor of an Israelite tribe. The 12th son, Benjamin (בנימין), is born to Rachel in 35:16–18. His name does not contain a theophoric element, but his name appears to mean 'son of the right hand'.

59. Contra Thomas L. Thompson ("Conflict Themes in the Jacob Narratives," *Semeia* 15 [1979] 19), who advances that the narrative is a fabrication and not meant to speak to the history of Israel's later tribes. The idea of history as a necessary prerequisite for the authenticity and import of these verses is unnecessary, however. Ancient Israel quite likely used this story as a means of explaining its understanding of the origin of the 12 tribes who come from Israel, who one must remember is Jacob!

60. Thomas Meurer, "Die Gebärwettstreit zwischen Lea und Rahel: Der Erzählaufbau von Gen 29:31–30:24 als Testfall der Erzählerischen Geschlossenheit einer zusammenhanglos wirkenden Einheit," *BN* 107–8 (2001) 95.

does not figure at all in these texts.[61] The sheer fact that several of these children—Dan, Isaachar, and Zebulon, specifically—have names associated with God immediately calls Meurer's statement into question. Another key verse, 30:8 about the birth of Naphtali, levels another challenge against seeing conflict as the sole central operative issue. Francis Andersen sees this verse as paralleling 32:29—"for you struggled with God; and with men you did succeed"—evidencing that in 30:8 Rachel relates a struggle with her sister and with God.[62] This translation makes great interpretive sense given that in 30:2 Jacob responds to Rachel's request for children with the harsh retort that God alone has withheld children from her. Conflict most assuredly contributes to the narrative flow in 29:31–30:24, and it is conflict with and amidst the activity of God.

The structure that Meurer identifies serves as an envelope, enclosing each intervening birth in a context in which the deity appears active in fulfilling one aspect of the ancestral promise: progeny. Within the inclusio, God *sees, hears, vindicates, struggles with, gives reward and gift, takes away,* and *adds.* God is also in the business of opening wombs (29:31; 30:22) and closing them (29:35?; 30:2). And the result of this burst of divine activity is, for the first time in Genesis, multiple children of the promise.

The wives are also vitally important characters who advance the promise. Both have problems at the outset. It is not inconsequential that this narrative unit begins with Yнwн's noticing Leah's unloved status and responding by opening her womb, while Rachel remains barren. Here one may observe an oddity within Genesis: this scene presents the only time that Yнwн shows a preference for the firstborn to the detriment of the secondborn. Sherwood appeals to a similar situation in which there are two wives—Sarah and Hagar—and poses a fascinating set of questions, especially the affinity between Rachel, Rebekah, and Sarah (all of whom were 'barren' [עקרה]) and whether this would necessitate Leah and her progeny's sharing a fate similar to Hagar, outside the promise.[63] Conversely, each wife "becomes" Hagar and Sarah at different moments. Leah shares Hagar's fertility yet "becomes" Sarah when she ceases bearing (29:35) and gives Zilpah to Jacob as a wife, just as Sarah gave her maidservant to Abraham.[64] Rachel begins like Sarah, barren, and likewise gives her maidservant

61. George W. Coats, "Strife without Reconciliation: A Narrative Theme in the Jacob Traditions," in *Werden und Wirken des Alten Testament. Festschrift für Claus Westermann zum 70. Geburtstag* (ed. Rainer Albertz; Göttingen: Vandenhoeck & Ruprecht, 1980) 83. See also his *Genesis, with an Introduction to Narrative Literature* (FOTL 1; Grand Rapids, MI: Eerdmans, 1983) 209, 216, where he calls this account a "digression" concerned only with articulating a conflict between sisters within the larger conflict between Jacob and Laban.

62. Francis I. Andersen, "Note on Gen 30:8," *JBL* 88 (1969) 200. See also Frank Crüsemann, "Die Gotteskämpferin: Genesis 30,8," in *Für Gerechtigkeit streiten: Theologie im Alltag einer bedröhten Welt* (ed. Dorothee Sölle; Gütersloh: Chr. Kaiser, 1994) 41–45.

63. Sherwood, *Had God Not Been on My Side*, 145.

64. Ibid., 146–147.

to Jacob. According to Sherwood, the compound effect is a tension in that Leah and Rachel find themselves "on equal footing."[65] It is not as though one is Hagar and the other Sarah; both women occupy both roles at various points in the narrative. Their birthing contest comes down to one common denominator: Yhwh works in and through both to bring about children for the bearer of the promise.

Deception also is not too far off in this narrative of incipient fulfillment. Were it not for Laban's deception of Jacob in 29:21–30, Jacob would have found himself married to the barren Rachel, not the fruitful and fertile Leah. His prospects for achieving numerous progeny would have become dismal at best. Through Laban's deception, the circumstances emerge that Yhwh employs to begin fulfilling the ancestral promise.

While deception may not figure explicitly into this scene, Yhwh remains a startlingly silent character. Perhaps he plays the role of trickster by upsetting what has seemingly become a new convention, preference for the younger, by instead electing Leah as the matriarch who will bear the majority of Jacob's children.[66] Perhaps his reluctance to respond to Leah's pleas for Jacob's love or Rachel's reason for barrenness casts him in a trickster light. A dark side certainly exists in the birth of Jacob's children, for Yhwh does not appear overly concerned with the plight and struggle into which the chosen family continues to be thrust. Yhwh does not seek to resolve the conflict but contributes to it by opening Leah's womb while Rachel remains barren. Meurer sums up the theological message of this passage by writing of the uncircumventable freedom with which Yhwh acts.[67] This freedom, however, is wholly bound up with a unique and unwavering concern for the ancestral promise. And it continues to be this context of strife and deception that Yhwh prefers.

The narrative, when read as a whole, depicts a rapid influx of children at God's behest, set in the context of a dispute between Jacob's two wives. Yet amidst and through this dispute, one finds a theologically loaded passage that begins to fulfill the ancestral promise of a great nation by the birth of Jacob's 12 children, who also become conduits of the blessing, not to mention deceivers themselves (Gen 34). God's activity in providing numerous descendants for Jacob, from whom will come the 'great nation' (גוי גדול) of 12:2, functions theologically to highlight God's presence with Jacob and to anticipate the blessing to all.

Trickster as Blessing (Genesis 30:27–30)

If Gen 29:31–30:24 establishes the circumstances necessary to realize the promise of progeny, then 30:27–30 presages the concept of blessing all

---

65. Ibid., 147.
66. Leah actually bears more children for Jacob than Rachel, Bilhah, and Zilpah combined!
67. Meurer, "Der Gebarwettstreit zwischen Lea und Rahel," 107.

nations by means of Jacob and his descendants. In 30:27, in the context of their renewed negotiation, Laban says to Jacob, 'If I have found favor in your eyes, I know by divination that Yʜᴡʜ blessed me on account of you' (אם־נא מצאתי הן בעיניך נחשתי ויברכני יהוה בגללך). This comment marks the first instance in the text in which the descendants of Abraham are explicitly said to be a blessing to a foreigner. The method by which Laban learns of this blessing, however, remains unclear. A potential meaning of the word נחשתי is indeed to learn by divination, as Gen 44:5, 15 shows.[68] Another possibility also exists. J. J. Finkelstein argues that the word may be cognate with the Akkadian *naḥāšu*, which means 'to prosper', with the resultant translation running something like '. . . I have prospered, and Yʜᴡʜ has blessed me on account of you'.[69] Laban's ambiguous speech—both meanings are equally plausible—shows the cunning trickster at work, perhaps availing himself of language that is overly fawning in order to guarantee that Jacob does not depart.[70] Each possible translation also emphasizes a different yet complementary way of reading the import of these verses.

If one opts to read with the Akkadian cognate *naḥāšu*, the contrast between an insolvent Jacob and the rich Laban becomes that much more potent. Laban has prospered by no work of his own hands but by Yʜᴡʜ through Jacob. Jacob has little materially to show for his 14 years of servitude; however, to reiterate, Jacob may arrive penniless, but he also arrives with God on his side. Therefore, reading *naḥāšu* in 30:27 presages the reversal of fortunes that will occur in short order, leaving Laban with the weakest of the flocks and Jacob with the strongest, which may be understood as an implication of Yʜᴡʜ's promise of presence and protection for Jacob. The agent of this reversal, as will be discussed in relation to Gen 31:1–16, is the trickster God Yʜᴡʜ.

Conversely, if one translates 'I have learned by divination', a whole host of theological implications present themselves. According to Lipton, Laban's use of divination casts him as an outsider, a foreigner.[71] While Laban is clearly genetically related to Jacob, the narrative begins to separate him from the chosen family in a variety of ways. Most telling is Laban's use

---

68. Hamilton, *Genesis 18–50*, 282. See Sherwood (*Had God Not Been on My Side*, 213–15) for a fine summary of the various positions.

69. J. J. Finkelstein, "An Old Babylonian Herding Contract and Genesis 31:38f.," *JAOS* 88 (1968) 34 n. 19.

70. Wenham (*Genesis 16–50*, 255) describes Laban's address as "an obsequious way of addressing a superior," while Sherwood (*Had God Not Been on My Side*, 212) notes the "exaggerated" nature of Laban's language, as well as its awkwardness. The initial clause has no clear apodosis, leading Sherwood to characterize Laban's speech here as "broken" and "stammering." On the fragmented nature of Laban's speech, see also Mathews, *Genesis 11:27–50:26*, 496.

71. Diana Lipton, *Revisions of the Night: Politics and Promises in the Patriarchal Dreams of Genesis* (JSOTSup 288; Sheffield: Sheffield Academic Press, 1999) 158–65, especially pp. 163–65.

of the personal name of Israel's God, Yʜwʜ. Claus Westermann incisively sees great significance in that one would expect Laban, a non-Israelite, to use the more generic אלהים in reference to God.[72] Westermann does not, however, comment on the significance of Laban's choice of words for God.

The theological importance conveyed by Laban's use of the personal name Yʜwʜ is that one should regard Laban's blessing as coming only from the personal God of Jacob. This point is punctuated all the more if Laban only learns of his blessed position vis-à-vis Jacob through divination of, arguably, Laban's own personal deities. The god of Laban is not the same God that he calls "Yʜwʜ" in 30:27. In 31:19, Rachel steals her father's household gods, perhaps out of fear that he will learn of Jacob's escape through divination, and in 31:47, 53, Laban swears in Aramaic by invoking the name of his own personal god.[73] Laban's deity (or deities) is unable to bestow the same profitable blessing on Laban as has Yʜwʜ, the God of Jacob. God's promise is thus at work here, and the theological impact becomes all the more palpable when the recognition comes for the first time from a foreigner. Fokkelman describes the theological nature of Laban's words succinctly:

> From the enemy's mouth we now hear that God's blessing has accompanied Jacob all the time. God has kept his promise made at Bethel, Jacob

---

72. Claus Westermann, *Genesis 12–36: A Continental Commentary* (trans. John J. Scullion; Minneapolis: Fortress, 1985) 481.

73. The identity of Laban's deity of choice by whom he swears here has evoked much scholarly discussion. The text-critical note to 31:53 complicates matters even further; the Samaritan Pentateuch and Greek have the singular form of the verb, ישפט (denoting that the God of Abraham and the God of Nahor are one and the same), while the MT has the plural ישפטו, understanding the God of Abraham and the God of Nahor as two distinct entities. Although I give preference to the MT, there are sound text-critical reasons for accepting the plural rendering of the MT as the more original reading. The primary evidence comes from another textual issue in the same verse, this time regarding the phrase 'the God of their father' (אלהי אביהם). Simply by merit of its odd placement in the overall syntax of the sentence, one may regard this description as an explanatory or clarifying gloss that is likely secondary to the original text. That the phrase is absent in two Hebrew manuscripts and the LXX buttresses this point even further. The phrase also creates a jarring interruption into Laban's first-person speech that begins in v. 51. One might also remain mindful of the possibility, though perhaps unlikely, that אלהי be translated as plural 'gods'. As it stands in the text, this gloss may serve to highlight the singularity of the God of Abraham and the God of Nahor, which is also probably the impetus behind the difference in singular and plural verb form earlier in the verse. It is thus not unlikely that these two textual issues belong together—though they need not come from the same hand—in the subsequent attempt to equate the God of Abraham with the God of Nahor. Heard (*Dynamics of Diselection*, 167–68) offers a helpful reminder: even the earliest interpreters and readers wrestled and struggled with this text. Ultimately, I agree with Westermann (*Genesis 12–36*, 500) that here Laban and Jacob swear by their own respective deities. Given the surrounding narrative context, combined with the textual issues here discussed, it seems clear that Laban's god(s) is not equivalent with the God of Jacob. On the familial import of the different deities, see Petersen, "Genesis and Family Values," 19.

creates prosperity wherever he appears. . . . The *bᵉrākā* shines about him. And who has benefited by it so far? Laban. . . .[74]

Fokkelman helpfully confirms the context of the ancestral promise as operative here, as well as noting that Laban, the other, stands to be blessed also by God. Here one sees the realization of Gen 12:3 (cf. 28:14) in miniature by means of Laban's acknowledgment that Y<small>HWH</small> blessed him through Jacob, just as Jacob's descendants will be a blessing to all nations.

This blessing is not a guarantee, however, for in what follows Y<small>HWH</small> transfers Laban's wealth to Jacob. How should one understand the quick succession of events? Laban at first is blessed by Y<small>HWH</small>, a comment to which Jacob staunchly agrees in v. 30, and by v. 43 Laban is left with the weakest of the flock while Jacob possesses the strongest. How should one make sense of the seeming unraveling of Laban's blessing? Reading within the context of the ancestral promise provides a solution. Central to Gen 28:13–15 is the promise of divine presence and protection 'until' (עד) God's purposes come to fruition. Thus far in the narrative, the promise is still in abeyance, awaiting the future fulfillment that until now has only been partially realized. In Laban, however, the promise finds not only an outlet for blessing but also an individual who potentially could harm the heir to the promise, Jacob, by prolonging his stay with Laban and thus minimizing— or perhaps wholly negating—the possibility for blessing to all nations purposed in 12:3 and 28:14. Laban may thus be trying to arrogate for himself the conduit of his blessing, Jacob, as a guarantee of continued prosperity. Aware of this potentially deceptive tactic, the narrative next moves to display God's intervention in accord with the promise of presence and protection, as will be discussed below in reference to Gen 31:1–16. The message, stemming from the conditional nature of the ancestral promise discussed in chap. 1—that blessing to the nations is contingent on the nations' not impeding the sharing of the blessing with other nations—is that Laban has failed to acknowledge that the divine blessing is for Abraham and his family, not exclusively for Laban.[75] Whether Laban speaks earnestly or not in 30:27 about his understanding of events, his blessing is quickly reversed by means of an overt act of divine deception.

The Great Escape and Y<small>HWH</small>'s Deception of Laban (Genesis 30:25–31:54)

Deception and fulfillment have proven to be pervasive and related themes in the Jacob/Laban narratives. Jacob has already acquired the multiple children who will ultimately become the progenitors of the people Israel, and I have just argued that blessing the nations occurs amidst and

---

74. Fokkelman, *Narrative Art in Genesis*, 142.

75. See chap. 1, pp. 40–44. Laban has not blessed Jacob, and thus he receives as he has given.

through deception. Now, in Gen 30:25–31:54 the Jacob/Laban narratives draw to a close with the primary concern being the final element of the ancestral promise that remains most fully unfulfilled: the return to the land. As one may expect, deception will figure prominently in bringing about the circumstances for its potential fulfillment.

In Gen 30:25–31:54 readers encounter a complex web of interrelated texts and deceptions that help both to clarify and to drive the narrative forward. Each section will be treated in turn. First, I will discuss Gen 30:25–43 both for how it depicts deception and for how it sets the stage for the bold revelation in 31:1–16 that Yʜwʜ is behind the deception of Laban. Second, Gen 31:1–16 will be the object of thorough scrutiny to show Yʜwʜ's role in the deception of Laban and the way that the deception furthers the ancestral promise.

Tricksters in Conflict (Genesis 30:25–43)

This narrative section comprises three interrelated scenes: vv. 25–34, 35–36, and 37–43. In 30:25–34, Jacob and Laban renegotiate the terms of their agreement, with Jacob first requesting to leave in order to care for his own family now (vv. 25–26, 30), followed by Laban's counteroffer of a wage of Jacob's choosing (vv. 28, 31).[76] Jacob accepts Laban's proposal, naming only the spotted and speckled goats and black sheep of Laban's flocks as payment. Westermann reminds the reader that in so doing Jacob has not merely named his wage but also agreed to continue working for Laban.[77] Laban quickly and unwaveringly assents to Jacob's terms, possibly because he knows that this request will yield only a very small number of animals for Jacob to take.[78] Moreover, given that he again offers the possibility for Jacob to name his own wage, as he did in 29:15 much to Laban's benefit, it is even more likely that the conniving and clever Laban already has a preemptive plan in mind, as the ensuing narrative reveals.

Verses 35–36 describe Laban's attempt to alter Jacob's wages by means of deception. Laban acts quickly (v. 35 states, 'on that day' [ביום ההוא]) by taking the spotted, speckled, and black of his herds and entrusting them to his sons to watch. Heard sees Laban's action in going through his flocks as ambiguous, lacking a clear sense from the narrator how one should un-

---

76. Brett (*Genesis,* 93) draws a connection with Jacob's request to leave in 30:25 and the ancestral promise given to him at Bethel. Jacob asks Laban to leave and return to 'my place' (מקומי). The same word that Jacob uses here, מקום, is used six times in the Bethel narrative, framing the ancestral promise.

77. Westermann, *Genesis 12–36,* 481.

78. Sarna (*Genesis,* 212) writes that Near Eastern sheep are often white and goats are dark brown or black. Therefore, Jacob's named wage is the abnormal of the flock; Laban therefore likely accepts because he believes he is getting a "bargain." The fact that Jacob names his wage as the oddities of the flock and the fact that they ultimately bear these in abundance highlight all the more not only the miraculous nature of what will happen but also God's participation.

derstand this episode.[79] Evidence exists within the narrative, however, that Laban has less-than-sterling intentions. Similarly, one should not regard Laban's actions here as does Westermann, seeing them merely as "precautionary measures" because he does not trust Jacob to separate the animals faithfully.[80] Instead, this act is clearly an act of deception, evidenced by the fact that Laban sets them at a distance of three-days' journey from Jacob.[81] George Coats also reads Laban's activity as deceptive, drawing a parallel with his earlier deception by switching Rachel for Leah.[82] In both cases, the deception involves a manipulation of Jacob's agreed-upon wage. Had Laban intended to select Jacob's wages himself, there would have been no reason for a vast separation. If Laban were acting in earnest, one would expect him to let Jacob know that his wage had been collected or perhaps to corral the animals in a space allotted to Jacob. The agreement to which Laban assents (v. 34) dictates that Jacob is to go through the flocks and pick out his wage, and then Laban is to come to Jacob to verify the wages (v. 33), not the other way around. Moreover, nothing in the narrative reveals Laban's intention to turn these animals over to Jacob as a wage. Therefore, Laban's actions can only be viewed as an attempt to alter the agreed-upon contract that he has established with Jacob.

Jacob appears to have learned from history, because the narrative portrays him as rightfully suspicious of Laban's allowing him to select his own wage. The first time resulted in Jacob's being hurtfully deceived. Laban had already proven himself untrustworthy in the giving of Leah as a wife before Rachel. Now Jacob takes measures to ensure that history will not repeat itself. Verses 37–43 narrate Jacob's coterminous deceptive activity while tending the rest of Laban's flocks. While Jacob's shenanigans may seem odd and unclear to contemporary readers, the text is graphic in its detail. Brueggemann gives this feature adequate voice, seeing the text as "embel-

---

79. Heard, *Dynamics of Diselection*, 155–56. Heard's assertion here that Laban's actions are ambiguous is odd. Only two pages earlier, Heard challenged Laban's credibility in appealing to local custom as an excuse for deceiving Jacob with Leah rather than Rachel, providing as a reason only that "Laban is a liar" (p. 153). It remains unclear why Heard makes judgments of this sort in some cases and not in others. Perhaps his words, "A man who would lie about his daughter's identity on her wedding night cannot be assumed to provide reliable information about local marriage customs" (p. 153), are applicable in 30:35: a man who would lie about Jacob's wage for the first seven years of work cannot be trusted to provide the agreed-upon wage for Jacob's subsequent work.

80. Westermann, *Genesis 12–36*, 482.

81. In the Pentateuch, a journey of three days is at times tied to an act of deception. For example, in Gen 31:22, it takes three days for Laban to realize that Jacob has fled; as will be discussed below, Laban regards this escape as a deception. Another example appears in Exod 3:18; 5:3; 8:23, where God suggests to Moses and he subsequently asks that Pharaoh let the Israelites venture only a three-days' journey into the wilderness to offer sacrifice to God, when in reality the intention is to flee Egyptian control and not return. See chap. 1, pp. 18–19 for a brief discussion of this latter scene as involving deception.

82. Coats, "Strife without Reconciliation," 88.

lishing [the story] with exaggerated (though not decipherable) vocabulary."[83] Jacob takes and peels back branches from the poplar, almond, and plane trees, revealing white (לבן) streaks on the branches (v. 37). He then places the peeled branches in the watering troughs, and when the flocks come to drink they also mate, giving rise by some elusive means not yet spelled out in the text—although clarified in 31:1–16 as an act of God—to spotted and speckled young (vv. 38–39).[84] He continues this technique with only the strong of the flocks, separating his take from Laban's (vv. 40–42). The results are unequivocal: Jacob's property and wealth increase at the expense of Laban (vv. 42–43).

This scene also bears striking resemblance to an earlier episode of deception: Laban's deception of Jacob in 29:21–30. Noegel deftly illustrates the numerous lexical and thematic connections between the two: Jacob is duped into receiving Leah, who is described as having "weak eyes" (29:17), and Jacob retaliates by ensuring that only the "weaker" members of Laban's flocks will reproduce.[85] The meaning of Rachel's and Leah's names may also connote the flocks: Rachel (רחל) means 'ewe lamb', and Leah (לאה) means 'wild cow'.[86] Both deceptions also involve drinking (29:22; 30:38) and birthing (29:34–35; 30:39).[87] Noegel identifies several other parallels, though the parallels listed here should provide adequate support for the view that these two scenes of deception relate to one another.[88] Jacob does not merely outwit Laban; he repays deception with deception. As the narrative continues, however, the agent of Jacob's deception comes in to focus in a most conspicuous way.

God's Deception of Laban (Genesis 31:1–16)

In Gen 31:1–16, readers encounter quite possibly the most potent example of divine deception in Genesis. God returns to the narrative scene

---

83. Brueggemann, *Genesis*, 251.

84. Scott B. Noegel ("Sex, Sticks, and the Trickster in Gen 30:31–43," *JANES* 25 [1997] 10–12) argues that Jacob fashions the rods to serve as *faux phalluses*, and that the herds mate 'upon (אל) the rods'. Noegel's analysis relies on a close reading of the text, yet he fails to provide any discussion of 31:1–16 as a hermeneutical lens that orients one's reading of 30:37–43.

85. Ibid., 14–15.

86. Ibid., 15. Noegel expands on this point, claiming that the narrative equates Laban's daughters with the flocks on several occasions, such as when Jacob first meets Rachel, who is approaching with the sheep (29:9), and in 31:4, when Jacob calls his wives to the field "to his flock."

87. Ibid., 16.

88. For deeper connections involving wordplays and puns, see idem, "Drinking Feasts and Deceptive Feats: Jacob and Laban's Double Talk," in *Puns and Pundits: Word Play in the Hebrew Bible and Ancient Near Eastern Literature* (ed. Scott B. Noegel; Bethesda, MD; CDL, 2000) 166–73; and most recently, Song-Mi Suzie Park, "Transformation and Demarcation of Jacob's 'Flocks' in Genesis 30:25–43: Identity, Election, and the Role of the Divine," *CBQ* 72 (2010) 668–71.

and dictates that the time has come for Jacob to return to his homeland. Jacob then summons his wives and summarily reflects on his sojourn with Laban, readily recognizing that God has indeed been with him as promised (v. 5) and protected him from Laban's perpetual duplicity (v. 7). Encapsulating this theological reflection is Jacob's acknowledgment that God has ensured his success even, seemingly, to the point of participating in the deception of Laban. Jacob, speaking to Rachel and Leah, quite candidly attributes the prior deception of Laban in chap. 30 to God. Verse 9 provides the clearest statement: "God has *caused* to be stripped away (יצל) the cattle of your father and given [them] to me." The text records that God, not Jacob, bears responsibility for the deception in 30:37–43.

Scholars have advanced various approaches to make sense of this difficult textual assertion. Any attempt to explain Jacob's manipulation of the flocks' breeding in 30:37–43 by appealing to contemporary understandings of genetics and prenatal care misses the overwhelming theological point the text is making.[89] Moreover, Taschner rightly cautions against the assumption that Jacob's use of the rods would have made sense to an ancient audience, noting that they may also have been puzzled and surprised at Jacob's success only to learn later of God's role.[90] Some commentators hold that Jacob does nothing more here than implicate the deity, a point to which I will return below, yet the narrative reveals that much more is going on in and behind Jacob's statement. Immediately thereafter in 31:10–13, God strikingly corroborates Jacob's claim in a dream. God says, effectively, that he has orchestrated the success of Jacob's endeavor with the rods, gesturing toward the spotted and speckled of the flock and noting that this result has come about not because of Jacob's own ingenuity but "because I have seen all that Laban did to you" (v. 12).[91]

Several rhetorical factors in the narrative further buttress God's participation in the deception of Laban. Primary among them is the verb יצל in v. 9, deriving from נצל 'take or snatch away'. According to Mathews, one

---

89. For examples of interpretations of this sort, see James Douglas Pearson, "A Mendelian Interpretation of Jacob's Sheep," *Science and Christian Belief* 13 (2001) 51–58; and more recently Joshua Backon, "Jacob and the Spotted Sheep: The Role of Prenatal Nutrition on Epigenetics of Fur Color," *JBQ* 36 (2008) 263–65. These appeals to science and history, however, also appear endemic in Genesis scholarship, with many commentators trying to discover the actual animal-husbandry practice leading to Jacob's results. See Gunkel, *Genesis*, 329; von Rad, *Genesis*, 302; Westermann, *Genesis 12–36*, 483; Sarna, *Genesis*, 212; Hamilton, *Genesis 18–50*, 284.

90. Johannes Taschner, *Verheissung und Erfüllung in der Jakoberzählung (Gen 25,19–33,17): Eine Analyse ihres Spannungsbogens* (Herders Biblische Studien 27; Freiburg: Herder, 2000) 113. One should not assume that this breeding technique is something lost only on contemporary readers, argues Taschner. For this reason, he sees these various perspectives as originally connected to one another and ultimately unfolding to reveal God's participation.

91. Taschner (ibid., 114) also deems God's intervention to be a result of Laban's unfair treatment of Jacob.

may instead have expected the more common לקח 'taken' as opposed to the much stronger 'take or snatch away'.[92] The Hiphil form in the text with God as the subject highlights all the more the causative aspect of what God has done.[93] Lipton draws an apt parallel to Exod 12:36: "And the Lord has disposed the Egyptians favourably toward the people, and they let them have their request; thus they stripped (וינצלו) the Egyptians."[94] Here again, the word occurs with God's involvement, yet the Exodus example softens God's role in that God is not the subject of the verb נצל as in Gen 31:9. In both instances, however, Yнwн allows for and creates the circumstances by which a given party obtains prosperity at the expense of another. In Gen 31:9, the impact is much more noticeable given God's obvious place as the subject of the verb. Likewise, the Qal form of נתן at the end of v. 9 has God as its subject. He is the one directly causing the stripping away of Laban's flocks and the one who grants them to Jacob. One should remain mindful also that in v. 16 Rachel and Leah respond, mimicking Jacob's use of the Hiphil: "all the riches that God has *caused* to be stripped away (הציל) from our father."

This reading creates several questions that one must address. First, how can one make sense of the obvious tensions that exist between Jacob's words in 31:1–16 and Jacob's actions in 30:37–43? Second, can Jacob's speech be trusted in 31:1–16? Third, how does this instance of divine deception connect with the larger theme of the ancestral promise and its furtherance? I will engage each question in turn.

Texts in Tension

Understanding the connection between 30:27–43 and 31:1–16 is seminal for grasping the import of God's intervention on behalf of Jacob. Von Rad holds that the two accounts belong to two different sources, J and E, respectively, with E presenting a "moral purification" of Jacob's earlier deception.[95] Can one instead read the two scenes together as a literarily cogent unit? At first glance, readers may acknowledge the presence of several seemingly insurmountable tensions between the two episodes. These tensions may be resolved, however, when read synchronically and with an understanding of the artistic nature of biblical narrative.

The first tension exists between 30:31–34 and 31:8. In the former, Jacob names his wage as the spotted and speckled goats and the black sheep, the anomalous animals of the herd. In the latter, Jacob reports to his wives that

92. Mathews, *Genesis 11:27–50:26*, 513.

93. Walter Brueggemann (*Theology of the Old Testament: Testimony, Dispute, Advocacy* [Minneapolis: Fortress, 1997] 123) notes in his description of ancient Israel's theology of rhetoric that Yнwн serves as the subject of strong, active verbs that are "transformative, intrusive, or inverting." Special attention, he says, may then be placed on moments in ancient Israel's rhetorical enterprise when Yнwн is the subject of causative, Hiphil verbs.

94. Lipton, *Revisions of the Night*, 124.

95. Von Rad, *Genesis*, 307.

Laban has variously named Jacob's wages as *either* the spotted *or* the speckled, and whichever Laban deemed the wage, this is what the flocks bore.
It may be easy to see a discrepancy between the terms of chap. 30 and the
actuality of chap. 31, yet this is not the case. In fact, the alleged discrepancy
is absolutely vital to the unfolding plot and confirms Jacob's words to his
wives in 31:1–16. Just one verse earlier, in 31:7, Jacob asserts that Laban
has changed the agreed-upon wage ten times, a point that scholars have
noted does not occur in the narrative and is thus, at best, a severe stretching of the truth.[96] Verse 8, then, in the mouth of a reflective Jacob looking
back on his years of service to Laban, shows the progression: the original
agreement was for the spotted, speckled, and black of the flocks, and upon
seeing Jacob prospering, Laban seeks to change the terms of the deal by
claiming that *only* the spotted were discussed as payment, and then only
the striped, and so on. This reading is most fully spelled out by Fokkelman,
who goes so far as to construct the imagined words of a bewildered Laban
to an ever-increasing Jacob: "'No, Jacob, we had agreed that the speckled
animals should be yours,' and a season later, 'but Jacob, you must be mistaken! I said the striped animals.'"[97]

One may thus make sense of this purported tension by appealing to the
literary artistry of biblical narrative. Alter notes that biblical narrative is
often "selectively silent in a purposeful way."[98] This narratorial reticence
carves out a niche for the reader, who is then left (in almost midrashic fashion) to fill in a story's or character's gaps. The narrator provides hints—for
instance, Jacob's statement that Laban has cheated him by changing his
wages ten times—and the task of discerning potential meanings resides
with the reader.[99]

Another potential tension lies in the intersection of Jacob's action in
30:37–43 and his report of God's action in 31:7–13. How is Jacob said to
be the actor in one scene and God the actor in the other? Here one must
consider again the literary artistry of biblical narrative, paying specific attention to *how* things are narrated as opposed strictly to *what* is narrated.
Alter has pointed out the propensity within the biblical text for dialogue
or direct speech as the means of driving the narrative forward as opposed
to simple narration.[100] In his view, narration serves largely as a connective
"bridge" between larger blocks of dialogue.[101] The absence of dialogue and
the presence of extended narration, therefore, become significant.

---

96. Heard (*Dynamics of Diselection*, 158) offers a brief bibliography of some representative positions.
97. Fokkelman, *Narrative Art in Genesis*, 153.
98. Alter, *The Art of Biblical Narrative*, 115.
99. See ibid., 126.
100. Ibid., 66.
101. Ibid., 65.

This point finds its outlet in 30:36–43, the only text in the entire Jacob cycle that is entirely narration.[102] Neither Jacob nor Laban speaks. What one finds, instead, is a meticulous narration of Jacob's practice of select breeding by employing the peeled, white branches. Nothing of Jacob's thoughts or the impetus behind this numinous practice receives any clarification or exposition. Scott Noegel regards the ambiguity evident in the text surrounding Jacob's measures as a purposeful mechanism to reinforce the idea of deception.[103] To press Noegel further, the ambiguity also allows for the subsequent clarification that Jacob will provide by means of dialogue with his wives. Only in 31:7, 9, 12, and 15 does one garner any sense of what has taken place. Here, Jacob shares with his wives that it is God who has been behind it all, just as he had promised in 28:13–15 at Bethel (cf. 31:3). Again, as promised, God comes to the fore, revealing his action behind the scenes on Jacob's behalf.

God's concealed advocacy of Jacob becomes more overt through an appreciation of the literary artistry of the narrative. Song-Mi Suzie Park has recently argued that the theme of "what you see is *not* what you get" pervades Jacob and Laban's dealings with one another.[104] The wife swap in Gen 29:21–30 provides the first example.[105] Through use of paronomasia involving the animal's descriptions in relation to their owners, Park maintains that a separation is being drawn between Jacob and Laban, their property, and their families. The appearance and color of the animal corresponds to and serves as an indicator for which of the two, Jacob or Laban, is the owner.[106] That the results of the animal's breeding produces not what one expects to *see* hints at the activity of the *unseen* God on Jacob's behalf. What the reader *sees* is Jacob attempting a ruse (30:37–43), yet what the reader *gets* is the *unseen* God who *sees* Jacob's plight and comes to his rescue (31:7–13).[107] Not *seeing* God at work thus does not pose an insurmountable problem; the immediate and wider context of Gen 29–31 has already deftly illustrated the idea that things are not always as they seem.

Adele Berlin is also instructive here in her view that biblical narrative may at times combine different points of view through repetition that

---

102. Fokkelman, *Narrative Art in Genesis*, 158.

103. Noegel, "Sex, Sticks, and the Trickster," 8, 16–17. Among the ambiguous facets of the text that Noegel draws attention to are words with unclear referents (that is, whose "flocks" are being manipulated and when?), the variety of different adjectives used to describe the multicolored animals, and how Jacob is employing the rods for his own benefit.

104. Park, "Transformation and Demarcation," 677.

105. Ibid., 674.

106. Ibid., 671–73. Park summarizes the puns as follows: "Jacob uses Laban's *lābān* flocks and the *lābān* shavings of the twigs to produce a flock that is not *lābān* and not Laban's, but *nāqōd* and Jacob's. The flock is transformed from white (לבן) to black (חום), from white (לבן) to speckled (נקד and עקד), and from Laban's (לבן) to Jacob's (יעקב)."

107. Park, "Transformation and Demarcation," 675–676.

may or may not deviate from an original utterance or narration.[108] The compound effect of these multiple and at times diverse points of view is a "unified, multi-dimensional narrative."[109] However, Berlin is only helpful inasmuch as she recognizes the importance of isolating and hearing the distinct points of view. It then falls to the reader to adjudicate matters of interpretation.

Johannes Taschner maintains a similar position, but it is a position that helps clarify *how* the text means and transition into *what* it means. He holds that the omniscient narrator presents for readers the same scene from three different perspectives, each with an increasing level of clarity. First, in 30:37–43 the story is recounted from the narrator's perspective, followed by a second report by Jacob to his wives in 31:5–13.[110] The third and final perspective comes from a divine point of view in Jacob's dream.[111] For Taschner, the dream stands as an interpretion of Jacob's activities in 30:37–43, bringing the proper subject into focus: God.[112] In this way, Taschner recognizes yet another occasion on which the protection of God (*Schutz Gottes*) assumes a preeminent place in response to Laban's plotting.[113] The narrative spanning these three perspectives begins vaguely and crescendos to this central theological affirmation that God has been behind it all.

According to Alter, this after-the-fact revelation is also endemic to biblical texts, which will often suppress important details until a critical and pertinent juncture in the narrative.[114] In Gen 30, it is not immediately relevant that God is at work in some mysterious way (although the attentive reader of the Jacob cycle may assume this to be the case), yet in Gen 31, with the threat of further internment to the bearer of the promise, it becomes immediately relevant. Brueggemann rightly notes the significance of the fact that this episode comes immediately on the heels of the birth of Jacob's children. For him, Gen 31:1–16 is the "theological summary" for the entirety of Gen 29–31, and therefore it succeeds in "affirm[ing] that all of Jacob's life is kept (cf. 28:20) and valued by this God who works inversion for the sake of the promise."[115] However, Brueggemann seemingly reduces the promise here solely to the return to the land, which is surely part of but not the entirety of the ancestral promise. In the ancestral narratives, the promise expands; it is not reduced. God's work in the deception of Laban is bound much more deeply to the various particulars of the promise than Brueggemann appears to suggest.

108. Adele Berlin, *Poetics and Interpretation of Biblical Narrative* (Bible and Literature 9; Sheffield: Almond, 1983) 73.

109. Ibid., 82.

110. Taschner, *Verheissung und Erfüllung*, 111–12.

111. Ibid., 112.

112. Ibid., 112–13.

113. Ibid., 113.

114. Alter, *The Art of Biblical Narrative*, 66. See also Fokkelman, *Narrative Art in Genesis*, 159, 162.

115. Brueggemann, *Genesis*, 258.

Similar language connects chaps. 30 and 31. Two of the three words used to describe the cattle that would become Jacob's wages in chap. 30 pose a neat parallel with 31:10, 12. The roots עקד and נקד both occur in 30:39 and 31:10, and נקד appears also in 30:32. Niditch sees this connection as evidence of the "new detail" that Jacob provides in 31:1–16 about the events of 30:37–43.[116] This affinity demonstrates not only a connection between the two chapters but a connection that focuses on the central action of 30:37–43: the coloring of the animals. Additionally, this connection highlights how the promise continues to be operative in Jacob's daily life. His deception will succeed, whereas Laban's will not, all because YHWH will ensure it to be so.

Jacob's attribution of the prior deception of Laban to God in 31:1–16 commends itself to another way of seeing the connection between chaps. 30 and 31. Niditch has outlined the traditional pattern of the "hero" based on her work in folklore.[117] A vital part of this pattern is the deceiving of the deceiver. The interactions between Jacob and Laban fall nicely into her schema, as she recognizes. Again, though, recalling Alter's insights about patterns and type scenes, this schema is adapted in a meaningful way. God's preemptive involvement on behalf of Jacob and to the detriment of Laban is unprecedented in any of the folklore parallels.[118] As such, God's role in Gen 30 and 31 stands as a unique part of the type scene and gives expression to a theologically loaded, unique, unrivaled, and inimitable experience with and understanding of a God who is not above deception as a means of achieving his ultimate ends.

In the final form of the biblical text, Gen 30 and 31 are meant to be read together as mutually informing texts. Erhard Blum avers this very point, affirming how difficult it would be to comprehend Jacob's intentions in Gen 31 if the particulars of Gen 30 had not already been narrated.[119] Similarly, Wenham describes the two scenes as two different perspectives on the same event: the author's in Gen 30 and Jacob's in Gen 31.[120] Tremper Longman suggests that the inexplicable oddity and enigma of Jacob's activities in 30:37–43 allow for but a single conclusion: that God is behind it all, which the text confirms in 31:9.[121] Genesis 31 is much more, however, than simply Jacob's own perspective on events. Here again, one sees a glimpse behind the curtain, from the divine perspective, albeit from the mouth of Jacob.

---

116. Susan Niditch, *A Prelude to Biblical Folklore: Underdogs and Tricksters* (Urbana: University of Illinois Press, 2000) 91.

117. See the helpful chart in ibid., 107.

118. Michael James Williams, *Deception in Genesis: An Investigation into the Morality of a Unique Biblical Phenomenon* (Studies in Biblical Literature 32; New York: Peter Lang, 2001) 199.

119. Erhard Blum, *Die Komposition der Vätergeschichte* (WMANT 57; Neukirchen-Vluyn: Neukirchener Verlag, 1984) 122.

120. Wenham, *Genesis 16–50*, 271.

121. Tremper Longman III, *How to Read Genesis* (Downers Grove, IL: InterVarsity Press Academic, 2005) 141.

God's activities redound to Jacob's benefit, and the story told in 31:1–16 is not solely another viewpoint on what Jacob accomplishes but, rather, what Yнwн accomplishes for and through Jacob.

Lipton's study of dreams in the ancestral narratives lends support to this line of reading. One may remember from chap. 2 above that one key element of these dreams is that they recast and revise previous events in terms that help clarify a divine hand at work. This is the case here, argues Lipton, as God accepts responsibility for the deception of Laban.[122] Lipton understands God's role against the backdrop of "dual causality," which she defines as follows:

> Briefly stated, 'dual causality' describes the complex interplay of human action and divine intervention employed by writers who were uncomfortable with anthropomorphic or other explicit expressions of divine intervention; who wished to convey a sense of historical realism; who sought to emphasize the role played by human strengths and weaknesses in the fulfilment of God's will; or who were motivated by a combination of all three concerns.[123]

Dual causality provides a helpful hermeneutical lens through which one may better understand this scene. This perspective has the benefit of recognizing that neither Jacob nor God is merely a bystander in the deception of Laban. Moreover, Lipton interestingly ponders whether "confusion" may serve as a characteristic of dual-causality narratives, noting the very opaque nature of Gen 30:37–43. She concludes that this confusion serves a narrative purpose, making readers receptive to the idea that God has been behind it all.[124] Her understanding of confusion as a lack of clarity about what is occurring exhibits certain parallels with the discussion of ambiguity and deception from my previous two chapters. It is perhaps fitting, then, that Lipton sees confusion (ambiguity) as fostering and fueling deception.

When read in tandem, Gen 30 and 31 achieve on a theological level an oft-ignored sentiment, though one that appears to be ubiquitous in the Jacob cycle: God's commitment to the ancestral promise is both unwavering and absolute. Chapter 31 brings the latent character, God, to the forefront, and it is God alone who the narrator shows can and does upset the equilibrium between the two deceivers Jacob and Laban. Fokkelman rightly calls God "the only effective 'factor' in the attack-counter-attack of the two sly men."[125] Susan Niditch further clarifies that, by choosing to reveal God's explicit participation in this way, God becomes "a part of the scene without intruding too heavily upon its trickster pattern."[126] Fokkelman perhaps summarizes the connections between the two chapters best:

---

122. Lipton, *Revisions of the Night*, 143–44.
123. Ibid., 133.
124. Ibid., 142.
125. Fokkelman, *Narrative Art in Genesis*, 161.
126. Niditch, *Prelude to Biblical Folklore*, 110.

The scope of Jacob's speech [in 31:1–16] is the precise complement of the scope of the report in Gen. 30. That is why the two texts are corresponding descriptions of the outside and the kernel of one and the same event.[127]

At base, the narrative expands and becomes increasingly provocative as new details emerge. Here, at the necessary moment, Jacob opts to make known the origin of his wealth, prosperity, and protection: the God of the promise he encountered at Bethel.

Trusting Jacob

One question still persists: can Jacob be trusted in what he relates about God's role in the deception of Laban, and if so, why? Jacob has already proven he has no misgivings about acting or even speaking deceptively. In fact, based on what the reader knows of Jacob at this stage in the narrative, one may wholly expect him to spout dubious speech without flinching.[128] One should proceed with caution, however, and not fall prey to the a priori assumption that Jacob can never speak truthfully. Just because he may speak deceptively in one circumstance does not mean that he is unable to speak honestly in another.[129]

Scholars' responses to this question run the gamut of possibilities. Brett accuses Jacob of "inflat[ing] the facts" in order to convince his wives that their father and not Jacob is at fault.[130] Coats holds a similar view, arguing that Jacob the deceiver here shines brightly, crafting a story to persuade his wives and not offering anything authentic.[131] Humphreys similarly contends that God is nothing more than a "rhetorical factor" adduced by Jacob in the interest of convincing his wives to join him in flight.[132] For Humphreys, the fact that it is Jacob and not the narrator who reports this dream complicates its viability all the more. To be sure, Jacob's speech does possess a rhetorical purpose—he does intend to and succeed in convincing his wives to come along—but rhetoric does not necessitate deception.[133] Humphreys's view also strains to accommodate the fact that God has

---

127. Fokkelman, *Narrative Art in Genesis*, 159.

128. See C. D. Evans, "The Patriarch Jacob: An 'Innocent Man,'" *BRev* 2 (1986) 34.

129. Fokkelman (*Narrative Art in Genesis*, 161) correctly cautions against this way of reading. He writes: "A correct literary analysis is not interested in a preconceived portrait of Jacob, but wants to elicit the image of Jacob from the story itself, line by line."

130. Brett, *Genesis*, 95.

131. Coats, "Strife without Reconciliation," 89.

132. Humphreys, *The Character of God in the Book of Genesis*, 180. Most recently, Bill T. Arnold (*Genesis* [NCBC; Cambridge: Cambridge University Press, 2009] 273) takes this sort of view. He writes: "God's protecting presence is a recurring them[e] in Jacob's speech." See also Turner, *Genesis*, 135.

133. On the dream as rhetoric and authentic, see Lipton, *Revisions of the Night*, 121–27, where she argues compellingly that Jacob does indeed use the dream in the hopes of persuading his wives, but in doing so he also makes a larger statement about God's role in the deception that has both forward- and backward-looking ramifications.

spoken *through the narrator* in 31:3, instructing Jacob to return home, and
that God will likewise speak *through the narrator* in 31:24 when he instructs
Laban to do Jacob no harm. Could not these two narratorial references to
God substantiate Jacob's story? Indeed, they accomplish precisely this, for
in 31:13 Jacob parrots God's command to return home, and in 31:7 and 12
Jacob speaks of God's unique protection of him. Moreover, Humphreys's
eager willingness to trust the narrator is problematic; one may equally ask
whether the narrator can be trusted! Shimon Bar-Efrat raises this very note
of caution. [134]

Westermann conversely sees "no contradiction" in Jacob's pointing to a
divine hand as the true, numinous actor of Gen 30. [135] Reflecting on a similar question, Kevin Walton concludes that at best one is unable to know
whether Jacob is speaking deceptively or not. [136] Lipton maintains that the
particulars of the dream are authentic, yet Jacob's claim that the dream is
of one piece is "fabricated." [137] Lipton attempts to establish a chronology
for the various elements of Jacob's dream report, arguing that the narrative
has reshaped them in order to recast previous events in a different light. [138]

Profound reasons exist for trusting Jacob's recollection of his dream
theophany. First, the thorough literary analysis above attests to the veracity of reading Gen 30 and 31 together as mutually illuminating texts. Readers and interpreters should not be overly credulous in believing that the
first account of a given story (30:37–43) is always more reliable than the
second (31:1–16). The answer to the question is not either/or but both/
and. The fact that both accounts exist alongside one another in the final
canonized form of the text prevents readers and interpreters from simply
picking and choosing. [139] One must ask how the two accounts fit together.
In this case, 31:1–16 supplements, clarifies, and expands on 30:37–43. Second, although Jacob is the speaker in 31:1–16, he does not remain entirely
autonomous; the narrator may opt to fashion Jacob's words in any particular way. Fokkelman thus rightly notices the scarcity of any narratorial
comments or cues that would cast Jacob's words in a deceptive tone. [140] The

---

134. Shimon Bar-Efrat (*Narrative Art in the Bible* [JSOTSup 70; Sheffield: Almond, 1989]
33) explains that despite the narrator's omniscience the narrator is neither "completely
objective" nor "impartial towards [his] protagonists." See also chap. 1 above, p. 6.

135. Westermann, *Genesis 12–36*, 491.

136. Kevin Walton, *Thou Traveller Unknown: The Presence and Absence of God in the Jacob
Narrative* (Carlisle: Paternoster, 2003) 118.

137. Lipton, *Revisions of the Night*, 130.

138. Lipton, *Revisions of the Night*, 132.

139. Sherwood (*Had God Not Been on My Side*, 300) adduces two other examples in the
Hebrew Bible in which "new information" stands in dissonance with a given character's
speech: the words of Jacob recounted by his sons upon his death (Gen 50:16–17) and
Bathsheba's avowal that David had promised her son Solomon was next in line for succession (1 Kgs 1:13).

140. Fokkelman, *Narrative Art in Genesis* 161.

narrative does, however, remove Jacob as an effectual agent in regard to the success of the ruse, which may be unfitting and unexpected of the brazen patriarch.[141]

Third, Jacob adduces Bethel, and according to Walton it would be puzzling for Jacob to lie while "swearing by his most sacred experience."[142] That experience not only corroborated his obtaining of the blessing and birthright at a most tumultuous time in his life but also saw him receiving the ancestral promise, which I have increasingly shown has served as a resounding force in his life ever since. Fourth, Jacob's wives serve as a sort of barometer against which the reader can measure the veracity of what Jacob says. Their agreement, then, in 31:14–16 confirms that Jacob's words conform to reality as they understand it. They do not learn anything new from what Jacob tells them except for the fact that God appeared to him with this information.[143] It is not incidental that these previously battling sisters now, for the first time, speak with one voice. Fifth, proponents of the view that Jacob does not warrant the reader's trust in this instance must explain why Jacob's dream theophany here is problematic, yet his dream theophany at Bethel is not. In both scenes, Jacob has a nocturnal experience with the divine. In both scenes, Jacob receives a word of promise. And most importantly, in both scenes, the narrative recounts the action from Jacob's perspective.[144] Why should readers not trust Jacob in Gen 31 yet trust him at Bethel? Are all of Jacob's experiences with God merely rhetorical or feigned? In the end, interpreters have not adequately addressed these central and important issues. In light of them, the quick dismissal of Jacob's reported dream theophany in Gen 31 is unwarranted.

One final consideration merits attention and upholds the authenticity of Jacob's words. In 31:5–13, Jacob takes over the role of narrator. George Savran argues persuasively that in such moments elsewhere in Genesis (for example, Abraham's servant in Gen 24 or Judah in 44:18–34) the character recedes into the background, assuming the usual inconspicuous though

---

141. Ibid., 158.

142. Walton, *Thou Traveller Unknown*, 118.

143. Fokkelman, *Narrative Art in Genesis*, 161–62.

144. While Gen 28:10–22 does not occur explicitly on the lips of Jacob, Fokkelman (ibid., 50–51) describes a sudden stylistic change in the description of Jacob's dream at Bethel. There the narrative switches to a repeated use of the particle הנה followed by participial forms, which results in a change in perspective. He writes: "Up till now he [the narrator] had been telling us all kinds of things from the superior point of the omniscient narrator, now he abandons this attitude; he withdraws behind his protagonist and in a subordinate position *he records what his, Jacob's eyes see.* . . . This has great consequences for the experiencing of time in the narration. There is no longer a narrator who looks back to a past; there is only the present *as Jacob experiences it*—there, a ladder! oh, angels! and look, the Lord himself! No more narratives but five participles one after another with the strength of a durative present" (italics mine). See also Berlin (*Poetics and Interpretation*, 43–82) on point of view, esp. p. 62, where she holds that הנה followed by a verb of perception may be taken as a hint at a change in perspective.

omniscient posture of the regular biblical narrator.[145] What results is an inverse relationship: "the more authority a character is given, the more self-effacing he becomes, and the more the ultimate control of God is emphasized."[146] Therefore, Jacob's position as narrator of his own history in 31:5–13 succeeds in accomplishing two things: first, it renders Jacob an authoritative witness to the truth; second, it propels God to the narrative foreground. At the strictly literary level, Jacob's report about God's activity in the deception of Laban gains another layer of complexity and legitimacy.

Connection with the Ancestral Promise

As has been seen to be the case with the many deceptions in the Jacob/ Laban narratives, this instance of divine deception both echoes and furthers the ancestral promise. Jacob Myers comes closer than most others in affirming an explicit connection between the previous deceptions and the resulting fulfillment. He writes: "From the tone of the text [31:3] as it now stands, it would appear that the convergence of circumstances was part of [Yhwh's] plan to fulfill the promise made to Abraham and to Isaac."[147] Myers's treatment, however, is tantalizingly brief and does not discuss the theological implications of this possibility.

God's command that Jacob "return to the land (אֶרֶץ) of your fathers (אֲבוֹתֶיךָ), to your birthplace (לְמוֹלַדְתֶּךָ), and I will be with you" (v. 3) is evocative of several aspects of the promise. At one level it recalls God's original uttering of the promise to Abraham in Gen 12:1: "Go, from your land (מֵאַרְצְךָ) and from your birthplace (מִמּוֹלַדְתְּךָ) and from the house of your father (מִבֵּית אָבִיךָ) to the land that I will show you." This constellation of similar words is telling. It achieves more than a mere recalling of the ancestral promise; it also seeks to reverse Jacob's 14+ years of exile by instructing him to return to the promised land. While Abraham is to go 'from' (-מ) his land, birthplace, and family, Jacob is to return 'to' (-ל) the land, his family, and his birthplace. Matthews and Mims deem this episode a parallel to Jacob's flight from his family to Haran; they note that when Jacob both enters and leaves Haran a theophany accompanied by the promise provides the proper theological orientation, showing that Jacob is not alone.[148] Additionally, Charles Mabee rightly notices that Yhwh's command "tells Jacob what to do, but no[t] how to do it."[149] While Mabee does not draw the connection, the same ambiguity is evident in Yhwh's command that Abraham up and leave everything. The text simply records that God commands and

---

145. George Savran, "The Character as Narrator in Biblical Narrative," *Prooftexts* 5 (1985) 14.

146. Ibid.

147. Jacob M. Myers, "The Way of the Fathers," *Int* 29 (1975) 135.

148. Victor H. Matthews and Frances Mims, "Jacob the Trickster and Heir of the Covenant: A Literary Interpretation," *PRSt* 12 (1985) 187.

149. Charles Mabee, "Jacob and Laban: The Structure of Judicial Proceedings (Genesis XXXI 25–42)," *VT* 30 (1980) 194.

Abraham departs. Read in this way, the incipient fulfillment of the promise of land comes into focus in Yʜwʜ's command that Jacob return *to the land.*

More specifically, Yʜwʜ's words to Jacob call to mind the ancestral promise granted to Jacob at Bethel. The final clause in 31:3, 'I will be with you' (אהיה עמך) recalls Yʜwʜ's reassurance in 28:15: 'I am with you (אנכי עמך). Gen 31:13 draws the connection even more explicitly. Yʜwʜ identifies himself as "the God of Bethel, where you anointed a pillar and where you made a vow to me." The resonances with Bethel, a pillar, and a vow should be clear.[150] One should also understand the deception itself, from the mouth of Yʜwʜ in 31:12, as an outworking of Yʜwʜ's promise at Bethel of presence and protection for Jacob. This point becomes especially evident given that Yʜwʜ couches discussion of the deception in terms of his maintaining a watchful eye over Jacob, taking special notice of what Laban has been doing to him (vv. 7, 12).

Yʜwʜ's insistence that Jacob depart now touches on the ancestral promise in one other way. Jacob's renewed flight requires confidence in the ancestral promise. The fact that Jacob prepares to leave so quickly upon hearing from God testifies to his trust in the promise. Turner gives even greater import to the necessity of Jacob's reliance on Yʜwʜ's fidelity to the ancestral promise by recognizing that a number of unanswered questions still persist for Jacob: Has Esau's anger abated? Is Rebekah still alive? What circumstances exist at home?[151] In the face of this plethora of unknowns, the ancestral promise, embodied by the trickster Jacob, forges onward, protected by the trickster God.

Divine Deception, Flight, and the Promise (Genesis 31:17–54)

Jacob's hastened departure does not end the deception. Rather, yet again the twin themes of deception and the ancestral promise appear together in ways that are less overt than some of the ways discussed above. Three issues warrant brief discussion: Yʜwʜ's command to depart as deception, Rachel's theft of the *teraphim*, and Yʜwʜ's protection of Jacob and his family in accordance with the ancestral promise.

Departure and Divine Deception

Laban is deceived not only by Jacob and Yʜwʜ's stealthy rigging of the wage agreement but also by the sheer fact that Jacob departs unannounced. On three occasions, the text regards Jacob's hastened departure as a means of deception, and two of these times Laban does the speaking. Verse 20 states that Jacob "stole the heart of Laban," a construction formed from some form of the verb 'steal away' (גנב) plus 'heart' (לב), commonly regarded as an idiom implying deception. In v. 26, the same construction

---

150. See Mathews, *Genesis 11:27–50:26*, 514.
151. Turner, *Genesis*, 134.

appears, but now Laban asks why it is that Jacob 'stole his heart'. Last, in v. 27, only the word גנב is used, which is oftentimes translated 'deceive'. In all three of these occurrences, the deception is associated no longer with Jacob's obtaining of great wealth but solely with Jacob's surreptitious exit. However, this exit was not of Jacob's choosing but instead was a response to God (31:3). Thus, the text again portrays YHWH as, in a way, deceiving Laban through the command that Jacob and his family leave and return home.[152] One should remain mindful also of the way that this deception connects with the ancestral promise, discussed above.

Rachel's Theft of the teraphim

Prior to the family's departure, the text records that Rachel steals (תגנב) her father's *teraphim*. Detailed investigation and discussion of the nature and background of the *teraphim* press beyond the bounds of the present study, but it is vital to recognize that both Laban (v. 30) and Jacob (v. 32) refer to them as "gods."[153] Anne-Marie Korte sees in this scene "a remarkable deconstruction of the theological dichotomy" between the God of the fathers and the *teraphim*.[154] For her, the point is not that the two concepts are so vastly different in regard to "corporeality, materiality or tangibility" but, rather, that each functions with varying degrees of inclusiveness.[155] Korte's conclusions react against traditional understandings of this scene that have great merit: namely, that YHWH is here juxtaposed with and shown to be superior to the *teraphim*. In this comparison, however, Korte is right that one should not equate Rachel with uncleanness or the state of taboo because she says she is menstruating as a means of covering her deception (v. 35). Her claim to be menstruating, however, does cast ridicule on the *teraphim*. Assuming that they were some sort of household god, we can see that this episode makes a larger theological statement: while YHWH is a God who delivers his chosen and protects them from oppression in line with the promise, the *teraphim* are nothingness and have no power or vitality.

That this theological statement is made in the context of a deception is significant. According to Esther Fuchs, given that Jacob's (and YHWH's)

---

152. Mabee ("Jacob and Laban," 194) correctly writes that nothing in the narrative indicates that YHWH takes umbrage at the method of leaving Jacob chooses.

153. This word occurs a number of times in the Hebrew Bible. All the biblical occurrences of the word (Gen 31:19, 34, 35; Judg 17:5; 18:14, 17, 18, 20; 1 Sam 15:23; 19:13, 16; 2 Kgs 23:24; Ezek 21:26; Hos 3:4; Zech 10:2) appear to represent some type of deity and perhaps connote its function as an instrument of divination; only the occurrences in 1 Samuel deviate from this function because there, the *teraphim* serve as a stand-in for the sleeping David. See Westermann (*Genesis 12–36*, 485, 493) for a brief yet helpful explanation of the term and a thorough bibliography, as well as Taschner (*Verheissung und Erfüllung*, 115–23) on the function, etymology, and other biblical attestations of the word.

154. Anne-Marie Korte, "Significance Obscured: Rachel's Theft of the Teraphim—Divinity and Corporeality in Gen 31," in *Begin with the Body: Corporeality, Religion and Gender* (ed. J. Bekkenkamp and M. de Haardt; Leuven: Peeters, 1998) 181.

155. Ibid., 179, 181.

deception of Laban by fleeing as well as Rachel's stealing of her father's *teraphim* both use the verb גנב, the two scenes are related though dissimilar.[156] Whereas גנב functions literally in reference to Rachel's theft, it is used figuratively for Jacob.[157] Fuchs does not mention v. 27, however, where גנב appears without the idiomatic accompanier לב in reference to Jacob. Technically, Jacob has not stolen anything from Laban, yet in v. 43 Laban clearly names the daughters, grandchildren, and flocks as his, leading to the possibility that he saw them as a sort of booty that Jacob had also taken. Matthews and Mims describe this scene as a scene in which YHWH functions as Rachel's "fellow trickster, who can demonstrate his superiority by protecting his people and discrediting the images and power of rival deities."[158] Matthews and Mims do not clarify precisely how YHWH is a trickster here, but Fuchs's insightful assertion that the two most recent deceptions are connected may provide some clarity.[159] She describes Rachel's deception as being laden with what Sternberg calls permanent gaps; in this scene, ambiguity is ubiquitous.[160] Based on what one has encountered thus far in the Jacob cycle, the prevalence of ambiguity in this scene may lead one to suspect deception. What Fuchs leaves unsaid, however, is that the keen reader may fill in these gaps so as to make sense of the narrative. Doing so, it seems, reveals one possible way of understanding YHWH as her co-trickster.

Rachel's theft occurs immediately after Jacob's speech to his wives (vv. 5–13) and their assent (vv. 14–16). Jacob states (and YHWH agrees) that it was YHWH who had taken Laban's possessions and granted them to Jacob. Laban's daughters, then, affirm the same in v. 16, but this time claim that all the wealth that YHWH has 'caused to be stripped away' (הציל) belongs not to Jacob but to them and their children. Against this broader backdrop, one may construe Rachel's theft of the *teraphim* as her acting in accordance with YHWH's words reported by Jacob in vv. 5–13. If she understands *all* (כל) of her father's property to belong to her and her sister, and YHWH is the mechanism by which this property is transferred from Laban to them, then Rachel's deception of her father extends beyond her insistence that she is menstruating in v. 35. Just as YHWH had taken all of Laban's flocks and

---

156. Esther Fuchs, "'For I Have the Way of Women': Deception, Gender, and Ideology in Biblical Narrative," *Semeia* 42 (1988) 74.

157. Ibid.

158. Matthews and Mims, "Jacob the Trickster," 189.

159. Fuchs ("For I Have the Way of Women," 70, 80) underscores the often-ignored fact that because Jacob does not know of Rachel's theft (v. 32b) she deceives not only Laban but also her husband, Jacob!

160. Ibid., 70, 79. For Fuchs, unlike when males deceive in the Hebrew Bible, Rachel's deception lacks an explicit motive, narratorial judgment, and any sense of closure. Of course, I disagree with Fuchs that each of these elements—especially a judgment issued by the narrator—serves a necessary or even recurring function in scenes depicting males engaged in deception. See chap. 1, pp. 39–40.

given them to Jacob, so too the narrative hints that Yʜᴡʜ has some hand in Rachel's stealing of her father's *teraphim*.

Genesis 31:24 and the Ancestral Promise

Further substantiating the point above that Yʜᴡʜ plays a part in the missing case of the *teraphim* is his reappearance in the narrative, now to Laban, with the instruction not to do anything good or evil to Jacob. The phrase "from good or evil" serves as a merism, covering the full range of possibilities that Laban may or may not do to Jacob; the Hebrew literally reads 'from good *to* evil' (מטוב עד־רע). This statement does not, however, censure Laban entirely, forbidding him to speak a word at all, as Honeyman suggests.[161] If this were the case, Laban certainly did not adhere to instruction well, for he did speak with and against Jacob, accusing him of deception and theft (vv. 25–30, 43–44, 51–52). Mathews correctly understands the merism as placing a limit on Laban's "authority."[162] The injunction against doing "*good* to evil" makes better sense when read this way; Yʜᴡʜ, not Laban, is the sole source of good and prosperity in Jacob's life. W. M. Clark and E. A. Speiser argue, based on parallels elsewhere in the Hebrew Bible, for a forensic understanding of the phrase, meaning that God forbids Laban to prosecute his accusation.[163] This line of reading is equally important, for the threat exists that Laban will uncover Rachel's theft, to which even Jacob is aloof. The fact that Laban cannot speak anything "good to evil" to Jacob thus obtains an additional dimension of protection against legal redress, given the prospect of Laban's discovery of Rachel's theft.

Yʜᴡʜ's words to Laban in 31:24 have several connections with the ancestral promise and concern for its perpetuation. First, as many have noticed, Laban's dream is reminiscent of Yʜᴡʜ's appearance to Abimelech in a dream in Gen 20:3.[164] In Gen 20, the scene relates to the promise by means of its concern for Sarah's well-being as the mother of the promised child. On both occasions, Yʜᴡʜ intervenes, appearing to the one whom the patriarch has deceived, in order to eliminate any attempt at reciprocation. Both situations find Yʜᴡʜ protecting the deceiver subsequent to the deception. Second, Fokkelman maintains that an obvious parallel exists with 24:50, where Laban and others respond to the providential journey of Abraham's servant by stating, "This comes from Yʜᴡʜ; we are not able to speak to you evil or good." Whereas in 24:50 Laban saw God's purposes at work

---

161. A. M. Honeyman ("*Merismus* in Biblical Hebrew," *JBL* 71 [1952] 12) translates the phrase 'not any word at all'.

162. Mathews, *Genesis 11:27–50:26*, 523.

163. W. Malcolm Clark, "A Legal Background to the Yahwist's Use of 'Good and Evil' in Genesis 2–3," *JBL* 88 (1969) 269; Speiser, *Genesis*, 246. This understanding fits within the larger context of Gen 31 established by Mabee ("Jacob and Laban," 194–205), who sees the prolonged discussion between Jacob and Laban as an example of a judicial proceeding.

164. Hamilton, *Genesis 18–50*, 299; Mathews, *Genesis 11:27–50:26*, 523; Lipton, *Revisions of the Night*, 150–52; Turner, *Genesis*, 137.

and said so, in 31:24 Yʜᴡʜ must inform him, with threats, that Jacob's deceptive flight also comes "from Yʜᴡʜ."[165] Third, God demands that Laban "take care (שמר) not to speak good to bad to Jacob." The verb used here (שמר) is used by Yʜᴡʜ at Bethel when conferring the ancestral promise on Jacob. Gen 28:15 says, 'I will *protect* you' (שמרתיך). The link between these two verses underscores that the ancestral promise is the operative interpretive context for Yʜᴡʜ's intercession on Jacob's behalf in 31:24. Driving this point home for us is the fact that Jacob clearly recognizes Yʜᴡʜ's protective presence in his final speech to Laban (v. 42).

Fourth, the protection afforded Jacob by Yʜᴡʜ results in Laban's eventual defeat. Lipton, as one may now expect, sees Laban's dream as casting its shadow back across the entire Jacob/Laban narratives (Gen 29–31), recasting the human conflict between Jacob and Laban as a conflict in which God has had a hand all along.[166] Upon failing to trump Jacob time and again, Laban can conclude only with a covenant over which Yʜᴡʜ will preside (vv. 49–50, 53). This covenant, argues Vera, has the twin concerns of protecting Jacob's newly acquired family and of imposing a protective limit for both parties, over which neither can transgress.[167] Petersen, recognizing the obvious familial dynamics operative in this scene, likens Jacob and Laban's formal separation to a divorce.[168] The two tricksters mark this geographical boundary with a stone (vv. 45–54). Jacob and Laban's erecting of a stone at Mizpah recalls the ancestral promise previously memorialized with a stone (28:18). The latter marks the giving of the covenant, the former Yʜᴡʜ's demonstrated commitment to it.

Understood from this perspective, Yʜᴡʜ's directive stands as an injunction against endangering the bearer of the promise in any way, and yet another example of Yʜᴡʜ's protection (שמר) amidst deception in line with the ancestral promise. By warning Laban to do Jacob and his family no harm, God creates and ensures a framework wherein the blessing can and will be spread to the west, east, north, and south (28:14).

Conclusion: Deception and Incipient Fulfillment of the Ancestral Promise

This chapter has investigated the way in which the ancestral promise begins to move toward fulfillment through the many deceptions occurring during Jacob's sojourn in Haran. The opening verses of Gen 29 function,

---

165. Fokkelman, *Narrative Art in Genesis*, 165.

166. Lipton, *Revisions of the Night*, 172. See also José Loza Vera ("La Berît entre Laban et Jacob (Gn 31.43–54)," in *World of the Aramaeans I: Biblical Studies in Honour of Paul-Eugène Dion* [ed. P. M. Michèle Daviau, J. W. Wevers, and M. Weigl; Sheffield: Sheffield Academic Press, 2001] 63–64) on the connection between Gen 31:43–51 and what precedes it.

167. Ibid., 66.

168. Petersen, "Genesis and Family Values," 20.

much akin to the analysis of the opening verses of the entire Jacob cycle, to reintroduce the centrality of the ancestral promise and Yʜᴡʜ's fidelity to it by means of his guiding Jacob safely to Laban's family. Second, I discussed Laban's notorious "wife swap" as a deception that succeeds in setting the stage for Jacob's acquiring two wives, as well as their maidservants, who end up bearing, with Yʜᴡʜ's help alone, 12 children of the promise. I also emphasized the way in which Laban's deception of Jacob does not necessitate a negative evaluation of Jacob's deception of his father, Isaac, in Gen 27 but instead may underscore the notion of fulfillment that arises as a concern in both scenes. Taken together with Gen 27, Gen 29 provides an overall orientation for the Jacob/Laban narratives. This perspective of promise related to deception helps to condition the reader to regard what befalls Jacob in Haran not as judgments for prior wrongs but as an outworking of Yʜᴡʜ's commitment to the ancestral promise.

Given this interpretive context, I treated three scenes of incipient fulfillment of the ancestral promise. First, in Gen 29:31–30:24, the narrative reports a rapid succession of 12 births to Jacob's wives, a circumstance afforded by Laban's previous deception in giving the fertile Leah in marriage prior to the barren Rachel. Emerging from this reading was also the highly theological nature of these birth narratives, evidenced by the preponderance of either theophoric names for the children or the mother's recognition that the child arose solely because of intercession to Yʜᴡʜ. Second, Gen 30:27–30 highlighted the fulfillment of the promise that Israel will serve as a blessing to the nations through Laban's avowal that Yʜᴡʜ had blessed him through Jacob. Whether Laban was here speaking deceptively or not is of little consequence, since his blessing was short-lived: in the final text treated, 30:25–31:54, Laban becomes the object of a deception, and the cost is his wealth accrued by attempting to exploit Jacob's services. This final scene is rife with deception and counterdeception, yet the final arbiter emerges in 31:1–16 when Jacob reports that Yʜᴡʜ, not he, had successfully manipulated the breeding of the flocks first narrated in 30:27–34. Concomitantly, it was shown that Yʜᴡʜ deceived Laban in another way, by instructing Jacob with his newly acquired wealth to depart and return to the land of the promise.

Taken in toto, the compound effect of these narrative movements reveals remarkable progress toward the end goals of the ancestral promise. Turner's thesis, with which I began this chapter—that within the Jacob cycle the ancestral promise sees advances only in the realm of progeny—is thus incorrect. Jacob leaves Haran with multiple children, who will eventuate in the entire people of Israel, but he is also the individual who has blessed Laban and the man who at Yʜᴡʜ's command begins the trek back to the promised land. The promise has certainly not reached fulfillment, yet it also is not stuck at an impasse, hanging in abeyance as Jacob and Laban attempt to outwit one another. Quite the opposite; just as the trickster oracle reaches fulfillment through deception (Gen 27; 28:13–15), so also the ancestral promise continues toward fulfillment through deception. While Jacob's stay in Haran may at times be unhappy, it is within and through all these experiences that the ancestral promise works itself out, guided at every turn by the trickster God.

Chapter 4

Replaying the Fool:
Esau versus Y<small>HWH</small> *and Jacob*
(Genesis 32–35)

Introductory Remarks

Traditional interpretations of this final section of the Jacob cycle settle
on the idea that these narratives depict a transformative moment in Jacob's
life. The nocturnal struggle and concomitant name change from 'Jacob'
(יעקב) the 'supplanter/deceiver' (cf. 25:26; 27:36) to 'Israel' (ישראל) the 'God-
wrestler' (32:29; cf. 35:10) is taken to solidify a change in Jacob's character
that allows for his successful reconciliation with Esau and suitability as a
viable candidate for the ancestral promise. Matthews and Mims are among
the foremost proponents of this reading. For them, the Jacob cycle is about
preparing Jacob to become the rightful heir to the promise.[1] Conflicts with
Esau, Laban, and God help to mold Jacob into a character worthy of receiving the promise.[2] It is this final encounter with God in Gen 32 that is
most formative for Jacob. With his new name, according to Matthews and
Mims, he at last reaches a level of maturation that allows him to become
the rightful heir to the covenant.[3] Other interpreters view Gen 32 in a
similar vein. Von Rad labels Jacob's new name "a name of honor" that
will now ensure God's recognition and acceptance of him.[4] Brueggemann
argues for a transference of power between God and humanity whereby
Jacob assumes a new identity as both a man and a community in relationship with God.[5] Kenneth Mathews sees Jacob's renaming as evidence of an
impending "metamorphosis" of his "moral character."[6] And Wenham goes
so far as to describe the renaming as a "rebaptism."[7]

---

1. Victor H. Matthews and Frances Mims, "Jacob the Trickster and Heir of the Covenant: A Literary Interpretation," *PRSt* 12 (1985) 186–87.

2. Ibid., 187.

3. Ibid., 193.

4. Gerhard von Rad, *Genesis* (OTL; rev. ed.; trans. J. H. Marks; Philadelphia: Westminster, 1973) 321.

5. Walter Brueggemann, *Genesis* (Interpretation; Atlanta: John Knox, 1982) 268–69.

6. Kenneth A. Mathews, *Genesis 11:27–50:26* (NAC 1B; Nashville: Broadman & Holman, 2005) 559.

7. Gordon J. Wenham, *Genesis 16–50* (WBC 2; Dallas: Word, 1994) 296.

130

As will become clear in the course of this chapter, the traditional interpretation outlined here is severely wanting. First, the view presented in Matthews and Mims misses crucial elements in the literary flow of the text. Jacob is not a character on the way toward earning the ancestral promise or becoming a fit candidate to receive it. God's selection of Jacob has occurred already at the beginning of the cycle, albeit in ambiguous terms (Gen 25:23), not at the end, and more importantly, Jacob has already received the promise at Bethel in 28:13–15. No preparation or testing as Matthews and Mims suggest is overt or even necessary in the text. All along, the promise belongs to Jacob. The promise to Jacob, just like the promise to Abraham, rests on the bedrock of God's own initiative and covenantal fidelity, not on the assumed merits of the patriarchs.

Second, a thorough scrutiny of the text leaves the reader pondering precisely how much Jacob truly changes after Gen 32. In fact, his renaming in 32:29 appears to do quite little to change his deceptive character as he unremittingly deceives Esau again in Gen 33 in a number of ways, including ambiguously offering to return the "blessing" (33:11; cf. 32:29) and reneging on his promise to follow Esau to Seir but instead journeying to and residing in Sukkoth (33:12–17). It is also not insignificant that the narrative continues to employ the name "Jacob" well beyond his renaming in Gen 32.[8]

A third difficulty also presents itself: the continued role of God in all that follows. As is evident above, the traditional interpretation sees Jacob as a character who must, in a way, become palatable to God before receiving the promise. In my analysis in the preceding chapters, however, I have leveled a strong critique against this posture of reading that seeks to place God outside Jacob's life and experiences. To reiterate the argument of chap. 2, Jacob is chosen by God from birth (25:23), a choice confirmed at Bethel, when God bestows the ancestral promise on him (28:13–15). To place these closing chapters of the Jacob cycle in the overall context of the interpretation presented in this book, chap. 2 focuses on how Jacob receives the ancestral promise through deception, while chap. 3 presents the multifarious ways in which the promise moves toward fulfillment amidst and through the various deceptions between Jacob and Laban. The operative question for chap. 4, then, is not how Jacob attains the promise despite deception but how God functions in Jacob's life through deception to guarantee the promise's perpetuation and bring the Jacob cycle to some type of resolution. To achieve any sense of resolution, Jacob must address the only remaining obstacle in the narrative: Esau. He exists as the final and most

---

8. See Fredrick C. Holmgren, "Holding Your Own against God! Genesis 32:22–32 (in the Context of Genesis 31–33)," *Int* 44 (1990) 11; Laurence A. Turner, *Genesis* (Readings; 2nd ed.; Sheffield: Sheffield Phoenix, 2009) 145. Among the relevant texts, one may consult Gen 32:29–30, 32; 33:1, 5, 8, 10, 17, 18; 34:3, 6, 7, 13, 27, 30; 35:1, 2, 4, 5, 6, 9, 10 (2x), 14, 15.

ominous threat to Jacob and thus, by extension, to the continuance of the ancestral promise.

This chapter will challenge the traditional interpretation, arguing specifically that Jacob by no means repents of his deceptive ways but continues in them, with God, for the sake of the promise and at the expense yet again of his brother, Esau. I will show that the encounter at the Jabbok (32:23–33), through its use of ambiguity and deception, functions not to transform Jacob's future but to commend his past dealings with the individuals whom he has deceived. As such, this struggle with God becomes concurrently a prefiguration of his deceptive reunion with Esau (Gen 33). But as was the case in Gen 25 and 27, the success of this trickery is not of Jacob's own making; the divine trickster is also at work for Jacob, not against him. In Gen 32–35, divine deception casts its glance both backward—in essence, again approving the successful deceptions of Isaac, Esau, and Laban—and forward—ensuring Jacob's continued success in his meeting with Esau to advance the ancestral promise toward fulfillment.

This chapter will unfold in three parts. First, I will examine Jacob's preparations for reconciliation with Esau, seeing in them the work of a consummate trickster whose goal is to allay Esau's presumed anger. Here I will give attention specifically to two encounters—(1) with the messengers of God at Mahanaim (33:2–3), and (2) the enigmatic wrestling match between Jacob and God (32:23–33)—to see how each sets the stage for Jacob's triumph over Esau in Gen 33. Second, I will analyze the reconciliation of the brothers in Gen 33 with the intent of showing that it is a text rife with deception. Through clever fawning and outright deception, Jacob reconciles with Esau, holds onto the promise, and most importantly, returns to the land. Last, Gen 34–35 will receive brief treatment as a sort of epilogue to the cycle in which deception persists. The result of the deception in Gen 34, however, is of insurmountable importance in the cycle, for it leads to God's directive that Jacob return not merely to the promised land but to the land *of the promise*, Bethel. It is here at Bethel that the ancestral promise will be reaffirmed, though now not only to Jacob but in the presence of the signs of the promise's fulfillment: his wealth, wives, and children.

Encounters: Preparations for Reconciliation (Genesis 32:1–33)

No sooner does Jacob escape the threat of Laban with the assistance of divine trickery then he is thrust into another impending conflict, this time with his brother, Esau, the object of the original act of divine trickery in Jacob's life (25:23). How will this scene play out? Has Esau's anger attenuated, or will he succumb to his earlier murderous intentions (27:41)? Jacob is uneasy, uncertain as to his brother's objectives, and so he sets in motion a litany of attempts to placate Esau with messengers, flattering words, and gifts (32:1–22). After he organizes all his wealth and family and situates them as a buffer between himself and the approaching Esau, an unnamed entity (only later identified as God) accosts Jacob (32:23–33). The outcome of this struggle is a blessing for Jacob, but this blessing comes with a price, won at the expense of a permanent injury to the recipient of the promise.

The ancestral promise remains at the fore in the narrative, a point that scholars have readily noted. However, what has not received adequate voice here are the manifest ways in which the narrative connects God to these events in a way that benefits Jacob. Although scholarship has been preoccupied largely with the question of what these narratives say about Jacob and his undergoing some sort of transformation, this question cannot be answered without attending to the concomitant question that forms the basis for this study: what does the text say about God? If Jacob experiences a change—a view already challenged above—then one might expect God likewise to change his approach in dealing with Jacob. What one finds, however, is that God remains steadfast, to the point of trickery, in his twin concerns for Jacob and the ancestral promise.

Divine Messengers and Fearful Flattery (Genesis 32:1–22)

Genesis 32–33 is a text of encounters. First with the messengers of God (32:2–3), then with God (32:23–33), and finally with Esau (33:1–20), these encounters hold the narrative together and help to orient the reader to the proper theological perspective: that God continues to be at work on Jacob's behalf. The encounter with the messengers of God and then with God give shape to Jacob's encounter with Esau, both affecting the way in which he will approach his brother and equipping him with the necessary arsenal to achieve success in the encounter.

The first encounter at Mahanaim (32:2–3) has long perplexed interpreters of the Jacob cycle. Among the most pressing issues seems to be what meaning and import these verses contribute to the surrounding narrative. The text is terse and to the point; it is the point, however, that remains unclear. Jacob and his family with their possessions leave Laban and press onward toward the land. Along the way, at some unnamed juncture, they chance upon two messengers of God (מלאכי אלהים), leading Jacob to identify the place as God's camp and name the place Mahanaim (מחנים). Immediately thereafter, Jacob is seen assiduously preparing for his meeting with Esau, and no subsequent mention of Mahanaim occurs anywhere else in the Jacob cycle.

Scholarly discussions have only added to the ambiguity of these few verses. Some scholars, most recently Tzemah Yoreh, have argued that vv. 2–3 were once attached to the scene of Jacob's struggle in vv. 23–33 and that the "man" with whom Jacob fought was in fact a member of this encampment.[9] Cornelis Houtman points out a number of questions that the text leaves unanswered: Is the meeting hostile or polite? Where are the messengers from? How did Jacob see the messengers? Whom do the two camps comprise?[10] Victor Hamilton similarly underscores the deafening silence in this brief scene: neither Jacob nor the messengers speak or react to one another.[11] Outwardly, the scene appears quite odd in its present context. What, then, is its purpose at the close of Jacob's sojourn with Laban and at the outset of his journey home?

Genesis 32:2–3 is of fundamental importance in our comprehending what lay ahead for Jacob. Westermann regards these verses as originally independent from the Jacob cycle, making their way into the text by the hand of J, who inserted them at a crucial point in the narrative.[12] While Westermann's explanation of the mechanism by which 32:2–3 enters the narrative may be prone to dispute, his final statement that the text is highly purposive in its present context is a necessary prerequisite to grasping its meaning. From this perspective, the point of the narrative begins to come into sharper focus.

Genesis 32:2–3 sets the stage for the impending encounter between Jacob and Esau by both recalling the ancestral promise bestowed on Jacob at Bethel and affording Jacob the insight regarding how to go about facing his brother. Concerns over the narrative's silence need not delay us; instead, we find here another fine example of the way in which biblical narrative is purposely silent in order to inform meaning. The task is left to the careful reader to draw the various connections between Jacob's encounter with the divine messengers at Mahanaim and his preparations for the encounter with Esau that follow. The importance of the Mahanaim encounter lies not

9. Tzemah Yoreh ("Jacob's Struggle," *ZAW* 117 [2005] 95–97) maintains that both episodes belong to the pentateuchal source E and were separated by a J redactor who desired that the identity of Jacob's opponent be obscured. Hosea 12 preserves a quite distilled version of the Jacob cycle, and v. 5 appears to share Yoreh's reading, recording Jacob's opponent as a 'messenger' (מַלְאָךְ). Yoreh's reading, however, requires a reconstructed text that eliminates v. 3b, the etiology for Mahanaim, ascribing it instead to the later J redactor. More problematic, Yoreh's thesis does not account for two seminal aspects of the final form of the Genesis text: (1) that a 'man' (אִישׁ) wrestles with Jacob, not an angel; (2) the final form of the text understands this being as God, which is evident in the fact that Jacob's new name is explained by the saying "you have wrestled *with God*" as well as Jacob's etiological statement explaining that his naming of the place as *Peniel* stems from his understanding that he has seen *God* face to face and survived. See also F. M. T. Böhl, "Volksetymologie en Woordspeling in de Genesis-Verhalen," *MKAW Letterkunde* 59A (1925) 23. For the most recent proponent of this reading, see Bill T. Arnold, *Genesis* (NCBC; Cambridge: Cambridge University Press, 2009) 280.

10. Cornelis Houtman, "Jacob at Mahanaim: Some Remarks on Genesis xxxii 2–3," *VT* 28 (1978) 37–38, 43.

11. Victor P. Hamilton, *The Book of Genesis: Chapters 18–50* (NICOT; Grand Rapids, MI: Eerdmans, 1995) 317.

12. Claus Westermann, *Genesis 12–36: A Continental Commentary* (trans. John J. Scullion; Minneapolis: Fortress, 1995) 505.

in its opacity but in how it reintroduces the recurrent theme of the ancestral promise while concurrently giving Jacob a strategy in facing Esau. I will
treat this relevance under two separate but related rubrics: Mahanaim and
the ancestral promise, and Mahanaim and Jacob's stratagem.

Mahanaim and the Ancestral Promise

The brief encounter at Mahanaim exhibits a number of telling lexical
links to the ancestral promise scene at Bethel in Gen 28.[13] The most potent
of these connections is the phrase 'messengers of God' (מלאכי אלהים). While
the singular form is ubiquitous in the biblical text, this particular plural
construction occurs only twice in the entire Hebrew Bible: at Mahanaim
(32:2) and at Bethel (28:12).[14] In the latter, Jacob observed the "messengers
of God" ascending and descending a stairway, with God stationed at its
top. God then spoke, granting the ancestral promise to Jacob. At Mahanaim, however, God and his emissaries are silent. But there are words from
Jacob that elucidate another facet shared by the two scenes.

Jacob responds to the sheer sight of the Mahanaim messengers by ex-
claiming that he has arrived at the camp of God. His exasperated utterance
in 32:3, '*This* is God's camp' (מחנה אלהים זה), mirrors the statement found
in 28:17, when he wakes from his dream and says, '*This* (הזה) is none other
than the house of God, and *this* (זה) is the gateway to Heaven'. The shared
emphatic use of 'this' (זה) in relation to Jacob's recognizing the true nature
and identity of an unknown locale ties the two scenes together.[15] Both
also employ nearly identical etiological naming formulas for a previously
unnamed place.[16] In 28:19, Jacob '*calls the name of that place* Bethel' (יקרא
את־שם־המקום ההוא בית־אל), and in 32:3 he '*calls the name of that place* Mahanaim' (יקרא שם־המקום ההוא מחנים).[17] These lexical affinities assist even further
in linking the two scenes together.[18]

Several other lexical parallels contribute to the context of promise. In
both scenes, the narrative uses a form of the verb 'encountered' (פגע); in
28:11, Jacob "encounters" the place that will become Bethel, while in 32:2
the messengers of God "encounter" Jacob.[19] Kenneth Mathews understands
the angels at Mahanaim as scouts surveying the lay of the land ahead of

---

13. Contra Mark G. Brett (*Genesis: Procreation and the Politics of Identity* [Old Testament
Readings; London: Routledge, 2000] 98), who contends that Jacob's separation is a self-
interested action motivated by fear, not by any resonances with Bethel.

14. Houtman. "Jacob at Mahanaim," 39; Hamilton, *Genesis 18–50*, 317.

15. Houtman, "Jacob at Mahanaim," 39.

16. Ibid. See also Hamilton, *Genesis 18–50*, 317.

17. In English, one notices no difference. The differences between the Hebrew in the
two statements are of no consequence; the only dissimilarity is the absence of the direct-
object marker את in the Mahanaim etiology.

18. Johannes Taschner (*Verheissung und Erfüllung in der Jakoberzählung (Gen 25,19–
33,17): Eine Analyse ihres Spannungsbogens* [Herders Biblische Studien; Freiburg: Herder,
1999] 141) also recognizes many of these same cross-references.

19. Hamilton, *Genesis 18–50*, 317.

Jacob and his family.[20] According to Westermann, the scene communicates God's awesome and unique power, which is especially evident in the image of God's (military?) encampment, in the face of Jacob's fear about meeting Esau.[21] Assuming that Mathews and Westermann are correct, one may view the messengers in line with the promise of presence and protection in 28:15. Both texts (33:3; cf. 28:11 [2x], 16, 17, 19) also describe Jacob's surroundings initially only as a 'place' (מקום).[22]

Fokkelman notes a parallel with Jacob's vow at Bethel in 28:20–22. There and in 32:2 one finds the only place where the words 'go' (הלך) and 'way' (דרך) appear together in the Jacob cycle.[23] This connection is most significant for the way that it unites the promise in theory (or, Jacob's understanding of it) with the promise experienced as a present reality for Jacob. In 28:20, Jacob seeks to clarify the divine word of promise, requesting that God protect him 'on this way (בדרך) that I am going (הולך)'. In 32:2, Jacob encounters the messengers while he is 'going on his way' (הלך לדרכו). I have already shown in chap. 3 that God is certainly with Jacob during his time with Laban. Now that Jacob has left Laban behind, God shows through the presence of two divine messengers that he continues to abide with Jacob at a time of similar apprehension: a looming encounter with Esau.[24]

One may discern also a vital thematic link between Bethel and Mahanaim. Brueggemann highlights a related scene in Josh 5:13–15, where Joshua, on the verge of leading the Israelites into the promised land, encounters a man who identifies himself as captain of the host of Yhwh.[25] Just as Joshua and the Israelites were about to enter the land, so also Jacob at Mahanaim is drawing near this sacred boundary. When we apply this comparison to the text under consideration here, a striking connection comes to the fore. While the Bethel theophany takes place on Jacob's way *out of* the land of promise, the Mahanaim encounter takes place on Jacob's *way back into* the land of promise.[26] At these two critical moments in his life, Jacob meets with the divine. During the first, he receives the ancestral promise, and during the second the confidence of Yhwh's continued presence and protection.

---

20. Mathews, *Genesis 11:27–50:26*, 547.

21. Westermann, *Genesis 12–36*, 505.

22. See Shimon Bar-Efrat, *Narrative Art in the Bible* (JSOTSup 70; Sheffield: Almond, 1989) 188.

23. J. P. Fokkelman, *Narrative Art in Genesis: Specimens of Stylistic and Structural Analysis* (Eugene, OR: Wipf & Stock, 1991) 197. See also Taschner, *Verheissung und Erfüllung*, 141.

24. Ibid.

25. Brueggemann, *Genesis*, 261. On the connection with Judg 5:13–15, see also Westermann, *Genesis 12–36*, 505.

26. Johann Marböck ("Heilige Orte im Jakobszyklus: Einige Beobachtungen und Aspekte," in *Die Väter Israels: Beiträge zur Theologie der Patriarchenüberlieferungen im Alten Testament* [ed. A. R. Müller and M. Görg; Stuttgart: Katholisches Bibelwerk, 1989] 220) notes that encounters with the divine separate the Jacob/Esau and the Jacob/Laban narratives.

Mahanaim and Jacob's Stratagem

The Mahanaim encounter does much more than simply recall the ancestral promise; it also looks forward to Jacob's impending encounter with Esau. Attempts to ascertain the meaning of this scene outside its larger surrounding narrative context yields only a frustratingly palpable silence on how this text helps make sense of Jacob's activities that follow. Within the final form of the text, Gen 32:2–3 is not a displaced, partial account meant to shed light on the identity of Jacob's opponent in vv. 23–33 but rather a fundamental piece of how the reader is to understand God's role in Jacob's preparations for meeting Esau. In fact, as the narrative continues, it will become clear that Jacob understands this encounter much more deeply than the narrative appears at first glance for its readers. These two short, seemingly innocuous verses present Jacob with two separate stratagies for his initial dealings with Esau. This point gains full voice through an analysis of two key words from 32:2–3: 'messengers' (מלאכי[ם]) and 'Mahanaim' (מחנים). I will treat each in turn.

The word 'messengers' (מלאכי[ם]) occurs 3 times within the span of only a few verses (32:1–9). First, the reference is to the messengers of God (v. 2), but the text then quickly transitions to human messengers (vv. 4, 7). By means of this echo, a connection between the 2 becomes evident. This point gains even greater support when one realizes that the word 'messenger(s)' occurs only 2 other times in the entire Jacob cycle—28:12 and 31:11—only the former of which is plural, in comparison with 11 occurrences elsewhere in Genesis.[27]

What then is the nature of this connection? Edward Curtis suggests that by repeating the word "messengers" the text shows Jacob mimicking what God has done.[28] Curtis goes on to acknowledge the possibility that Jacob may have viewed the camp at Mahanaim as a sign of God's willingness to help, but then rejects this possibility, citing that Jacob shows no interest in availing himself of any divine assistance.[29] This conclusion seems odd for a number of reasons, among them the fact that Jacob's journey homeward has begun as a direct result of God's command (31:3), to which Jacob demonstrates unwavering obedience.[30] Additionally, God protected Jacob from any threat that Laban may have posed after his flight (31:24, 29). More immediate to the context, the messengers in vv. 2–3 do not display any overt hostility toward Jacob, and Jacob's response at seeing them hardly implies

---

27. These 11 occurrences are found in Gen 16:7, 9, 10, 11; 19:1, 15; 21:17; 22:11, 15; 24:7, 40; 48:16.

28. Edward M. Curtis, "Structure, Style and Context as a Key to Interpreting Jacob's Encounter at Peniel," *JETS* 30 (1987) 132.

29. Ibid., 133.

30. Brett (*Genesis*, 100) insightfully notes that in 31:3 Yhwh commands Jacob to return to both land *and family*. Esau is without doubt a member of that family. Might the divine command in 31:3 already hint that Jacob will succeed in encountering Esau?

any negativity or ambivalence. Looking forward, Jacob utters a prayer to God in vv. 10–13, showing that he is not beyond seeking God's help when needed. Curtis's argument appears to rely on an unfortunate a priori assumption that Jacob is perpetually a self-interested villain with a strained relationship with God. Although Curtis is correct that Jacob takes his cue in sending his own messengers to Esau from God, he is incorrect in claiming that in doing so Jacob displays an arrogant aversion to the offer of divine assistance.

It is better to understand the "messengers" connection in terms of divine guidance and protection in accordance with the promise at Bethel. If the previous discussion on the resonances between the Mahanaim and Bethel scenes has merit, then the appearance of the "messengers of God" gives Jacob the idea to send his own messengers to Esau as a preemptive move affording him the ability to gauge Esau's demeanor and intentions.[31] Mathews couches the connection in terms of "encourage[ment]" for Jacob to make the first contact with Esau.[32] The narrative shrouds precisely how Jacob concocts this plan, yet the literary proximity between God's messengers and Jacob's messengers creates an unspoken link between the two. For Mathews, however, the silence regarding how Jacob comes to this decision does not pose a problem; just as Jacob credits God with giving him the idea regarding the breeding of Laban's herds in 31:10, so also Jacob receives an idea about how to protect himself and his property from Esau in 32:8.[33] Jacob indeed does what God does, not as a matter of haughty presumption in the attempt to handle matters himself. Jacob instead does what God does simply *because* God does it; God gives Jacob the idea to initiate first contact with Esau. God has proven trustworthy and steadfast thus far for Jacob; there is no reason to presume that this changes at Mahanaim. Just as YHWH allayed any fears Jacob may have had at Bethel, after the deception of Esau, by conferring on him the ancestral promise, now at Mahanaim, YHWH addresses Jacob's fears at meeting his deceived brother by giving him a method to ensure his protection. Jacob makes the initial contact, but one must then inquire about the nature of this contact.

At the narrative level, Jacob's employment of "messengers" recalls his previous trickery in a number of ways. The clearest example is found in v. 4, when Jacob sends his messengers ahead not to an unnamed place but to 'the land of Seir, the field of Edom' (ארצה שעיר שדה אדום). Nearly every one of these words is reminiscent of a particular trait endemic to Esau that led to his being deceived. Seir recalls Esau's hairiness (שער) mentioned at birth and by Jacob in the deception of Isaac (25:25; 27:11), a characteristic that Jacob would exploit in his pursuit and successful acquiring of the paternal

31. Houtman, "Jacob at Mahanaim," 42.
32. Mathews, *Genesis 11:27–50:26*, 549.
33. Ibid., 550–51.

blessing. The field also recalls the description of the grown Esau as a 'man of the field' (אִישׁ שָׂדֶה) in 25:29, another facet of Esau's character used at his expense. And 'Edom' quite clearly hearks back to Esau's ruddy appearance at birth as well as the 'red' (אָדֹם) lentil stew for which he sold his birthright to Jacob (25:25, 30). Hamilton regards these parallels as referring to three specific areas of "tension" that exist between the two brothers: birth, birthright, and blessing.[34] But all three were tensions because they were part of the deceptions by which Jacob attained prominence over his brother with the help of Yhwh.

A similar case may be made for "Mahanaim." Grammatically, the form in v. 3, מַחֲנָיִם, is dual, likely referring to 'two camps'. Houtman points out the peculiarity of the dual form, given that Jacob equates the place with only one camp, the 'camp of God' (מַחֲנֵה אֱלֹהִים).[35] Again, however, this brief encounter finds its outlet in a subsequent act of the patriarch given that in v. 8 Jacob divides all the people and animals with him into two 'camps' (מַחֲנוֹת). While not an exact parallel, the semantic affinity plus the fact that the narrative seems to envisage two camps in both vv. 3 and 8 attest to the veracity of reading the dual camps (of God?) as influencing Jacob's decision to separate his own party. Mathews strengthens the connection by appealing to the dual, seeing each of Jacob's two camps as being under the watchful eye of the two messengers of God from v. 2.[36] And Wenham astutely points out the theme of God's protective presence here in that the Hebrew word for camp, מַחֲנֶה, includes the consonants חֵן that spell 'grace, favor', thus hinting at the word used in v. 6.[37] To find 'favor' (חֵן) is Jacob's express desire in sending messengers to Esau (v. 6). No worry is necessary, however, for God's favor will ensure that Jacob is met with favor from Esau.

Laurence Turner adroitly explains the significance of the connections between Mahanaim and the following narrative in terms of a movement from divine to human.[38] One first meets divine "messengers" and only subsequently "human messengers"; likewise, "Mahanaim" denotes a divine encampment that secondarily gives rise to Jacob's separation of all that is with him into two camps. Turner rightly sees that this "easy movement" between heaven and earth and between divine and human typifies the Jacob cycle and has already received graphic representation with the Bethel staircase.[39] That Jacob's activities mirror those of the divine serves to solidify "divine involvement" in readying Jacob for encounter with Esau.[40]

---

34. Hamilton, *Genesis 18–50*, 320.
35. Houtman, "Jacob at Mahanaim," 41.
36. Mathews, *Gen 11:27–50:26*, 550.
37. Wenham, *Gen 16–50*, 290.
38. Turner, *Genesis*, 139.
39. Ibid.
40. Ibid., 139–40.

As one might expect, however, trickery continues to loom. Taschner writes that Jacob undertakes two specific, calculated measures in response to the encroaching Esau: dividing his 'camp' (מחנה) and sending livestock ahead as a 'gift' (מנחה).[41] Scholars are largely in agreement that this gift is an attempt to "buy off" Esau and thus depicts Jacob acting as trickster.[42] A clever wordplay between 'camp' and 'gift' reinforces this idea of trickery. Taschner notices that the two letters interchanged in each word are נ and ח, the same two letters that form the word 'favor' (חן), which Jacob desires from Esau.[43] For Taschner, this paronomasia parallels an earlier play in which the two final letters are switched, in Gen 25 and 27, between 'birthright' (בכר) and 'blessing' (ברך).[44] Since Gen 25 and 27 are rife with deceptions, this new wordplay may indicate the presence of deception tied to Mahanaim and what Jacob gleans from his encounter here.

Given the phonetic and consonantal similarity between מחנה and מנחה, it is possible that the narrative wishes to communicate that the camp-of-God theophany gives Jacob the idea to separate himself into two camps and to send a gift in hopes of appeasing Esau. Both ideas come from God. In the treatment of Gen 33, it will become apparent how a "gift" evokes deception; it seems clear from the text, however, that in 32:14–22 Jacob sends a series of gifts not as an honest expression of sorrow or guilt at the shattered relationship with his brother but simply to placate Esau. Two deceptions are evident here.

First, Jacob withholds from Esau his true motivation behind the multiple gifts. One may discern this point by a comparison between Jacob's preliminary and subsequent communications with Esau in Gen 32. Upon sending the original batch of messengers to Esau so as to learn his intentions in v. 6, Jacob instructs them to tell Esau his purpose is to find "favor (חן) in [Esau's] eyes," a noble and transparent enough goal. The messengers return with news that a band of 400 men accompany Esau, which Jacob—despite the fact that Esau allows the messengers to return unharmed—understandably interprets as a formidable threat.[45] Chris Heard advances the possibility that the 400 men represent nothing more than Esau's extended seminomadic family group coming to welcome Jacob home.[46] While the

---

41. Taschner, *Verheissung und Erfüllung*, 145.

42. See Hermann Gunkel, *Genesis* (trans. Mark E. Biddle; Macon, GA: Mercer University Press, 1997) 355; S. R. Driver, *The Book of Genesis* (Westminster Commentaries; London: Methuen, 1915) 299.

43. Taschner, *Verheissung und Erfüllung*, 146.

44. Ibid.

45. The vastness of Esau's entourage coupled with his refusal of Jacob's gift in v. 10—because he has enough—lends credence to my interpretation presented in chap. 2 that Isaac's blessing of Esau is not a curse or anti-blessing. See chap. 2, p. 80.

46. R. Christopher Heard, *Dynamics of Diselection: Ambiguity in Genesis 12–36 and Ethnic Boundaries in Post-exilic Judah* (Semeia Studies; Atlanta: Society of Biblical Literature, 2001) 129–30.

reader never gains a clear insight into Esau's temperament, given that the promised word from Rebekah never comes (cf. 27:45), Jacob's pessimistic view of the situation is defensible. The narrative quickly picks up and resumes the tension five chapters later; like Jacob, the reader probably expects the same homicidal Esau who was last seen in 27:41.

As a result, Jacob sends several caravans as a gift, this time telling his servants only to say that the animals are a gift and that Jacob "is behind us" (32:19, 21). Esau receives no rationale for the gifts. Buttressing the deception even further, the latter half of v. 21 has Jacob speaking to himself, saying, "Let me appease him [lit., 'cover his face'] with a gift going before me, and afterwards I will see his face; perhaps he will accept me [lit., 'lift my face']."[47] Jacob's express motive is not to gain Esau's favor by an honest gesture but to bribe him into meeting Jacob with favor so as not to seek retribution. Moreover, whereas previously Jacob plainly limned the reason for the messenger's visit to Esau (32:6), here he deceptively withholds this information from Esau. The gift shows Jacob to be concerned solely with Jacob; he merely wants to mollify Esau so as to save his own skin. The gift also, however, shows God's concern for Jacob, in that the idea for the strategy comes from the divine.

A second deception arising out of the insight that Jacob gains from the Mahanaim encounter has gone unnoticed by scholars. The scene has already been set: Jacob's telling his servants how they should address Esau. Each is to indicate that the herds are a gift from Jacob *and* that "he [Jacob] is behind us" (vv. 19, 21). At first glance, this statement comes across as quite innocuous, but couched within the surrounding narrative, it becomes an example of deception. Verse 20 shows Jacob coaching a second, third, and countless other successive groups with the same words. Therefore, assuming all goes according to plan, the first dispatch responds to Esau as commanded and then summarily says Jacob is behind them. Presumably Esau will then expect Jacob to arrive next, but instead, he will be met by another installment from Jacob's camp, who will summarily say Jacob is behind them, only to be followed by another group from Jacob's camp, and another. One may only conjecture regarding the net outcome, but perhaps Esau will become increasingly more frustrated or even confused with each successive arrival. This plan also runs the risk of backfiring, for, in sending such a large retinue to his brother, Jacob in effect shows Esau that the

---

47. That this speech is part of Jacob's inner monologue gains support in several ways. First, and perhaps most telling, the speech lacks Jacob's calling Esau "my lord" and his self-deprecating posture as "your servant," instead employing simple pronouns through pronominal suffixes. Second, the speech is introduced by another "and he said," causing a separation. Third, the text is in first person, but elsewhere when Jacob addresses Esau it is in second person (compare with "you will say" in vv. 19, 21). Fourth, the cohortative style with which the line begins ("let me cover his face") is jarring and discontinuous when compared with Jacob's instructions to his servants about how to address Esau.

birthright and blessing have come to fruition.[48] Lending further support to this possibility, v. 22 resolutely concludes that "the gift crossed over before him [Jacob], and he stayed that night in camp." It is not as though Jacob stations himself somewhere between his various dispatches, as he has his servants say to Esau; rather, he spends the night in the safety of camp (מחנה). Here again, one sees the wordplay between "gift" and "camp." The 'gift' (מנחה) passes on ahead of Jacob and into "enemy" territory, while he stays within the confines and security of 'camp' (מחנה).[49]

The ensuing narrative creates a geographical puzzle for readers. Verse 23 shows Jacob, on the same night that he sends the gifts ahead to Esau, crossing the Jabbok with his wives, their maidservants, and his 11 children (*sans* Dinah!). He possibly crosses another stream (v. 24) and then sends all his possessions across ahead of him. The text here is nearly incomprehensible, as Skinner has rightly noted.[50] Are the wives and children part of the possessions that he sends/takes to cross over after the first crossing? Does Jacob join them, only to return to the banks of the Jabbok in solitude? Or does Jacob remain behind on the banks? The text's geography is problematic, yet two items stand out. First, as Serge Frolov maintains, Jacob has placed his entire family and possessions—the results of the promise—as a buffer between himself and Esau.[51] Frolov describes Jacob's activities:

> He begins with endangering his messengers (Esau could kill them), continues with making his camp more vulnerable in order to get a 50 per cent chance of escape, then relinquishes part of his cattle, and finally abandons his wives and children—to say nothing of the remaining servants and cattle—to the mercy of Esau (whom he accused a little earlier of being capable of murdering 'the mother with the children').[52]

To be sure, Jacob does not make a very good impression here. Not only does he deceive Esau by separating himself at a great distance from his brother, he also endangers all that he has received as a result of the promise because of his own fear.[53]

---

48. Jeffrey M. Cohen, "The Jacob-Esau Reunion," *JBQ* 21 (1993) 160.

49. The text is unclear regarding whether Jacob stays in his own camp, or perhaps more convincingly, at the camp of the messengers of God. Since that first encounter in 32:2, Jacob has seemingly not moved.

50. John Skinner, *A Critical and Exegetical Commentary on Genesis* (ICC 1; Edinburgh: T. & T. Clark, 1930) 408.

51. Serge Frolov, "The Other Side of the Jabbok: Genesis 32 as a Fiasco of Patriarchy," *JSOT* 91 (2000) 42, 56.

52. Ibid., 56.

53. Frolov (ibid., 56 n. 39) further notes Jacob's failure to live up to the promise made to Laban in 31:50 to protect Leah and Rachel from any and all danger. I wonder, however, whether this arrangement may have been a bit perplexing to Jacob as well. Certainly the "human shield" that Frolov sees Jacob placing between himself and Esau serves as a more-than-adequate buffer but, if Esau were to attack, Jacob's options are quite limited. He cannot retreat to Haran lest he incur Laban's anger and vengeance at breaking the boundary

But a second point requires attention. In this arrangement, Jacob is now alone (v. 25). Having sent 'messengers' (מלאכים) ahead and divided his family and possessions into two camps, Jacob can now be described as being his own 'camp' (מחנה). He has thus far done what he understands God to have instructed him to do based upon the encounter at Mahanaim. Now alone, he turns to God.

Jacob's Prayer

Amid all this posturing and plotting, Jacob offers a prayer in vv. 10–13 that warrants brief mention because it aids in couching the adjacent narratives in terms of God's fealty to the ancestral promise. Jacob appeals to the history of the promise between himself and God. Jacob opens the prayer with an address to the "God of my father Abraham, God of my father Isaac, YHWH" (v. 10), which clearly evokes YHWH's self-revelation to Jacob in 28:13 at Bethel. Wenham notes that extended epithets such as these often do not appear in the speech of humans about or addressing God; the rhetorical effect is that Jacob appeals to God based not only on his own merits but also on the long history between God and Jacob's father and grandfather.[54]

At various points in the prayer, Jacob openly quotes or paraphrases the ancestral promise, in essence aiming to convince YHWH that it will prove worthwhile for him to intervene. He begins with reference to the promise of land, evident in the phrase "return to your land," which likely refers back to 31:3 and the divine command that Jacob leave Laban. Jacob therefore reminds YHWH that he is simply following a divine order by returning home. In v. 13, Jacob repeats the promise of protection (Jacob reports YHWH as having said, "I will surely do good for you," which Hamilton points out YHWH has never said; it is likely, however, with Wenham, that here Jacob is simply paraphrasing the additional promise of presence and protection in 28:15)[55] and progeny. Earlier in the prayer, Jacob makes plain the threat to the promise of progeny by requesting God's help, "lest he [Esau] come and kill me, mothers, and children" (32:12). Jacob in effect calls on YHWH to intercede not merely for his own sake but for the sake of the promise, for

---

that they established (or perhaps even another seven years of labor), nor would moving forward toward an incoming Esau and his army make much sense. A lateral movement might prove efficacious, but one assumes that, were Esau's army to attack, Jacob would be their main objective (not the numerous flocks, children, or wives). Indeed, all the aforementioned family and property are being put at grave risk, but one should not then assume that Jacob has exempted himself from all risk either.

54. Wenham, *Genesis 16–50*, 291. W. Lee Humphreys (*The Character of God in the Book of Genesis: A Narrative Appraisal* [Louisville: Westminster John Knox, 2001] 188) argues that Jacob omits from his prayer the fact that Esau is also the son of Isaac and grandson of Abraham, meaning that Esau may possess an equally probable right to these promises. Where Humphreys errs, in my estimation, is his apparent forgetfulness that, while Esau may share with Jacob these genetic relationships to Abraham and Isaac, YHWH has already decided the matter, selecting Jacob and "dis-electing" Esau.

55. Hamilton, *Genesis 18–50*, 323; Wenham, *Genesis 16–50*, 291.

of what value is the promise and all that Y<small>HWH</small> has done up to this point if it is now allowed to be destroyed, especially by the brother whom Y<small>HWH</small> did not choose? The mention of offspring as numerous "as the sands of the sea" (v. 13) recalls the only other use of the same phrase, in 22:17, when Y<small>HWH</small> likewise intervenes to save Isaac's life.[56]

Some interpreters regard Jacob's prayer as little more than a rhetorical ploy to persuade God to participate. Spina disparagingly calls it "a quintessential 'foxhole' prayer."[57] Humphreys goes further, holding that Jacob crafts his prayer so carefully that God is left with little room to maneuver. He writes: "Jacob co-opts God's assurance and promise into his own terms for the specific future he seeks."[58] It remains unclear specifically how Humphreys believes that Jacob can or will force God's hand, but this sort of cynical reading of the prayer is problematic. Brueggemann claims that amid all the rhetorical shaping that Jacob does in the prayer, fundamentally, "he is only asking that what is rightly his from God should now be given."[59] Indeed, the prayer does speak with "a candor that presumes upon God," but this presumption still takes the form of a request.[60] Additionally, in matters of form Jacob's prayer differs very little from prayers beseeching God's help found in the Psalter that set out to persuade God with an equal boldness and vigor.[61] One may adduce other biblical examples of daring speech directed (successfully) at God: Abraham's bartering with God on behalf of Sodom and Gomorrah (Gen 18:22–33) or Moses' insistence that God not destroy the Israelites after the Golden Calf incident (Exod 32:1–14). The latter example offers an apt parallel to Jacob's prayer, in that Moses appealed to God's fidelity to the promise to "Abraham, Isaac, and Jacob, your servants" (32:13) as the impetus for the way that Y<small>HWH</small> should act in that situation.

The prayer does operate at another, deeper level in the narrative, a level that ties Jacob's request for divine assistance to a history of his deceptions guided by God. Four specific occurrences draw the reader's attention. First, the word usually translated 'staff' (מַקֵּל) in v. 11 has important resonances. Frolov notes that this word appears in the entire Hebrew Bible only 18 times, one-third of which are located in Gen 30:37–43, the perplexing story of Jacob's attempt to manipulate the breeding of Laban's flocks with

56. Arnold, *Genesis*, 282. See also Wenham, *Genesis 16–50*, 291.

57. Frank Anthony Spina, "The 'Face of God': Esau in Canonical Context," in *The Quest for Context and Meaning: Studies in Biblical Intertextuality in Honor of James A. Sanders* (ed. Craig A. Evans and Shemaryahu Talmon; Leiden: Brill, 1997) 14.

58. Humphreys, *The Character of God in the Book of Genesis*, 188.

59. Walter Brueggemann, "A Case Study in Daring Prayer: Genesis 32:9–12," *Living Pulpit* 2 (1993) 12.

60. Ibid.

61. Josef Schreiner, "Das Gebet Jakobs (Gen 32,10–13)," in *Die Väter Israels: Beiträge zur Theologie der Patriarchenüberlieferungen im Alten Testament* (ed. A. R. Müller and M. Görg; Stuttgart: Katholisches Bibelwerk, 1989) 296.

rods (מקל).[62] According to Frolov, this semantic overlap highlights the "un-finished" nature of Jacob's return.[63] But another possibility exists: the word is reminiscent of the successful deception of Laban, perpetrated jointly by Jacob and Yhwh.[64] Placed in the context of Jacob's prayer, the line "with my staff (במקלי), I crossed this Jordan" may be heard by Yhwh on two different levels: (1) the once destitute Jacob has grown exceedingly wealthy through Yhwh's fidelity to the promise, and (2) the method by which Yhwh has demonstrated this fidelity in the past was by using deception.

A second example builds on this same previous deception. The word meaning 'deliver' (נצל) in Gen 32:11 is the same root that appears in 31:9, 16 with the meaning "snatched/stripped away" in reference to God's giving to Jacob at Laban's expense by ensuring the success of Jacob's plan with the rods. Thus, in his prayer, Jacob makes certain that his request resonates with the divine ear through a meaningful wordplay. Brueggemann sums up the essential message: "As God has 'snatched' property for Jacob from Laban, so Jacob prays to be 'snatched' from the power of Esau."[65]

Two final examples are perhaps even more germane to the present discussion in that they recall Jacob's original deceptions in Gen 25:27–34 and 27:1–45, of which Esau was the victim. At the beginning of 32:11, Jacob makes a statement that most translations construe with regard to his 'un-worthiness' before God. In the Hebrew, however, the resonances are much richer. The word usually translated 'unworthy' comes from the root קטן, which I argued in chap. 2 means 'little, younger'. Genesis 27:15 and 42 employ this same root to identify Jacob as the younger son of Rebekah. One should thus not take Jacob's statement that he is קטן as an admission that he is undeserving but, rather, as a reference to Jacob's age in relation to Esau. This one word conjures up Yhwh's original election of Jacob prior to birth (25:23), along with the deceptions that ensued as a result, and solicits Yhwh's help in line with that election. Just as Yhwh had chosen and watched over Jacob earlier, despite his being קטן, so now Jacob asks that Yhwh again take account of him as קטן and protect him from his older brother, from Esau.

Last, Jacob's double mention of the word 'hand' (יד) in v. 12—asking for deliverance "from the hand of my brother, from the hand of Esau"—recalls the frequency with which this word occurs as part of Jacob's deceptions of his brother. Turner provides an excellent list:

---

62. Frolov, "The Other Side of the Jabbok," 48.
63. Ibid., 50.
64. See the discussion in chap. 3 above, pp. 108–123. To be fair, Frolov does relegate this possibility to a footnote, though he describes Jacob as the master manipulator here and not God. The מקל is ultimately for Frolov a sign of Jacob's "social status." See ibid., 50 n. 22.
65. Brueggemann, *Genesis*, 265.

This request is somewhat ironic, since the 'hand' motif has been used to good effect previously when Jacob had been acting against Esau. Jacob's hand gripped Esau's heel (25.26), his hands were covered with goats' skins (27.16), the savoury food and bread were given into his hand (27.17), and Isaac believed Jacob to have the hands of Esau (27.22–23).[66]

In the past, Jacob's "hand" had deceptively triumphed over Esau with God's help; now Jacob asks that God make certain that Esau's hand does not triumph over him.

This analysis of Jacob's prayer, imploring God for assistance through appeal to a joint history of promise and deception, shows that the prayer functions on two levels of meaning. On one level, Jacob seeks to persuade God to deliver him from Esau for the sake of the ancestral promise, lest it be decimated in one fierce attack by Esau and his band. On a more subtle, deeper level, Jacob uses words connected with his past tricks, of which YHWH has been a part, to provide concrete examples of occasions on which YHWH deceives for Jacob's betterment. When read in tandem, Jacob's prayer creates for the reader a tension and an expectation: will God answer Jacob's prayer, and if so, how? At this stage, however, all the reader can do is wait alongside Jacob in the hope that God will in some way hear his prayer and deliver him from the presumed wrath of Esau. As the text continues, the initial tension over whether God intervenes is quickly replaced by a new tension centered on *how* God sets out to deliver Jacob. This divine assistance comes in a much more foreboding form than Jacob or the reader could anticipate: an encounter with the divine that quickly takes on a terrifyingly violent tenor. What kind of deliverance is this that includes God's assault on the bearer of the promise?

Trickster Wrestling (Genesis 32:23–33)

Genesis 32:23–33 is one of the most enigmatic scenes in the entire Bible. Jacob remains alone on the banks of the Jabbok, having sent all his family and possessions on ahead of himself. Suddenly an abstruse, unnamed entity identified only as a "man" attacks him, and the two struggle until daybreak, at which time his assailant requests that Jacob let him go. In the midst of the contest, Jacob's hip is wounded by a simple touch, yet he hangs on long enough to receive both a new name and another blessing from the being. The text retains a startling ambiguity about the identity of this figure, but Jacob quite clearly understands him to be God. After the encounter, Jacob limps onward toward his brother, Esau, with both a new name and another blessing.

Many commentators have understood Gen 32:23–33 as a story that is unbefitting to its wider context. Ostensibly, it appears to have little to do with the looming Jacob/Esau encounter with which the surrounding narra-

---

66. Turner, *Genesis*, 141.

tives express concern. The preponderance of etiologies—for Israel, Peniel, and the dietary restriction pertaining to the hip sinew—in these few verses has led some scholars to similar conclusions. For example, John L. McKenzie writes that a connection with its surrounding context "is not skillfully made in the final form of the text."[67] Perhaps more noteworthy, Martin Noth describes the scene as occupying an "infelicitous place in the midst of the story of Jacob's encounter with Esau."[68] Noth later expands on the implications of this statement:

> The Peniel episode (Gen. 32:23–33 [J]), which is bound very firmly to a specific place, was inserted still later in a rather loose fashion and intrinsically has nothing at all to do with the narrative theme 'Jacob and Esau.' Rather, it is a distinctly separate narrative which originally was concerned with cultic matters and all sorts of etiological secondary interests.[69]

Subsequently, von Rad has rightly said that the text "interrupts" the overall narrative flow of the Jacob/Esau reunion, yet this interruption is a vital aspect for construing and understanding the whole.[70] In the analysis that follows, I wish to challenge Noth's notion that 32:23–33 have no relation to the larger drama of the Jacob/Esau reunion and to expand on and demonstrate von Rad's contention that the story is a prerequisite for a proper sense of Gen 32–33. Genesis 32:23–33 is a carefully crafted story that is integral to the encounter with Esau.

In its present literary context, the story functions much akin to the Mahanaim scene treated above, highlighting God's involvement in the imminent encounter with Esau. Here however God adopts a more direct, threatening, even menacing stance in relation to Jacob. God, who all along has served as Jacob's benefactor, ensuring his success even in and through deception, now seemingly becomes Jacob's opposition.[71] As I discussed in the introduction to this chapter, much has been made of this scene by scholars who see it as a turning point in the narrative, one in which God becomes Jacob's adversary in order to purify Jacob's less-than-stellar character; I have already demonstrated that this line of interpretation is wanting. Despite this equivocation, the text may still stand as a turning point. This encounter with the divine is the one toward which all previous encounters build. At Bethel, Jacob sees God on top of a staircase; and during Jacob's

---

67. John L. McKenzie, "Jacob at Peniel: Gn 32, 24–32," *CBQ* 25 (1963) 71.

68. Martin Noth, *A History of Pentateuchal Traditions* (trans. B. W. Anderson; Englewood Cliffs, NJ: Prentice-Hall, 1972) 7.

69. Ibid., 95.

70. Von Rad, *Genesis*, 320.

71. Humphreys (*The Character of God in the Book of Genesis*, 193–94) deems God's attack on Jacob as a sort of punishment. He maintains that throughout the Jacob cycle God has been a character that Jacob has constructed to suit his own needs. Now, at Peniel, the narrative seeks to put Jacob in his place. Humphreys writes: "It is time for God to reconstruct Jacob."

time with Laban, God appears to Jacob in a dream. At Mahanaim, it is God's messengers whom Jacob meets. Now, for the first time in the text, Jacob literally encounters the deity "face to face," with whom he now engages in hand-to-hand combat. The turn in the narrative has two foci: first, Jacob limps from Peniel with the confidence that Yʜwʜ fights on his behalf and that he will prevail over Esau, the most potent threat to the promise. Second, with this encounter, the final element of the ancestral promise moves toward incipient fulfillment: Jacob returns to the land.

Another question, seldom asked, appears equally if not more valid: what if God is here acting not *against* Jacob but rather *on his behalf*? What emerges if one reads God's attack on Jacob in line with the contours of the ancestral promise, which Jacob already possesses (cf. 28:13–15), and not as a method through which Jacob becomes a fitting candidate for the accolade of receiving the ancestral promise? In the following analysis, I will seek to make this point explicit.

Here the goal is not to delineate a full interpretation of the multifarious nuances and aspects of Gen 32:23–33, as though this sort of task were possible in so small a space; one may consult critical commentaries for that purpose. Rather, here the intention is to underscore the theological dimensions of this recondite encounter from another perspective—namely, its deployment of trickery in the interest of the ancestral promise and how doing this ultimately equips Jacob with the necessary "arsenal" of tactics with which to face Esau. I will achieve this goal through attention to three specific topics: the encounter as the answer to Jacob's prayer; the scene's ambiguity about Jacob's opponent and about who does what to whom; the particulars of the scene as tied to deception.

An Unexpected "Deliverance"

Is God's assault on Jacob in dissonance with the divine fealty to the ancestral promise that I have been emphasizing? Must there be discontinuity? Some think so. Marböck claims that in vv. 23–33 Jacob has a completely different experience with God than he had at Bethel.[72] McKenzie similarly notes the problematic nature of this encounter in relation to the promise, in that God seemingly obstructs its fulfillment by blocking Jacob's entrance into the promised land.[73] Otto Kaiser argues that the prayer and ensuing divine onslaught demonstrate that even prayer cannot always protect one from God.[74] The text itself, however, provides compelling reasons for equating the wrestling match with the ancestral promise, seeing

---

72. Marböck, "Heilige Orte im Jakobszyklus," 222.

73. McKenzie, "Jacob at Peniel," 76.

74. Otto Kaiser, "*Deus absconditus* and *Deus revelatus*: Three Difficult Narratives in the Pentateuch," in *Shall Not the Judge of All the Earth Do What Is Right? Studies on the Nature of God in Tribute to James L. Crenshaw* (ed. David Penchansky and Paul L. Redditt; Winona Lake, IN: Eisenbrauns, 2000) 81.

Jacob's struggle with God as a startling mode of deliverance in line with the promise. This point is borne out structurally by Fishbane, whose meticulous chiastic outline of the Jacob cycle shows that the Bethel theophany (28:10–22) balances the entirety of Gen 32.[75] John G. Gammie presents a similar schematic.[76] In a related vein, Brueggemann details a concentric, inclusive structure in which Bethel corresponds specifically to the Peniel encounter in 32:23–33.[77] It stands to reason, then, that both episodes contain a word of promise and function *for* Jacob, not to his detriment.

One may wonder what this word of promise is in vv. 23–33. Karl Elliger offers a unique perspective, rightly seeing v. 31b as a reference to Jacob's prayer, yet proffering that God's answer is that he will 'smash' (*zerschmettern*) Jacob.[78] This manner of response would be out of character in the God-Jacob relationship, and if smashing Jacob is God's objective, it appears it is one he fails to accomplish. Additionally, Elliger's view does not account for how divine "smashing" becomes divine blessing (v. 30). It is more convincing, in light of the structural analyses of Fishbane and Brueggemann cited above, to regard this encounter as God answering Jacob's prayer.

If this encounter is meant to function as a type of rescue for Jacob, one may ask rescue from what? The traditional interpretation outlined at the outset of this chapter presents one possibility: that Jacob is rescued, in essence, from himself and from his old ways. Both Fishbane and Brueggemann lean in this direction. For Fishbane, the parallel lies in Jacob's receiving a blessing or sign of favor in each story.[79] For Brueggemann, Jacob obtains "a new identity through an assault from God."[80] Still others advance that Jacob confronts himself by answering with his name in v. 28, a tacit admission of guilt; *Jacob* is 'Deceiver/Supplanter'.[81] That the name *Jacob* continues well after Jacob's receiving a new name poses a problem for this interpretation. Another way of viewing the text, however, appears

---

75. Michael Fishbane, "Composition and Structure in the Jacob Cycle (Gen. 25:19–35:22)," *JJS* 26 (1975) 20, 28–30.

76. John G. Gammie, "Theological Interpretation By Way of Literary and Tradition Analysis: Genesis 25–36," in *Encounter with the Text: Form and History in the Hebrew Bible* (ed. Martin J. Buss; Philadelphia: Fortress, 1979) 121–22.

77. Brueggemann, *Genesis*, 211–12. See also his graphic presentation of this schema on p. 213.

78. Karl Elliger, "Der Jakobskampf am Jabbok: Gen 32, 33ff. als hermeneutisches Problem," *ZTK* 48 (1951) 22.

79. Fishbane, "Composition and Structure," 34, 36.

80. Brueggemann, *Genesis*, 268. Brueggemann, however, is rightly more cautious than others in making too much of Jacob's supposed new identity, asking after the reconciliation scene in Gen 33 the following question: "Has the whole notion of a transformed Jacob been a ploy without substance? Or is it serious? Probably, we are not meant to know. We do not know whether Jacob is genuinely changed or if this is more of his posturing" (p. 272). The fact remains, however, that Brueggemann does ascribe some sort of transformative power to vv. 23–33 regarding Jacob's life.

81. Holmgren, "Holding Your Own against God," 9; Hamilton, *Genesis 18–50*, 333.

more convincing. Jacob's dangerous encounter with the divine rescues him not from himself but from the danger that Esau allegedly poses.

Perhaps the most striking facet of the text demonstrating this very point is the way in which it becomes an answer to Jacob's prayer in 32:10–13. In explaining this prayer above, I have argued that Jacob implores God to act in accord with the ancestral promise. One key word in the prayer is most germane for my purposes here: 'deliver' (נצל). In v. 12, Jacob employs the imperative form הצילני ('deliver me'), very clearly seeking relief from Esau. At the conclusion of the nocturnal struggle in v. 31, Jacob acknowledges two things about his encounter: that it was with God and that, through it, his life has been 'delivered' (תנצל). Both verses use the root נצל.[82] When read together, the text indicates that the struggle with the divine is in some way the answer to Jacob's earlier prayer for deliverance from Esau.

But how is this so? Why portray Jacob's deliverance in such violent fashion? On this question, the text appears resolutely silent, yet this reticence seems to be the entire point of the narrative, for it is through this opacity that Jacob gains the confidence at last to face Esau. Jacob's deliverance indeed comes through combat, yet with whom? In answering this question, one may begin to make sense of the alacrity with which Jacob suddenly forges onward in Gen 33. The reason for this burst of confidence is that his opponent, I will show, is at one and the same time the trickster God *and* Esau.

Wrestling God, Wrestling Esau

Genesis 32:23–33 conceals much more than it reveals. The reader's eyes see as dimly in the night as do Jacob's, unable to ascertain "who is who," let alone the identity of Jacob's accoster. This ambiguity, however, conforms to the overall artistic quality of the narrative, which is replete with meaning. By allowing the attacker's identity to unfold as the story progresses, the text manifests a duality or tension that informs the larger complex of Jacob's impending encounter with Esau. Most interpreters regard Jacob's statement in 32:31 that he has seen "the face of God" and its echo in 33:10, where he acknowledges that seeing Esau's face is like seeing "the face of God," as indicating that in encountering Esau Jacob encounters God.[83] I suggest that the obverse is equally, if not more accurate: that in encountering God in Gen 32, Jacob meets Esau.

In line with this reversal of the usual trajectory, I will here argue that Gen 32:23–33 employs ambiguity as a vector of interpretation. The scene's

---

82. Fokkelman, *Narrative Art in Genesis*, 220. See also Allen P. Ross, "Jacob at the Jabbok, Israel at Peniel," *BSac* 142 (1985) 349; Mark S. Smith, "Remembering God: Collective Memory in Israelite Religion," *CBQ* 64 (2002) 643; Hamilton, *Genesis 18–50*, 337.

83. See Jerome Kodell, "Jacob Wrestles with Esau (Gen 32:23–32)," *BTB* 10 (1980) 69; J. Glen Taylor, "Decoding Jacob at the Jabbok and Genesis 32: From Crude Solar Mythology to Profound Hebrew Theology," *La Société Canadienne des Études Bibliques* 3 (2008) 21; Hamilton, *Genesis 18–50*, 345–46.

ambiguity creates dual yet interwoven planes of battle on which Jacob's struggle with—and victory over—God becomes concomitantly a struggle with—and victory over—Esau.[84] This victory creates the circumstances whereby Jacob will both face his brother with the surety of success and continue to avail himself of trickery in the reconciliation with Esau.

The narrative most potently captures this ambiguity through a blurring of the boundary between divine and human pertaining to Jacob's opponent.[85] At the outset in 32:25, it is quite simply a 'man' (אִישׁ) who jumps Jacob. Readers have been conditioned to expect (and perhaps rightly so) the man to be Esau; at this point, he is the only "man" on Jacob's radar.[86] Yet toward the end of the battle in v. 31, as morning begins to break, Jacob understands the entity to be 'God' (אֱלֹהִים). Which is he, man or God?

Compounding the enigma is the way the narrative portrays the opponent throughout. Although he is identified as a mere "man" at first, what man is able to dislodge Jacob's hip with a simple touch (נגע, v. 26)? From another vantage point, why would God need to resort to the described tactics to gain victory over a mortal? Or, why does this maneuver ostensibly fail to incapacitate Jacob, who ardently persists and is successful in holding onto him (v. 27)? One may discern other confounding examples, among them the ability to bless—which the reader of the Jacob cycle knows belongs to both humans (27:28–29) and God (28:13–15; 30:27)—and the ability to rename, which lies solely with God.

Another facet of the text pointing to a divine identity for Jacob's attacker is the being's urgent request to leave at the sight of daylight. Gunkel is the first to advance the idea that this demand shows that in the earliest version of the story Jacob was wrestling with a nocturnal River-god.[87] Johannes Bauer isolates five criteria held in common between Gen 32:23–33 and other literature depicting similar scenes, leading him to conclude that Jacob's struggle is with a river demon (*Flußdämon*).[88] Most recently,

---

84. In Gen 32:29, Jacob's opponent announces that Jacob has 'prevailed' (תוכל). Whether Jacob has indeed prevailed, persevered, or only barely survived (though Jacob clearly holds his own in combat), he is not destroyed by an encounter with God. Additionally, that Jacob survives the blow to his hip, and that his prowess results in the opponent's ultimately asking for release, unable to escape Jacob's grasp, points to Jacob as victor. He prevails over his opponent, and wrests for himself a new blessing.

85. Contra McKenzie ("Jacob at Peniel," 72), who argues that the scene is not a theophany, evidenced by the sheer absence of the divine name and any divine attributes ascribed to Jacob's opponent.

86. Of course, the "man" could just as well be a furious Laban, opting to disregard the covenantal agreement made with Jacob; however, the fact that Laban has already restrained himself from harming Jacob—in response to divine fiat—makes this possibility less persuasive. Laban does not again figure into the narrative, and Esau has returned as the primary antagonist.

87. Gunkel, *Genesis*, 349, 352.

88. Johannes B. Bauer, "Jakobs Kampf mit dem Dämon (Gen 32,23–33)," in *Die Väter Israels: Beiträge zur Theologie der Patriarchenüberlieferungen im Alten Testament* (ed. A. R.

J. Glen Taylor argues that the appropriate background for comprehending the scene is Egyptian solar imagery, and Jacob's opponent is the emerging sun.[89] While Gunkel, Bauer, and Taylor may be correct regarding the origins and background of the story, the fact remains that in the final form of the text it is not a river demon or the sun but, rather, man and/or God who assaults Jacob.[90] The text makes this point explicit at both its beginning and its ending. Furthermore, arguments over what type of divinity the being is miss the point; this question resides solely with the reader, not Jacob. Jacob's view and thus the final view of the text is unequivocal: he has wrestled with God and been delivered. The more poignant question, which is rarely asked, is how to negotiate the divine and human attributes of Jacob's opponent so that neither obliterates the other.

Stephen Geller offers a helpful treatment. He suggests that the text operates around two binary oppositions: victory-defeat and human-divine.[91] Concerning the latter, the text progresses in a way that is commensurate with its narrative purpose. Geller divides the story into three sections: 32:25–26, where Jacob's opponent is most clearly human; vv. 27–30, where the explanation attached to the name *Israel* meaning 'you have wrestled with God and with men' allows for both options; and vv. 31–33, where Jacob's struggle is with God.[92] The trajectory man → God/man → God functions for Geller as a part of a biblical type scene in which a human is unable to identify a divine figure until the figure does something wondrous; the revealing act Geller isolates here is the renaming of Jacob.[93] Other instances of this type scene appear in Gen 18–19, Judg 6, and especially Judg 13.[94] Geller uses this type scene as a tool to exegete the narrative's unraveling of the identity of Jacob's opponent; here I wish to emphasize instead, as Alter notes, what innovation the narrative affords vv. 23–33 in constructing this type scene.

I contend that what marks the portrayal of the type scene in Gen 32 as unique is the *literary* hybridity of the unknown entity. In each of the three

---

Müller and M. Görg; Stuttgart: Katholisches Bibelwerk, 1989) 18–19. The five criteria are (i) it is evening; (ii) the attack takes place during a time of trepidation; (iii) daylight results in a loss of power for the entity; (iv) a sudden 'magical' act occurs; (v) there is a lasting effect for one of the participants.

89. Taylor, "Decoding Jacob at the Jabbok," 5–6.

90. R. W. L. Moberly (*Genesis 12–50* [OTG; Sheffield: JSOT Press, 1992] 31) suggests a more inclusive approach, citing the fact that the narrative is evocative of this litany of possible interpretations (God, Esau, night spirit, river spirit, Jacob himself). All, he argues, are true in their mysterious communicative power.

91. Stephen A. Geller, "The Struggle at the Jabbok: The Uses of Enigma in a Biblical Narrative," *JANES* 14 (1982) 45.

92. Ibid. On this point, see also Turner, *Genesis*, 143.

93. Geller, "The Struggle at the Jabbok," 45–46.

94. Ibid., 45. The Judg 13 text bears striking similarities to the Genesis text. In Judg 13:15–18, Manoah asks the name of the "messenger of Yhwh," who in turn replies, "Why do you ask my name? It is wonderful/incomprehensible."

occurrences of this type scene just cited, there is no equivocation in the text *for the reader* that the unknown entity represents a divine messenger.[95] Only the characters encountering them are uncertain of their identity. Judges 13 provides the most compelling parallel. In Judg 13, despite the figure's being called a "man" at several points (vv. 10, 11 [2x]) or a "man of God" (vv. 6, 8) at others, the text first introduces him as undeniably a "messenger of Yhwh" (v. 3).[96] Buttressing this point from a narrative perspective, on every occasion when the divine being talks to either Manoah or his wife, the speech is prefixed with the introductory phrase 'the messenger of Yhwh said (ויאמר מלאך יהוה, vv. 3, 13, 16, 19).[97] Conversely, in Gen 32:23–33, as I will demonstrate, the text is ambiguous about who speaks and acts. The only hints provided regarding the opponent's identity come from the narrator in v. 25 ("a man") and Jacob in v. 31 ("God").[98] The reader is as ignorant as Jacob is at the beginning of the confrontation.

Within the Genesis text, then, the reader gets the sense that the figure could be either a man or God. However, the final form of the text does not allow for an either/or choice, for in the process of selecting one identity the reader loses vital aspects of the other. He appears at the narrative level to be both man and God, manifesting in some places distinct traits endemic to one and then vacillating to traits endemic to the other. This dual nature is not meant to suggest a new identity for Jacob's attacker as some semi-divine, God-man creature, nor should it be taken as an argument in favor of seeing Jacob's opponent as an angel. The Hebrew text avoids the Hebrew word for 'angel' (or 'messenger', as I have translated מלאך).[99] Similarly, this is not some sort of inner-psychological battle that Jacob wages in his own mind or perhaps during a dream.[100] Gunkel already correctly cautioned

---

95. Admittedly, in Gen 18–19 the reader does not learn of the men's identity until 19:1, though there and increasingly in what follows, the text is clear in its articulation that the men are not simply human but are divine agents sent for the purpose of protecting Abraham's family. They do not share the literary hybridity evident in Gen 32:23–33.

96. One also should not overlook the fact that Manoah's wife seemingly has some idea of who the figure is, saying in v. 6 that he looked like 'an angel of God' (מלאך האלהים).

97. Verse 18 only calls the figure a "messenger." The text also makes this point abundantly transparent in v. 16b: "For Manoah did not know that he was a messenger of Yhwh."

98. Fokkelman (*Narrative Art in Genesis*, 220) correctly states that there is no reason not to trust Jacob's assessment of the situation in v. 31. He writes: "Again Jacob is the first and the best interpreter of his own history; again he produces his authoritative interpretation on the spot." See also Mark D. Wessner ("Toward a Literary Understanding of 'Face to Face' in Genesis 32:23–32," *ResQ* 42 [2000] 170), who argues that the phrase "for I have seen *Elohim* face to face" is reserved for meetings between God and humans. Contra Taylor ("Decoding Jacob at the Jabbok," 4–5) and Hamilton (*Genesis 18–50*, 336), who puzzle over Jacob's naming the place *Peniel* ('face of God') when all he had encountered was a "man."

99. Geller, "The Struggle at the Jabbok," 54. This silence is all the more striking given that Geller rightly sees the word as a *Leitwörter* elsewhere in Gen 32.

100. Jeffrey M. Cohen ("Struggling with Angels and Men," *JBQ* 31 [2003] 128) writes: "One does not have to be a professional psychologist to see Jacob as a man beset, suffering

against this reading at the turn of the twentieth century, cleverly writing: "One's hip does not become disjointed in a prayer struggle."[101] Rather, the contest is very real in regard to two fronts: God most immediately, and Esau imminently in Gen 33. The narrative's ambiguity should not and cannot be so easily overcome or dismissed; when the ambiguity is retained, Jacob's meeting with God becomes proleptic of his meeting with Esau.

One may wish to compare this type scene with others in which Yhwh becomes adversary. Hendel outlines several texts that may warrant investigation, among them Gen 22 and Exod 4:24–26.[102] This latter example, the ever-evasive bridegroom-of-blood passage, serves as an especially apt and illuminating comparison. Geller recognizes several affinities: a nocturnal attack and touching a leg.[103] Hamilton isolates another: both assaults occur at a border region during a return trip, to Canaan and Egypt, respectively.[104] One also wonders whether the near inexplicability of the passage forms the crux of another similarity. Again, however, a key difference exists: in the Exodus passage, the opponent is unabashedly portrayed as Yhwh. The same may be said for Gen 22, if one accepts the view that Yhwh operates as Abraham's opponent.[105] In Gen 32:23–33, however, Jacob's opponent is at once both man and God.

Who, then, is the "man" with whom Jacob wages metaphysical battle in his contest with God? Within the story world of Genesis, the most likely candidate is obviously Esau. Jacob has prayed for deliverance "from the hand of my brother, from the hand of Esau" (32:12), and I have demonstrated how vv. 23–33 serve as God's answer to the prayer. Moreover, in what follows, the focus will be on the way in which this encounter with God prepares and equips Jacob for his encounter with Esau.

Roland Barthes's seminal article on this scene from a semiotics/structuralist point of view provides further corroboration that vv. 23–33 have Esau readily in mind. He argues that Jacob's victory upsets the expected "bal-

---

from psychic distress that is real and not invention. Perhaps his anxieties surface again, hypostasized in the forms of hostile angels." Steve Molen ("The Identity of Jacob's Opponent: Wrestling with Ambiguity in Genesis 32:22–32," *Dialogue* 26 [1993] 197) wonders about the possibility of seeing the contest "as Jacob's dream rehearsal for what transpires the next morning."

101. Gunkel, *Genesis*, 349. Wenham (*Genesis 16–50*, 295) also argues against the interpretation that the encounter was a dream or "wrestling in prayer."

102. Ron Hendel, *The Epic of the Patriarch: The Jacob Cycle and the Narrative Traditions of Canaan and Israel* (HSM 42; Atlanta: Scholars Press, 1987) 105–6.

103. Geller, "The Struggle at the Jabbok," 58.

104. Hamilton, *Genesis 18–50*, 343.

105. That Gen 22 uses "elohim" rather than "Yhwh" need not present an insurmountable problem. If anything, the Gen 22 passage and its use of "elohim" provide a close parallel with Gen 32:23–33, which also uses "elohim," albeit in a context that suggests both human and divine qualities for the figure.

ance" of the scene; weaker (Jacob) overcomes stronger (God).[106] However, this balance does not arise out of nowhere, for earlier in the story of Jacob and Esau a similar inversion occurs with the younger Jacob overcoming the older Esau (27:36). God had a hand in that instance as well. Based on this history of inversion, in the wrestling scene God becomes a "stand-in" for Esau. Barthes sums up the essential implication: "Jacob having just been marked in his struggle with God, we can say in a sense that A (God) is the substitute of the oldest Brother, who is once against defeated by the youngest."[107]

Building on this resonance with the first block of Jacob/Esau narratives in Gen 25 and 27, Steven Molen advances additional compelling reasons for seeing the "man" as Esau. Countless scholars have recognized that Jacob's name (יעקב) sounds remarkably similar to the name of the river, 'Jabbok' (יבק), and the activity, 'wrestling' (יאבק), that occurs there.[108] Looking at the Jacob cycle more broadly, the reader knows that Jacob's name also means 'deceiver' (27:36), a nuance given by his brother Esau. Molen describes the connection: "his [Jacob's] thoughts on the night of the river conflict are revolving around his brother. If phonetically speaking Jacob is at the appropriate place involved in the activity appropriate to his name, thematically speaking whom else but Esau would Jacob wrestle?"[109]

Molen also insightfully situates his reading of vv. 23–33 in relation to the prenatal (trickster) oracle with which the Jacob cycle begins (25:23). He writes:

> And just as the abrupt introduction to the struggle might reflect Jacob's ever-present fears of what will transpire the next morning, the setting and circumstances of the struggle could hark back to how the two brothers began their rivalry. The rushing water of the Jabbok, the darkness, the length of the struggle, and almost symbiotic conflation of the contestants all suggest a return to that first struggle in the womb.[110]

More than Jacob's surroundings create the possibility for a proleptic encounter with Esau. At the beginning of the wrestling match, the reader loses any sense of who is doing what to whom. In v. 25. the "man" attacks, yet v. 26 begins simply with 'and he saw' (וירא); no explicit subject

---

106. Roland Barthes, "Wrestling with the Angel: Textual Analysis of Genesis 32:23–33," in *The Semiotic Challenge* (ed. Roland Barthes; trans. Richard Howard; Oxford: Blackwell, 1988) 254.

107. Ibid. Fokkelman (*Narrative Art in Genesis*, 208) likewise says the scene comports with Gen 25:29–34 in that both speak of a conflict between two men.

108. Molen, "The Identity of Jacob's Opponent," 190; Fokkelman, *Narrative Art in Genesis*, 210; Hamilton, *Genesis 18–50*, 329; Mathews, *Genesis 11:27–50:26*, 556; Wenham, *Genesis 16–50*, 295.

109. Molen, "The Identity of Jacob's Opponent," 190.

110. Ibid.

is supplied, nor is the antecedent of "he" clear. Not until the latter half of v. 26 does the reader learn that Jacob's opponent is the proper subject, but the reader again quickly experiences another disorientation at the start of v. 27 and continuing to v. 28. The phrase 'and he said' (ויאמר) occurs no less than four times in half as many verses—a section of text that Molen describes as "covered in a thicket of 'he's' and 'him's'"[111]—never with a clear subject or antecedent. Only at the end of v. 29, when Jacob answers with his name, is the reader able retroactively to reconstruct what has happened. Molen likens the ambiguity latent in the struggle at the Jabbok with the ambiguity in the prenatal wrestling of the twins in 25:23.[112]

Through carefully crafted paronomasia, type scenes, and ambiguity, Gen 32:23–33 recasts Jacob's encounter with God as concurrently an encounter with his besmirched brother, Esau. This posture of reading the wrestling match, seldom recognized, gives depth to the narrative, creating two interrelated planes of combat. In "reality," on one of these planes Jacob defeats God (vv. 26, 31), and on another the narrative presages what will become for Jacob an equally successful victory over Esau. Thus far, however, I have only told half the story; there exists also the dark underside to this battle of tricksters. As my treatment of Gen 33 will highlight, Jacob attains victory over Esau yet again via deception, but the means and methods by which he carries out these deceptions are not of Jacob's own making. They are, instead, the gifts of a divine trickster and are indelibly connected to vv. 23–33 and to the ancestral promise. In the next section, I will look at the various ways in which vv. 23–33 portray God as trickster in combat with his chosen trickster, Jacob.

Wrestling the Divine Trickster

Scant attention has been paid to the way that the wrestling match proceeds through deception and trickery. Acknowledgment of deception in this scene will prove to be a vital prerequisite to a proper understanding of Jacob's persistence in deceiving Esau in Gen 33, given that the two stories are so closely interwoven with one another. Here I will give brief attention to four specific instances: the initial attack, the blow to Jacob's hip, the request for one's name, and Jacob's new name, *Israel*.

I have already noted the wordplay with Jacob, Jabbok, and the Hebrew word used in v. 25 for 'wrestle' (יאבק). This play has led Wenham to paraphrase v. 25 as "he Jacobed him!"[113] While Wenham is correct that the nature and form of the contest remain elusive, this wordplay may help shed some light on the matter. Broadening the perspective to encompass the whole cycle, the reader knows well that Jacob's name means 'deceiver'. His name also derives from his activity of clutching Esau's "heel" at birth.

---

111. Ibid., 195.
112. Ibid., 191.
113. Wenham, *Genesis 16–50*, 295.

Therefore, if at the outset of the struggle Jacob gets "Jacobed," is it not possible that the narrative, through this homophony, communicates that the attack should be interpreted as a trick from Jacob's perspective? After all, Jacob is clearly taken by surprise. He is alone. He is ignorant of the looming attack; he is told nothing. This information is withheld from him. If one may regard this wordplay as hinting at a deception, it accomplishes two things: first, placed at the beginning of the account, it helps orient the reader to look out for subsequent deceptions; and second, it anticipates another similar-sounding word that will create a fundamental link to Gen 33: חבק ('embrace') in v. 4, used to describe Esau's initial response to his first sight of Jacob in nearly 20 years.

A second example, the violent touch to Jacob's hip, is an act of deception with covenantal overtones. Gunkel proffers that the original, earlier version of the story depicts Jacob as the one employing dirty tactics to achieve victory—that is, Jacob is the deliverer of the blow to his opponent's hip, not its recipient.[114] Presumably Gunkel understands this scene as one of trickery based on his description of Jacob's maneuver as "a wrestler's trick."[115] If one may draw an analogy to the contemporary world of professional wrestling, by this logic the deity fells Jacob with a proverbial (and illegal) "low-blow." In fact, several scholars argue for just such an interpretation. Stanley Gevirtz holds that God strikes Jacob not on the hip socket but on his genitals, arguing that the Hebrew usually rendered 'hollow of the thigh' (כף־ירך) is a euphemism for this area of the body.[116] One wonders how an attack of this type could leave Jacob with a permanent limp, but I have already shown that this story operates on multiple planes of meaning. Steve McKenzie similarly sees deception as operative in this instance, though he unfortunately does not extrapolate on his assessment.[117] It is sufficient to label this maneuver an underhanded tactic that Jacob could hardly have anticipated, and a move that should have signaled his defeat. To be sure, God's maneuver is an odd means of deliverance for Jacob; if Jacob was not prone before, he most certainly is now.

There is, however, another dimension to the blow received by Jacob, one that hearks back to the ancestral promise. Those who emphasize that Jacob is struck on the genitals see this as an attack on his procreative abilities;

---

114. Gunkel (*Genesis*, 349) argues that a redactor adds v. 33b, thus attributing the blow to God. On this problem, see also Johannes P. Floß, "Wer schlägt wen? Textanalytische Interpretation von Gen 32,23–33," *BN* 20 (1983) 92–132.

115. Gunkel, *Genesis*, 349.

116. Stanley Gevirtz, "Of Patriarchs and Puns: Joseph at the Fountain, Jacob at the Ford," *HUCA* 46 (1975) 52, 53. See also S. H. Smith, "'Heel' and 'Thigh': The Concept of Sexuality in the Jacob-Esau Narratives," *VT* 40 (1990) 466–69; Taylor, "Decoding Jacob at the Jabbok," 19; Hamilton, *Genesis 18–50*, 331.

117. Steve McKenzie, "You Have Prevailed: The Function of Jacob's Encounter at Peniel in the Jacob Cycle," *ResQ* 23 (1980) 229. Mathews (*Genesis 11:27–50:26*, 558) also describes this maneuver as "trickery."

it acts as a firm reminder that God alone grants children of the promise.[118]
Not only does this interpretation err by assuming that Jacob obtains the
promise through this encounter, it makes little sense, given that Jacob has
already become the father of multiple children of the promise, evident in
29:31–30:24. In my discussion of that passage, I showed that the narrative
recognizes Yнwн's sovereignty over this aspect of Jacob's life through its ty-
ing of several names of Jacob's children to acts of God. A more compelling
perspective arises if one sees language of the 'thigh' (ירך) as evocative of
biblical oath-taking, which is associated with the gesture of placing one's
hand under the thigh. The word ירך occurs in Gen 24:2, 9 (in reference to
Abraham's servant), and 47:29. This latter passage, Geller notes, attaches
the action of taking an oath with the covenantal language 'steadfast love
and faithfulness' (חסד ואמת), which appears also in Jacob's prayer in 32:11.[119]
Based on this view, one may regard God's touching of Jacob's "thigh" as
a symbolic action whereby God swears an oath to Jacob that his prayer
for deliverance from Esau will be answered. Through this motion, Jacob
receives not only assurance of the promise; his limp serves as a permanent
reminder of it as he marches to face Esau. Jacob, through this divine gesture, comes to embody the ancestral promise and God's fidelity to it.

Two final instances of divine deception involve naming. The first recalls
the deception of Isaac in Gen 27, the decisive moment that eventuated in
the twins' separation. In 32:28, the opponent asks Jacob's name, and he responds, "Jacob." A unique angle emerges if one focuses not on what Jacob
says but on what his opponent leaves unsaid. Verse 30 records Jacob asking
his opponent's name; he is met only with an evasive response: 'Why do you
ask my name?' (למה זה תשאל לשמי). In 27:18, Isaac asked a disguised Jacob a
similar question: 'Who are you, my son?' (מי אתה בני). Just as Isaac, whose
eyes are darkened by blindness, asks who is before him, Jacob, whose eyes
are blinded by darkness, inquires about who struggles with him. Father and
son ask the same question. The results, however, are remarkably different.
In asking his question, Isaac is deceived and gives away his prized blessing,
while in asking his question, Jacob too is deceived—the deity does not
supply this information—but receives (another) blessing (32:30b). Again,
blessing is transmitted through deception.

Second, Jacob's new name, *Israel*, attests to the prevalence of deception
in Jacob's life. The etymology of the name is disputed and need not detain
us.[120] My focus is on the interpretation that God gives the name in 32:29:
"For you have struggled with God *and with men* and have prevailed." Here

---

118. Smith, "'Heel' and 'Thigh,'" 469.
119. Geller, "The Struggle at the Jabbok," 50.
120. For the various treatments of the name's etymology, see W. F. Albright, "The
Names 'Israel' and 'Judah' with an Excursus on the Etymology of Tôdâh and Tôrâh," *JBL*
46 (1927) 154–68; Martin Noth, *Die israelitischen Personennamen im Rahmen der gemeinsemitischen Namengebung* (Hildesheim: Olms, 1966) 207–8; Robert Coote, "The Meaning of
the Name Israel," *HTR* 65 (1972) 137–46.

the traditional interpretation outlined at the beginning of this chapter—that this new name signals a new, purified Jacob—again comes under fire. The concern lies not in forecasting a new destiny for Jacob; the name instead speaks of Jacob's past.[121] It is significant that the phrase "and with men" does not find a correspondence in the name *Israel*.[122] This addition casts an approving backward glance over the entirety of Jacob's life, relating his success with "men." The name can hardly attest Jacob's strong interpersonal and communication skills! Rather, the men who come to mind most quickly are Isaac, Laban, and most importantly, Esau—all objects of Jacob's deceptions. God therefore states that Jacob has 'prevailed' (תוכל) through deception. One should not, however, take this statement as God's indictment of Jacob. The explanation reveals that Jacob struggles 'with God' (עם־אלהים) as well. Jacob's new name then announces that, as he has succeeded in the past, so also will he succeed in the future. God wrestles with, and for Jacob.[123]

A final cursory mention of the blessing that Jacob receives is in order. It is important to recognize that the blessing is not restricted only to the new name that Jacob receives.[124] Speiser is one scholar who takes this position, opting to translate ויברך אתו שם in v. 30b as 'He, then, bade him farewell'.[125] This translation is problematic, primarily given that the root ברך meaning 'to bless' clearly appears here as well as throughout the Jacob cycle. Given the discussion above relating Gen 32:23–33 to Jacob's earlier deceptions of Esau, one quickly sees that a blessing figures prominently in both scenes. Indeed, the blessing will also play a significant role in the reconciliation with Esau (33:11).

This brief foray into the use of deception in 32:23–33 provides another necessary dimension to the interpretational context of Gen 33. The two scenes, as I have shown and scholars have long recognized, are indissolubly linked. The inability to see deception in the struggle leads to the unfortunate failure to see it in Gen 33. Jacob will again deceive Esau during their

---

121. Hamilton, *Genesis 18–50*, 335; Turner, *Genesis*, 144–145; Brett, *Genesis*, 99.

122. See von Rad (*Genesis*, 322) for other, less-convincing alternatives.

123. This notion of God's wrestling *for* Jacob may in fact be precisely the significance of the name *Israel*. Fokkelman (*Narrative Art in Genesis*, 217) writes: "The name 'God fights' [Israel] may then mean: God fights with you, because he is forced to by your stubbornness and pride. And also: henceforth God will fight for you, for he appreciates your absolutely sincere and undivided commitment." I disagree with Fokkelman's temporal insinuation that it is only at this moment that God begins to fight for Jacob; the trajectory of this study thus far has shown that God has worked on Jacob's behalf since the utterance of Gen 25:23. Fokkelman's point, however, that the name may connote God fighting as Jacob's ally is illuminating for much of what follows in Gen 33.

124. Hermann Eising (*Formgeschichtliche Untersuchung zur Jakobserzählung der Genesis* [Emsdetten, 1940] 128–29) understands the blessing as the ancestral promise, which would not be unusual, given that God has already reaffirmed the promise at various points along the way (cf. 31:3, 12–13).

125. E. A. Speiser, *Genesis: Introduction, Translation, and Notes* (AB 1; New York: Doubleday, 1964) 255.

reconciliation. No apologetic is necessary. Coming out of Peniel, Jacob possesses a renewed sense not of who he is to become but of who he has been all along. Jacob is and remains a trickster because the God who calls him and wrestles with him, is a trickster as well.

Reconciliation and Deception
(Genesis 33)

In Gen 33, the Jacob cycle reaches its highest arc of tension. A reunion nearly 20 years in the making looms. All the questions that the reader has carried along the way are about to be answered. What is Esau's mental disposition? How will Jacob and his family fare? Will the estranged twins reconcile? The narrative has conditioned the reader to expect certain answers to these questions. The reader probably anticipates that Esau will retaliate with the same murderous vengeance with which the narrative left him (cf. 27:41; 32:7), that Jacob and his family will be slaughtered or, at best, taken hostage (cf. 32:12), and that the prospects for reconciliation are thus not very promising. The fact that the narrative presents the polar opposite of what the reader most likely expects attests to the literary artistry of the story. Readers may therefore believe Jacob also to have undergone a radical change, though nothing could be further from the truth. He is the one constant in the story.

Interpreters almost uniformly deem Jacob to be a changed man coming out of his encounter with God in Gen 32:23–33.[126] He has shed his old mischievous ways. A modicum of scholars hold to a medial position, contending Jacob has gained a profound new outlook on life, but his almost immediate failure to act in accordance with this outlook simply signifies that one cannot change overnight.[127] The deceptions are residual. Here I wish to press the opposite side of the continuum, arguing that the reconciliation between Jacob and Esau is a narrative fraught with deceptions. What these deceptions achieve is the incipient fulfillment of the final aspect of the promise left hanging from Jacob's sojourn with Laban: return to the promised land.

Jacob Deceives Esau, Again

At last, Jacob limps forward to encounter his brother, Esau. Along with the reader, Jacob remains uncertain how Esau will respond, but the encounter with God (and "Esau") in 32:23–33 has imbued him with a sense

---

126. See among others Hamilton, *Genesis 18–50*, 347; Mathews, *Genesis 11:27–50:26*, 561; Wenham, *Genesis 16–50*, 301, 304; Westermann, *Genesis 12–36*, 530; Fokkelman, *Narrative Art in Genesis*, 221; Sarna, *Genesis*, 403–4; Speiser, *Genesis*, 257; Curtis, "Structure, Style, and Context," 135, 136; Jeffrey M. Cohen, "Struggling with Angels and Men," *JBQ* 31 (2003) 128.

127. Kodell, "Jacob Wrestles with Esau," 69; Holmgren, "Holding Your Own against God," 9.

of confidence in himself and trust that God accompanies him into this fateful encounter. It is against this backdrop that one must interpret much of Jacob's activities in Gen 33.[128]

Jacob begins the reconciliation with what can only be described as a carefully orchestrated show to earn Esau's favor (חן). In fact, this is the precise reason Jacob offers in response to Esau's question in v. 8. At the sight of Esau and the 400 accompanying him, Jacob quickly returns to an old stratagem: dividing his family into multiple "camps" (cf. 32:2–9). Attention has readily been given to the fact that Jacob shrewdly situates his family in relation to Esau in the inverse order of his affection for them—Bilhah, Zilpah, and their children first; Leah and her children second; and Rachel and Joseph last—and that Jacob assumes the front position, a stark contrast to his using his family as a buffer in 32:4–22. What has not received adequate attention, however, is that this arrangement shows Jacob still up to his old tricks. By placing the maidservants and their children first, the text communicates that Jacob deems them most expendable. This point receives potent voice from Jacob himself when in vv. 8–10 he offers them without hesitancy as a gift for Esau. Never does Jacob make this known to them, nor does he solicit their advice in the matter.

Jacob's posture in approaching Esau also helps couch this scene in the context of deception. Jacob bows to the ground seven times, a gesture that has led Turner to aver that Jacob's blessing has come to naught.[129] In 27:29, Isaac had stated in the context of blessing that others would 'serve' (עבד) Jacob and that his brother would 'bow (חוה) before him, but in the Jacob cycle עבד is used only in reference to Jacob and, most strikingly here, *by Jacob* as a description of his inferior status before Esau (cf. 32:5; 33:5, 8, 13, 14).[130] Moreover, the only other occurrences of חוה in the cycle are when Jacob and his family bow to Esau in Gen 33. Even Turner must admit, however, that this procession may be nothing more than "an insincere act of self-deprecation to save his [Jacob's] own skin."[131] In his more recent commentary, Turner appears to espouse just this position, writing: "If his [Jacob's] words cannot be trusted [in Gen 33:12–17; see below], then his actions of bowing before Esau can hardly be taken at face value."[132] In fact,

---

128. Both Fishbane ("Composition and Structure," 26–27) and Gunkel (*Genesis*, 354–55) interpret the reconciliation scene as a scene in which Jacob continues to deceive Esau. Gunkel goes so far as to describe Esau in Gen 33 as "a good-natured buffoon who can be won over by beautiful speeches and gifts" (p. 354). Concurrently, the reader is to "rejoice" at Jacob's cunning outwitting of his brother.

129. Laurence A. Turner, *Announcements of Plot in Genesis* (JSOTSup 96; Sheffield: JSOT Press, 1990) 123.

130. Bar-Efrat (*Narrative Art in the Bible*, 67) notes that brothers regularly address one another as "my brother" in the Hebrew Bible. Jacob's self-deprecating manner of address then is not without import.

131. Turner, *Announcements of Plot in Genesis*, 123.

132. Idem, *Genesis*, 148.

this interpretation appears quite likely to be based on Jacob's response that he has done this all to earn Esau's "favor." It is a deceptive and disingenuous ploy.

Another possibility also has gone unnoticed by scholars. Esau knows the basic content of Jacob's blessing, having been told by Isaac on the heels of Jacob's timely escape (27:37); there Isaac told his favorite son Esau that the blessing made him servant to his brother. Now, for Jacob to assume this posture may recall to Esau's mind the blessing that he had lost. Jacob's clever ruse in bowing to Esau may have made it seem to Esau as though he was the one who had received the blessing as planned. As I will show, Jacob's calculated offer of 'my blessing' (בּרכתי) in v. 11 lends further credence to this possibility.

Another part of Jacob's charade that is often neglected is the manner in which he approaches Esau. Readers must remain mindful that, since Peniel, Jacob now walks with a noticeable limp. Depending on the severity of the injury, for Jacob to prostrate himself not once but seven times in drawing near to Esau must have been physically taxing for the patriarch.[133] Concurrently, however, Benno Jacob has suggested that this pitiful sight of obeisance may have aroused compassion in Esau.[134] Here one sees an instance in which Jacob avails himself of the outcome of the encounter with God in 32:23–33 to assist in protecting himself from Esau.

The initial theatrics seemingly pay off, yet the narrative provides one final glimmer of tension. Jacob, limping and genuflecting, is met by Esau running (רוץ) directly at him. But for what reason? The narrative only reports that he runs 'to encounter/meet' (לקראתו) his brother.[135] The next verb used of Esau is that he 'embraces' (חבק) Jacob; however, this verb exhibits strong phonetic similarities to the 'wrestling' (עבק) that Jacob had experienced the previous night.[136] Have Jacob's worst fears come true? Has Esau attacked? It is only with the successive flurry of verbs to describe Esau's actions that one learns that Esau greets Jacob not with vengeful anger but with authentic kindness. What, though, has brought about this change in Esau's demeanor? The text is silent on this point, yet this homophony

---

133. Shubert Spero ("Jacob and Esau: The Relationship Reconsidered," *JBQ* 32 [2004] 250) says that Jacob "must have cut a truly pathetic figure."

134. Benno Jacob, *The First Book of the Bible: Genesis* (trans. Ernest I. Jacob and Walter Jacob; New York: Ktav, 1974) 226. Leon R. Kass (*The Beginning of Wisdom: Reading Genesis* [New York: Free Press, 2003] 467) muses over Esau's interior monologue: "My hated brother, my rival, the conniving supplanter paying me supreme homage, abasing himself supremely! Is this not a confession of his guilt, an acknowledgement of my rightful superior standing? See how he places himself at my mercy, trusting me with his life? And look how he has aged and how he limps along! Does he not begin to resemble Father?"

135. It is interesting that the exact same form, לקראתו, is used of Laban's running "to meet" Jacob in 29:13, in a scene where Laban arguably has ulterior motives (cf. 24:28–33).

136. Hamilton, *Genesis 18–50*, 343.

connects Esau's activity in 33:4 with God's activity in 32:25. For Jacob, the violent embrace of God somehow allows for the loving embrace of Esau.

Evidence exists that readers may be correct in still approaching Esau with a healthy dose of suspicion. His magnanimous and passionate gesture of embracing Jacob leads to a 'kiss' (נשק) in v. 4. The Hebrew word 'kiss' is *suprapunctuated*, with small dots placed above each letter, leading some to regard the kiss as especially passionate, while others deem it a "'Judas' kiss."[137] This "kiss" is the last in a string of five nearly successive verbs describing how Esau greets Jacob: he 'runs' (רץ), 'meets' (קרא), 'embraces' (חבק), 'falls' upon the neck of (נפל), and 'kisses' (נשק) Jacob—all within the span of a single verse. This rapid string of verbs is reminiscent and evocative of the last time that five consecutive verbs were used of Esau, when he "ate, drank, rose, went," and "spurned" his birthright in 25:34.[138] In meeting Jacob, Esau again shows himself to be overly impetuous, suddenly emotional, an individual living for the moment. That his activities here mirror his activities when Jacob first deceived him suggests the possibility of reading the two scenes in tandem: in both, Esau's perfunctory and overly credulous behavior allows for him to be deceived.

Jacob remains guarded, and consequently he continues to trick Esau by choosing his words carefully. In the procession of his family, Jacob essentially flaunts the outcome of the ancestral promise that he has received on account of his obtaining the blessing, yet when Esau inquires about who these all are in relation to his brother, Jacob plainly states that they are "the *children* (הילדים) with whom God has *favored* (חנן) your servant" (v. 5). Two points are important. First, Hamilton rightly recognizes that Jacob makes no mention of his wives, lest he incur Esau's wrath by reminding him of the disastrous bid to earn his parents' *favor* by marrying an Ishmaelite wife (28:8–9).[139] Second, Jacob cleverly does not attribute his wives and children to the success of God's "blessing" but only to God's 'favor' (חנן).[140] These two calculated moves recall the shrewdness of Jacob's speech in Gen 25:27–34 and signify that the trickster Jacob is up to his old tricks.

Note also that during their reunion Jacob continues to attempt to buy off Esau (vv. 8–11).[141] He is still uncertain of Esau's objectives, and his speech reveals this fact. Jacob avoids all pleasantries (one might surmise that he

---

137. Holmgren ("Holding Your Own against God," 14) cites Prov 27:6: "Profuse are the kisses of an enemy." Kass (*The Beginning of Wisdom*, 467) says the rabbis believed that God changed Esau's heart.

138. Hendel, *The Epic of the Patriarch*, 130.

139. Hamilton, *Genesis 18–50*, 344.

140. The reader of the cycle knows well that Jacob's wives and children are the result of the promise. See chap. 3 above, "Divine Deception and Incipient Fulfillment of the Ancestral Promise."

141. In what the reader may regard as another deception, Esau asks what Jacob means by parading everyone in front of him, to which Jacob replies, "to find favor in the eyes of my lord." Here Jacob quotes the same reason he had instructed his servants to tell Esau in

would inquire about his father, Isaac, who has been on his deathbed for 20 years, or about his mother, Rebekah, who loved him so dearly and has failed to send word that Esau's demeanor has changed) and continues in his mendacious ways.[142] Perhaps Rebekah's failure to inform Jacob of Esau's change of heart is a deafening silence that the patriarch cannot overcome. Within the family unit, he learned that he could trust only his mother. That she, and she alone has not sent the promised word leaves Jacob understandably speculative of Esau's aims.[143]

All of this posturing eventually gives way to two more potent, blatant deceptions: the return of the "blessing" in vv. 10–11 and Jacob's failure to meet Esau in Seir as promised (vv. 12–17). I will treat each in turn.

When the encounter with Esau was looming, Jacob had persistently tried to propitiate Esau with lavish 'gifts' (מנחה) that his brother would repeatedly decline. Now face to face, Jacob attempts the strategy again. In v. 10, Jacob again offers Esau a 'gift' (מנחה) that his brother declines, yet suddenly in v. 11 Esau moves to accept. Why has this gift so suddenly piqued Esau's interest? The shift in Esau's receptivity matches a shift in Jacob's vocabulary. In v. 11, Jacob offers not a 'gift' (מנחה) but a 'blessing' (ברכה). This is not just any ordinary blessing; Jacob calls it 'my blessing' (ברכתי). Using this word conjures up Gen 27 and the stolen blessing, and there is little reason to presume that this memory is beyond Esau's recognition, especially since it is what ultimately leads to his acceptance. Commentators often see Jacob here as returning the blessing that he had stolen so long ago, in an attempt to make amends.[144] Within the larger context of the Jacob cycle specifically and Genesis more broadly, however, this view cannot be sustained and is instead another deception of which Esau is the victim.

The point that seems lost on Esau in his eager acceptance of the blessing is that, once uttered, the blessing is irrevocable.[145] Isaac indicates as much after Esau uncovers the deception (27:33). Presumably Jacob is aware of this little known fact, if not because he was the one blessed and thus he has a deeper understanding of the blessing's intricacies, then for the fact that he,

---

32:6. I have argued above that this is an instance of deception, given that neither there nor here does Jacob reveal his true aims: to appease Esau with gifts (32:21).

142. One may perhaps take Jacob's reticence to ask about his family as another example of his fearful choice of words, since Esau had planned to kill Jacob once Isaac died (27:31).

143. Holmgren ("Holding Your Own against God," 12, 14) muses over whether Esau is in fact acting deceptively here.

144. Westermann, *Genesis 25–36*, 526; Wenham, *Genesis 16–50*, 299; Hamilton, *Genesis 18–50*, 346; Sarna (*Genesis*, 230) calls it a "reparation." Gammie ("Theological Interpretation," 123–24) maintains that Jacob comes up with this idea at the moment he persists in holding onto his opponent until he is blessed in 32:27; Esau similarly will not release Jacob until he blesses him.

145. Claus Westermann (*Blessing in the Bible and the Life of the Church* [trans. Keith Crim; Philadelphia: Fortress, 1978] 54) writes: "Blessing cannot be recalled, and it works unconditionally."

not Uncle Esau, passes on the ancestral blessing to each of his children in Gen 49:1–27 with a manner and content reminiscent of Isaac's blessing.[146] Additionally, Jacob's history of deception with God's sanction had endured far too much to pass off one of his most cherished possessions so blithely. One must also remain mindful that Jacob's possession of the blessing, not Esau, is precisely how Yʜwʜ wants it (25:23; cf. 28:13–15).

Probing more deeply into the story, especially the connection between Gen 32 and 33, one may remember that Jacob has another blessing now at his disposal: the blessing that he wrestled from God in 32:30.[147] Jacob never once specifies to Esau which blessing he intends, though the considerations just outlined make it viable that Jacob gives Esau this "empty" additional blessing—the content of which the reader is never told—rather than the blessing of their father, Isaac.

Conceivably the most patent example of Jacob's outright deception of Esau during their reconciliation occurs in 33:12–17. Now reconciled, Esau suggests that they journey on together, and Esau is willing to accommodate Jacob's pace (v. 12). Without hesitation, Jacob demurs by appealing to the frailty of his children and the nursing of his flocks (v. 13). Hamilton points out the oddity in Jacob's referring to his children as "frail" given that "they seem to have weathered the journey thus far with no ill effects"; out of his entire party, Jacob is the person limping, which clearly qualifies him as the most frail.[148] Is Jacob merely making excuses? The narrative reveals that much more is operative when in v. 14 Jacob insists that Esau venture on ahead of him while he follows at the speed of the children and cattle until he meets Esau again 'in Seir' (שׂעירה). After Jacob turns down Esau's offer to have some of his men accompany him (v. 15), which would force Jacob to come to Seir,[149] the text resolutely and unabashedly states that Esau makes his way to Seir, but Jacob sets out for and settles in Sukkot (vv. 16–17). Jacob deceives Esau again!

Some commentators have sought to soften this deception in various ways; however, the narrative expresses no concern for such apologetics. Heard avers that Jacob's hesitancy stems from fear that Esau will discover his disability, but it is probable that Jacob's multiple prostrations have already made his handicap readily apparent to his brother.[150] Hamilton

---

146. The various individual blessings in Gen 49 similarly speak of cursing (v. 7), division/separation (v. 7), brothers bowing down (v. 8), specific locales for dwelling (v. 13), supremacy over a people (v. 16), election of a particular brother (v. 26). Jacob's blessing of Joseph's sons, Ephraim and Manasseh, also recalls the dual promises given to Jacob and Esau, respectively, in Gen 27. Note also the dimness of Jacob's eyes later in life, which matches the dimness of Isaac's eyes at the time of blessing.

147. Geller ("The Struggle at the Jabbok," 42) sees Jacob's mention of "my blessing" in 33:11 as hearking back to 32:27 and Jacob's request for a blessing. Jacob's statement, "Seeing your face is like seeing the face of God," links these two scenes dramatically.

148. Hamilton, *Genesis 18–50*, 347.

149. Ibid., 348.

150. Heard, *Dynamics of Diselection*, 132.

expressly argues against the view that this deception shows that Jacob has not undergone a change, yet he provides no support for this argument.[151] Alfred Agyenta appeals to Jacob's fear of his brother as the rationale behind his tentativeness, yet the fact remains that fear may motivate deception; it does not, however, apologize for it.[152] Westermann uniquely sees Jacob's words to Esau as a genuinely honest expression of the differences between the two, which require that they not live adjacent to one another.[153] For Westermann, the phrase "until I come to my lord in Seir" is Jacob's way of courteously not "contradict[ing]" Esau.[154] One wonders, however, what Jacob would have thought he might contradict. Note that it is Jacob who originally suggests coming to Seir, not Esau.

This reading of Gen 33 shows that Jacob does not appear to have changed as much as scholarship has suggested. Throughout the reunion, Jacob deceives Esau with flattering speech and gestures, ostentatious and ambiguous gifts, and a bald-faced lie. Those who wish to maintain that Peniel transforms Jacob must make sense of these aspects of his character in some other way. Actually, it is striking that Jacob's penultimate encounter with Esau in a sense replays their first encounter years before: Jacob deceives, and Esau is the object of this deception.

Reconciliation and Deception in Tension?

A final consideration warranting inquiry may arise out of this analysis: how is the reader to resolve the idea that the brothers reconcile during Jacob's continued deception of Esau? Does this interpretive posture temper the authenticity of this reconciliation? I suggest that authentic reconciliation occurs during deception in Gen 33, the successful outcome of which is the final step moving toward the inchoate fulfillment of the ancestral promise of land.

Several approaches have been put forward in response to this issue. Perhaps the most well known is the approach of George Coats, who posits that the overriding narrative theme in the Jacob cycle is "strife without reconciliation."[155] This theme is not only predominant but also primary;

---

151. Hamilton (*Genesis 18–50*, 347) cites a quotation by E. M. Good ("Deception and Women: A Response," *Semeia* 42 [1988] 129) that presumably serves as his rationale: "Though he became Israel, he is not 'upright' Israel but, throughout chs. 32–33, 'uptight' Israel." I have already sought to show that Jacob has ample reason to be "uptight" since he does not know of Esau's mental disposition, and Rebekah has not sent any word that Esau has rescinded his anger. While Jacob may be "uptight," this fact does not mitigate the presence of deception in 33:12–17.

152. Alfred Agyenta, "When Reconciliation Means More than the 'Re-Membering' of Former Enemies: The Problem of the Conclusion to the Jacob-Esau Story from a Narrative Perspective (Gen 33,1–17)," *ETL* 83 (2007) 131.

153. Westermann, *Genesis 12–36*, 526–27. See also Wenham, *Genesis 16–50*, 299–300.

154. Westermann, *Genesis 12–36*, 526–27.

155. George W. Coats, "Strife without Reconciliation: A Narrative Theme in the Jacob Traditions," in *Werden und Wirken des Alten Testament: Festschrift für Claus Westermann zum 70. Geburtstag* (ed. Rainer Albertz; Göttingen: Vandenhoeck & Ruprecht, 1980) 83.

even the theme of promise, he contends, is subordinate to it.[156] Coats maintains that Esau extends an offer of genuine reconciliation in 33:4, which is met by Jacob's qualified hesitancy and uneasiness at the thought of accompanying his brother to Seir.[157] For Coats, true reconciliation is occasioned only when the reconciling parties dwell together.[158] This linking of reconciliation and residence is Coats's main flaw. There is no reason to assume that reconciliation requires a shared dwelling space.

Other scholars attempt to give the problem a historical dimension by attending to the national import of the narrative. Proponents of this way of reading emphasize the fact that Jacob and Esau are the eponymous ancestors of the nations Israel and Edom, and thus for them to reside together would make little sense. For instance, Frank Crüsemann regards Gen 33 as a text ultimately bound to the political realities of its time, with the impetus behind the reconciliation and separation of the brothers being concerned to show two separate national entities that are both free and at peace with one another.[159] As a result, the (trickster) oracle (25:23) forecasting a history of enmity goes unfulfilled.[160] Erhard Blum similarly regards the primary motivation of the text as being tethered to the formation of Israel as a political reality with a unique identity, which could only be maintained by separation from other nations and peoples.[161] Konrad Schmid defends a similar view of peaceful coexistence between two peoples requiring separate dwellings, though he couches it in more literary than historical terms; he does, however, appear to make a historical application in his judgment that peace requires separation of territories.[162]

In each of these readings, separation does not mitigate reconciliation but exists as a natural outcome of the larger national concerns of the text. Although they are helpful in providing evidence that reconciliation may persist despite the tensions latent in the narrative, these interpretations run the risk of oversimplifying the historical relationship between Israel and Edom. The biblical account presents a quite complex and vacillating relationship that some consider to be evident in the larger Jacob cycle as

---

156. Ibid., 82–83.

157. Ibid., 103.

158. Coats (ibid.) writes: "Reconciliation should apparently be symbolized by physical community. What good is reconciliation if brothers do not live together?"

159. Frank Crüsemann, "Dominion, Guilt, and Reconciliation: The Contribution of the Jacob Narrative in Genesis to Political Ethics," *Semeia* 66 (1994) 72.

160. Ibid., 74.

161. Erhard Blum, "Genesis 33,12–20: Die Wege Trennen Sich," in *Jacob: Commentaire à plusieurs voix de, Ein mehrstimmiger Kommentar zu, A Plural Commentary of Gen 25–36: Melanges offerts à Albert de Pury* (MdB 44; ed. J. D. Macchi and T. Römer; Geneva: Labor et Fides, 2001) 229.

162. Konrad Schmid, "Die Versöhnung zwischen Jakob und Esau (Gen 33,1–11)," in *Jacob: Commentaire à plusieurs voix de, Ein mehrstimmiger Kommentar zu, A Plural Commentary of Gen 25–36: Melanges offerts a Albert de Pury* (MdB 44; ed. J. D. Macchi and T. Römer; Geneva: Labor et Fides, 2001) 225.

well.[163] These political readings also commit an error similar to the error of which they accuse Coats: reducing the text to the simple equation of separation as being concomitant with peace.

What is needed is a narrative appraisal of this question, an appraisal that takes into account the various perspectives in Gen 32–33. Agyenta is one of the very few who attempt a reading of this sort, but he relies heavily on the assumption that the Jacob of Gen 33 is a new and different man.[164] My proposal is more modest. One should consider three perspectives. For Esau, reconciliation has taken place. For Jacob, Esau has been reconciled to him. These two points gain fullest expression in Gen 35:29, where Esau and Jacob reunite without narrated incident one final time, to bury their father Isaac. These two perspectives converge in the third perspective: God's perspective. The divine concern throughout the Jacob cycle has been intimately bound up with the perpetuation and incipient fulfillment of the ancestral promise. Through the deception of Esau in Gen 33, this promise reaches its apogee in the Jacob cycle. Jacob does not go to Seir but instead to Sukkot and eventually on to Shechem, where YHWH had reiterated the promise of land to Abraham (12:6). For the first time since he fled from Esau nearly 20 years before, Jacob is back in Cisjordan, back in the land of the promise.[165] That he arrives 'peacefully' (שלם) is of great consequence; at Bethel, Jacob had asked that YHWH guide him to the house of his father 'in peace' (בשלום).[166] He proceeds to purchase a parcel of land and establish an altar on it to "El, the God of Israel." God has fulfilled his part in Jacob's life, and now Jacob fulfills his. Had Jacob resided with Esau in Seir, there would be no advancement toward the promise of land. It is through deception that Jacob is able to enter the land again. This movement toward

---

163. To be sure, there are accounts of diplomatic, nonviolent cooperation, such as 2 Kgs 3:8–9, 12, 20, 26, where Edom joins with Israel and Judah against Moab, and the injunction in Deut 23:8–9 that "you are not to abhor an Edomite, for he is your brother." Accompanying the Deuteronomy text is the allowance for Edomites to enter the temple. See Diana Edelman, ed. (*You Shall Not Abhor an Edomite for He Is Your Brother: Edom and Seir in History and Tradition* [Archaeology and Biblical Studies 3; Atlanta: Scholars Press, 1995]). In the Hebrew Bible, however, the Israel-Edom relationship is hardly univocally peaceful. In Num 20:14–21, Edom refuses to grant the wandering Israelites safe passage into the land, which seems to have generated a long history of hostility between these two "brother" nations. See 1 Sam 14:47; 2 Sam 8:14; 1 Kgs 11:14–16; 2 Kgs 8:20–22; 14:7, 10; 1 Chr 18:11–13; 2 Chr 21:8–10; 25:19–20; Isa 11:14; 34:5–6; 63:1; Jer 9:24–25; 25:21; 49:7–22; Ezek 25:12–14; 32:29; 35:1–15; 36:1–7; Joel 4:19; Amos 1:6, 9, 11–12; 9:12; Obadiah; Mal 1:2–4. If the emphasis lies on these nations' living peacefully with one another, the less-than-flattering portrayal of Esau in Gen 25 and 27—where he is, not incidentally, actually given the name "Edom"—presents another problem. See also Schmid ("Die Versöhnung zwischen Jakob und Esau," 226), who admits the complexity inherent in reconstructing the historical background of the narrative and its attendant interests.

164. See Agyenta, "Reconciliation," 127–33, esp. pp. 127–29 on viewpoint.

165. Hamilton, *Genesis 18–50*, 349.

166. Ibid., 350; Wenham, *Genesis 16–50*, 300.

fulfillment has been God's purpose all along. In this way, just as Turner may speak of "separation within reconciliation,"[167] I may adequately speak of reconciliation within deception.

Deception and the Ancestral Promise, Reprise (Genesis 34–35)

The final two chapters of the Jacob cycle present a miscellany of various postreconciliation experiences of the patriarch and his family. Related are stories of the rape of Dinah, Simeon and Levi's murderous revenge, God's command that Jacob return to Bethel, Benjamin's birth and Rachel's death, Reuben's intercourse with Bilhah, a second recounting of Jacob's renaming, and the death and burial of Isaac. Here my focus, however, is quite narrow and the treatment quite cursory: I will be looking at how these chapters— specifically the response to Dinah's rape and the return to Bethel—continue the Jacob story in a way that shows the interconnectedness of deception and the perpetuation of the ancestral promise one final time.

Some of Jacob's children appear equally as deceptive as their father. In 34:13, after the rape of Dinah, the narrative recounts that two of Jacob's sons speak with Shechem and Hamor 'in deceit' (במרמה), saying that they will assent to the marriage to their sister if only the men of Shechem will agree to be circumcised. Shortly thereafter, in v. 25, Simeon and Levi act on this deception, slaughtering all the Shechemite males before they have recovered.

It is striking that God does not appear in this chapter, potentially leading one to believe that he fails to find much humor in this deception. Interestingly, James Kugel adduces a number of later Jewish texts that understand the brothers' impetus in killing the Shechemite males as arising out of an ordinance from God.[168] According to Kugel, this interpretation comes about as a desire to tidy up the problematic nature of Simeon and Levi's activities.[169] What Kugel leaves unstated is the implication that arises from this way of reading: in saying that Simeon and Levi act as God's instruments in punishing the Shechemites, God in turn becomes complicit in their deception! While these texts press beyond the bounds of the canon, they do buttress an underlying point of this study that within early Judaism the idea of God as using deception is not entirely unpalatable.

In the final form of the text, however, God does play a pivotal role. Genesis 34 closes with Jacob's lament over the danger in which Simeon and Levi have placed their family, and chap. 35 opens with a theophany—as

---

167. Turner, *Genesis*, 148.

168. James L. Kugel, *The Ladder of Jacob: Ancient Interpretations of the Biblical Story of Jacob and His Children* (Princeton: Princeton University Press, 2006) 65–66. Among the texts cited are *T. Levi* 5:3; 6:8, 11; Jdt 9:2–4; *Jub.* 30:5–6; *Jos. Asen.* 23:14.

169. Kugel, *The Ladder of Jacob*, 66.

always, at quite an opportune moment—in which God instructs Jacob and his family to go to Bethel and build an altar there. Theologically, Gen 35:1 achieves more than just delivering Jacob from a dangerous situation (although no doubt the promise of divine presence in 28:15 is evident here); it also hearks back to the theophany at Bethel where Jacob inherited this very promise. Therefore, God's appearance at the outset of Gen 35 confirms his choice of Jacob and his heirs, made at Bethel in Gen 28, on the very heels of a deadly act of deception.

Rounding out the Jacob cycle are narrative hints at the patriarch's previous deceptions. First, the deception of Esau is recalled by God in 35:1b, where God prods Jacob's memory by couching his instruction about a return to Bethel in terms of the time during which Jacob "was fleeing from Esau, [his] brother." There, at Bethel in 28:10–22, Yhwh had made the choice for Jacob abundantly clear by giving Jacob the ancestral promise after two deceptions of Jacob's own family (25:27–34; 27:1–45). Second, Jacob takes the initiative in requiring his family members to rid themselves of any foreign deities. Hamilton conjectures that the *teraphim* Rachel stole from Laban would surely be included.[170] Jacob's injunction against any other deities may evoke his deception of Laban with the rods—and God's help— in 30:37–31:16, as well as the divine command to depart, which Laban regards as a deception. These two seemingly innocuous references bring to mind the long history between the trickster Jacob, the trickster God, and the ancestral promise. In fact, now at the close of the cycle God reiterates the promise to Jacob yet again; albeit in somewhat different terms, the particulars are present. Verses 11–12 relate the promise of progeny and nationhood as well as land. The list of Jacob's 12 sons, from whom the entire people Israel will descend, are enumerated in vv. 22b–26, highlighting a transition from promise potential to promise realized. Just as Jacob is "Israel," so too will they become "Israel." By this stage in the narrative, "Israel" is a polyvalent word. The name points to much more than the isolated incident in 32:28. It now references an entire complex history, from Abraham to Jacob, in which deception, blessing, and the promise have intermingled in order to achieve the divine prerogative.

The final scene that the narrative leaves with the reader is the image of the twins Jacob and Esau, for the first time working as a unit, burying their father Isaac (vv. 27–29). Lying behind these two brothers is a shared history of strife and deception. That they work together is not merely a matter of Jacob's ingenuity or Esau's dim-wittedness. Just as their separation occurs by divine fiat (25:23), so also their reconciliation is orchestrated by the trickster God (32:23–33). And just as at the beginning of their lives the twins are very different from one another (25:25–34), so too they now remain distinct. Commentators readily point out the similarity between

---

170. Hamilton, *Genesis 18–50*, 375.

35:27–29 and 25:9, where Isaac and Ishmael reunite to bury their father, Abraham.[171] In both cases, however, unspoken inequality exists. Ishmael and Esau are outside the promise. Isaac and Jacob, conversely, are emblems of the promise, the result of God's own choice. Indeed, Jacob's life is paradigmatic of its incipient fulfillment.

Conclusion: Tricky Encounters

In this second block of Jacob/Esau narratives, the Jacob cycle has truly come full circle. Whereas Jacob had previously fled his home and family due to his brother Esau's homicidal plotting, he has now returned to his homeland and family, having reaped the benefits of the ancestral promise along the way. Upon his return, however, the promise again meets its most ominous threat: Esau.

This chapter has leveled a serious challenge at the hegemonic, traditional interpretation of Gen 32–33, which is that Jacob's life and ethics are transformed through a violent encounter with God in 32:23–33, making him a suitable prospect to receive the ancestral promise. Jacob, I remind the reader, is elect from birth (25:23) and obtains the promise by a free gift from God at Bethel (28:13–15) near the beginning of the cycle, not at its end, and following several acts of deception. Additionally, the prevalence of the name *Jacob* even after 32:23–33 serves as a narrative clue that the "old Jacob" indeed may not be as far removed as most scholars have suggested.

Through careful attention to three specific encounters—Jacob's encounters with the messengers of God (32:2–3), God (32:23–33), and Esau (33:1–17)—I have emphasized a way of reading that shows Jacob and God working in tandem to thwart Esau and any threat he may pose to the promise. These encounters frame the narrative, orienting the reader to see God's purposes as operative throughout: in Jacob's sending messengers and a gift ahead to Esau (32:4–9, 14–22) and in Jacob's proleptic defeat of Esau (32:23–33). At each stage, God's fealty to the ancestral promise was intertwined with past, present, and future deceptions, ultimately allowing for Jacob to outwit Esau one final time and, in so doing, to return after a nearly 20-year hiatus to the promised land. In the end, Jacob really does not change much. He is a trickster from beginning to end. But to recognize Jacob alone is to recognize only half the equation: Yнwн also is also a trickster from beginning to end.

---

171. Gunkel, *Genesis*, 374; Heard, *Dynamics of Diselection*, 133; Hamilton, *Genesis 18–50*, 389–90; Wenham, *Genesis 16–50*, 328.

Chapter 5

Concluding Remarks and Prospects for Further Study

Introductory Remarks

With the previous chapters' reading of the Jacob cycle now in place, chap. 5 will examine the conclusions that one may draw from this investigation as well as suggest several areas for further fruitful study. Special attention will be paid to the theological implications of divine deception in the Jacob cycle and how this phenomenon relates to the perpetuation of the ancestral promise in Genesis.

A Theology of Deception in the Jacob Cycle

Summary and Conclusions

The overriding thesis of this book is that Yʜwʜ engages in deception in the Jacob cycle in order to advance the ancestral promise (Gen 12:1–3; cf. 26:4–5; 28:13–15) toward incipient fulfillment. Chapter 1 established the context for the study. In scholarly research, divine deception has received some attention, particularly in the Deuteronomistic History and the prophetic books (Isaiah and Jeremiah especially), though no sustained treatments exist for Genesis more broadly or the Jacob cycle more specifically. Regarding divine deception in the Jacob cycle, scholars have taken three distinct positions. First, there are those who wish to separate Yʜwʜ from any complicity or role in deception, often arguing that the Jacob cycle presents a series of unedifying tales of an unethical patriarch, whom Yʜwʜ chastises and punishes for his deceptions. Second, one may discern within the work of some scholars various implicit references to Yʜwʜ as deceiver. Third, a few scholars have noted several instances where divine deception appears in the Jacob cycle, though these statements are often tantalizingly brief and undeveloped. Given this basis, I surveyed a number of texts from the ancient Near East that unabashedly depict deities—among them Ea/Enki, Inanna, Rē, Isis, Horus, Seth, Inaraš, Athena, Prometheus, Zeus, and Hermes—who act deceptively, and I noted the presence of trickster deities in modern anthropological studies.

I have argued that the most profitable method for investigating a theology of deception is a synchronic, literary hermeneutic with theological aims, emphasizing both *how* the text means and *what* the text means. Only then is one able to appreciate the rich literary artistry of the text while still giving pride of place to the final canonical form of the text; appeals to source criticism or other diachronic methodologies explain these issues by hypothesizing about different layers of tradition or editorial growth. Although this mechanism is probably the means by which the biblical text came into being, these aproaches do not address the topic fully, for the final form of the text is a multifaceted, multivocal whole that has been shaped in a particular way and with a particular purpose. Attention to the shape of the canonical form of the book of Genesis allows one to make sense of the whole, not its constituent parts.

Chapter 2 centers on the first block of Jacob/Esau narratives (Gen 25–28), covering a swath of history from womb (*beten*) to Bethel. Yhwh's oracle in 25:23 is central here; almost every translation renders the line 'the elder will serve the younger', which fails to give adequate attention to the ambiguity of the Hebrew. I argue for a better translation that is more reflective of the ambiguity inherent in the Hebrew: 'the greater will serve the lesser'. Through its use of ambiguity in matters of diction, syntax, and context in the book of Genesis, Yhwh's word to Rebekah becomes a trickster oracle in which Yhwh withholds vital information from the matriarch about the fate of her twin sons. Because of this ambiguity—and because of Rebekah's special love for Jacob—two deceptions take place. First, in 25:27–34 Jacob tricks Esau into exchanging his coveted right of the firstborn for nothing more than a bowl of lentil stew. Second, Rebekah and Jacob deceive an aged and blind Isaac into blessing Jacob rather than the intended Esau (27:1–45). God is not outside these events. The trickster oracle casts its shadow over these narratives as well, and God plays a role behind the scenes that comes to the fore at Bethel (28:10–22, esp. vv. 13–15). Here Yhwh does not lambast or judge Jacob in any way for the previous deceptions; rather, Jacob receives, of Yhwh's own volition, the ancestral promise, thus affirming the deceptive means by which Jacob obtained both birthright and blessing. Bethel, therefore, from the perspective of the literary flow of the narrative, stands as the theological pivot of the entire Jacob cycle.

Chapter 3 treats Jacob's sojourn in Haran at the residence of his uncle Laban (Gen 29–31). During this tumultuous time in Jacob's life, Yhwh's fealty to the promise continues to be in evidence. Yhwh uses deception to advance each element of the ancestral promise toward fulfillment. First, Laban's deceptive wife-swap, switching Leah for Rachel (29:15–30), results in Jacob's having two wives with two maidservants, all of whom together give birth to 12 children of the promise, from whom the entire *people* Israel evolves (29:31–30:24). Second, as a representative of the nations, Laban affirms that Yhwh has *blessed* him through Jacob (30:27). Third, Yhwh commands Jacob and his newly acquired family (with their wealth) to return to the *land* (31:3), a flight that Laban regards as a deception (31:27). Gen 30:37–31:16 stands out as perhaps the most potent act of divine deception.

In 30:37–43, Jacob employs rods to affect the breeding of the flocks, a tactic that results by some mysterious circumstances in a plethora of spotted and speckled animals, precisely the animals that Laban had agreed would be Jacob's wages. In Gen 31:1–16, however, Jacob ascribes credit for the success of the ruse to God rather than his own ingenuity.

Chapter 4 addresses the final meeting with Esau and Jacob's subsequent return to Bethel (Gen 32–35). In Gen 32–33, which I have described as a text of encounters, Jacob comes face to face with the "messengers of God" (32:2–3), God (32:23–33), and ultimately Esau (33:1–17). The first two of these encounters provide the proper theological orientation, assisting the reader in seeing the plan of God being acted out in order to achieve the incipient fulfillment of the promise: Jacob's return to the land. This final section of the Jacob cycle is not meant to establish a purified and transformed Jacob but instead depicts Jacob and Yhwh both performing their old trickster antics. Jacob deceives Esau in preparation for their encounter. Even after the wrestling match with God (32:23–33) Jacob persists in deceiving Esau by trying to buy Esau's "favor" with an unidentified "blessing" (33:8–11), by citing his own childrens' frailty as the reason that he cannot venture on with Esau when he is really trying to separate himself from his brother (33:12–14), and by telling Esau that he will meet him in Seir but then taking up residence in Sukkot (33:15–17). Jacob changes very little over the course of the narrative. The nocturnal encounter with God, traditionally understood as the decisive event leading Jacob to "change his stripes," is instead a scene replete with ambiguity. Jacob's opponent possesses qualities and acts in a way that causes readers to be uncertain whether he is a human or God. The rhetorical effect of this ambiguous portrayal creates two separate planes of combat: on one plane, Jacob battles and bests God; however, on another plane, his struggle is a prequel to the inevitable meeting with Esau. Just as Jacob prevails over God/Esau, so also Jacob will prevail over Esau in their final meeting. Jacob's deception of his brother allows him to return to the promised land.

Theological Implications

The analysis in the foregoing chapters shows that one cannot divorce Yhwh from Jacob's many deceptions. On some occasions, Yhwh operates behind the scenes (Gen 27:7, 20, 28); on others, Yhwh avails himself of the deceptions of another individual (29:15–30, cf. 29:31–30:24); and still in others, Yhwh is the primary deceiver (30:37–31:16). What theological implications arise from this sort of portrait? I will suggest four that I deem most important for the task of Old Testament theology, though no doubt there are more.

First, and most germane, God's unique fidelity to the (ancestral) promise comprises surprising and unexpected modes of fulfillment. The primary mode emphasized in this study is deception. When Yhwh deceives or uses deception in the Jacob cycle, it is always for the betterment of Yhwh's chosen, yet the individuals who are deceived are not debilitated or obliterated by the deception without due cause. For example, Esau, despite being duped out of the promise, meets Jacob some 20 years later as an extremely wealthy man. By comparison, I have identified Laban as a figure whose blessing turns into a curse, in line with the penultimate statement in Gen 12:3 that Yhwh will bless those who bless Israel and curse those who curse Israel. At the same time, this divine devotion does not mean trouble will not befall the elect, which is evident during Jacob's time in Haran, but it does reveal that Yhwh remains steadfast even in Haran. Yhwh is not disinterested when it comes to the promise, and the Hebrew Bible does not limit Yhwh to a single mode of operating. Old Testament theology must remain attentive and receptive to startling new ways in which God engages humanity.

Some of these methods may appear unpalatable to contemporary readers, yet the conclusions of this study raise an important issue: perhaps what Eric Seibert has called "disturbing divine behavior" is only disturbing to our contemporary sensibilities and has very little to do with the actual portrait of God gleaned from the Hebrew Bible.[1] I have sought in this book to advance a descriptive theology of the book of Genesis, outlining not what I wish the text said—in conformity with my own ethical sensibilities and *mores*—but, rather, what the text communicates and how it does so. Reading the Bible should not be an easy enterprise. Readers of the Bible are invited to participate in the conversation occurring across time within its pages. This conversation should be unsettling at points. It should raise questions. It should prompt self-reflection. It should press us to think "outside the box," to reevaluate who we are and who God is. Eryl Davies offers a worthwhile caution on this point:

> Besides, if we read the Hebrew Bible simply in order to take issue with its more unsavoury aspects, while appealing to its more positive, life-enhancing statements to confirm and corroborate values we already hold anyway, why bother reading the Bible at all?[2]

This sort of openness to the transformative and sometimes disquieting aspects of the biblical text, as I hope to have shown in this book, can produce rich and essential theological insights that may otherwise be missed or neglected.

In the Hebrew Bible, one may in fact discern a trajectory of continuity in which Yhwh's fealty to this chosen *family* is extrapolated to this chosen *people*, and Yhwh exhibits no qualms about defending this people through

---

1. See Eric A. Seibert, *Disturbing Divine Behavior: Troubling Old Testament Images of God* (Minneapolis: Fortress, 2009).

2. Eryl W. Davies, *The Immoral Bible: Approaches to Biblical Ethics* (London: T. & T. Clark, 2010) 132.

troubling measures such as the death of the firstborn (Exod 12:29), utter destruction of enemy nations (Deut 7:1–2; 20:16–18; Josh 10:40), and deception (2 Sam 17:14; 1 Kgs 22:19–23, 2 Kgs 6:15–20; 7:6–7). Yhwh's tampering with *our* conventional mores testifies not only to Yhwh's steadfastness but also to the divine freedom to traverse any bounds in the interest of the promise. The Jacob narrative stresses God's unique sovereignty, even to the point of deception.

Second, and related, this reading underscores the centripetal force of the ancestral promise. Yhwh demonstrates an unbridled passion for the promise as the overarching norm governing life. All other claims to power outside the divine prerogative prove only to be illusory and fleeting. Neither Laban nor Esau poses a legitimate threat to the promise that Yhwh is unable to overcome. There exists no situation in Jacob's life that is outside the bounds of the promise, be it the deception of his brother and father, his internment with Laban, or the purported threat of a reconciliation with Esau. One cannot separate Yhwh's activities and interventions from the divine word of promise, nor can one contend that the promise is secondary in the narrative. The promise and Yhwh's fidelity to it hold the narrative together. The lengths to which Yhwh goes show that the divine resolve for the promise is unflinching, unyielding, and resolute.

Third, there is a certain level of destabilization that accompanies this portrait of Yhwh as trickster. This God has subversive tendencies. One may readily discern this point in the divine proclivity throughout Genesis for the secondborn as opposed to the firstborn child. But this image extends further and is much broader in scope. God is a God of inversion, who is not circumscribed by the strictures imposed by the various power brokers of the narrative. The subversive nature of Yhwh attested in the Jacob cycle manifests a dogged insistence that Yhwh is free to undermine any sense of propriety, decorum, and convention as is deemed fitting to the situation at hand. For example, although I have not sought to chart a particular historical development or appropriation of these traditions about the trickster God, one can readily imagine that an image of this sort could be of great meaning and encouragement in response to ancient Israel's unrelenting experience with empire: Assyria, Babylon, and Persia most specifically. One may surmise that a trickster God would have been attractive to ancient Israel for this very reason; one has less use for a trickster God if one is in a position of power and authority. In Genesis, God (and Jacob) redraw the boundaries of what is expected and what is possible through their deceptions. The limits become limitless, for what is possible extends as far as God's and Jacob's aptitude for tricking. Yhwh is a God of inversion and subversion.

Fourth, and perhaps most important, this portrait of God resists any absolute claims that seek to whitewash, sanitize, or domesticate God. Yhwh is, as David Carr indicates, "untamable."[3] The God of the Hebrew Bible is beyond codification; God is unsettling. As an unpredictable character, Yʜᴡʜ acts in ways that often fly in the face of what readers may expect of God. Both good and bad, joy and pain, blessing and curse come from God.[4] The Jacob cycle gives ample voice to this perspective. Yʜᴡʜ serves as Jacob's benefactor, championing the patriarch's cause, yet this great care for Jacob does not mitigate the possibility of a violent encounter with Yʜᴡʜ (Gen 32:23–33). How should we reconcile the diverse portraits of God in the Hebrew Bible, or should we? This book proposes a way that does not jettison one image for another by reading divine promise and deception in tandem.

This perspective has potential ramifications for the way one goes about doing Old Testament theology. The Old Testament's way of doing theology is not systematic and attempts to systematize what is unsystematic inherently run the risk of a selective picking and choosing of the portraits of God that one will treat and not treat. An honest theological engagement with Israel's Scriptures must take them into account in toto, recognizing the diverse voices with which the text speaks.[5] An approach of this sort will not produce a unified, consistent, coherent picture of Old Testament theology, but it will at the very least recognize the fullness of the rich theological reflection of ancient Israel's God in all facets of being. The method employed in this study provides a helpful hermeneutic toward this end. Paying attention to the symbiotic relationship between *how* a text means and *what* it means—emphasizing a synthesis of literary and theological concerns—may prove beneficial in advancing the task of Old Testament theology with an appreciation for our postmodern context.

Trustworthy Deception

The single greatest theological issue that arises from this study is undoubtedly how to hold together the Hebrew Bible's descriptions of Yʜᴡʜ as deceptive and Yʜᴡʜ as trustworthy. The Hebrew Bible is adamant at several points that Yʜᴡʜ does not lie. Num 23:19 reads, "God is not a human

---

3. See David M. Carr, "Untamable Text of an Untamable God: Genesis and Rethinking the Character of Scripture," *Int* 54 (2000) 347–62.

4. Walter Brueggemann sees this tension expressed in Exod 34:6–7, his central credo for understanding Old Testament theology. For a canonical appropriation of this credo, see most recently Nathan C. Lane, *The Compassionate, but Punishing God: A Canonical Analysis of Exodus 34:6–7* (Eugene, OR: Pickwick, 2010).

5. Within the last quarter of a century, Old Testament theology has seen a shift from seeking a "center" to the Old Testament (see Walther Eichrodt, *Theology of the Old Testament* [trans. J. A. Baker; 2 vols.; Philadelphia: Westminster, 1961]) to appreciating multiple theologies in the Hebrew Bible. See especially Erhard Gerstenberger, *Theologies in the Old Testament* (trans. John Bowden; Minneapolis: Fortress, 2002) and Walter Brueggemann, "A Shape for Old Testament Theology, I: Structure Legitimation," *CBQ* 47 (1985) 28–46; idem, "A Shape for Old Testament Theology, II: Embrace of Pain," *CBQ* 47 (1985) 395–415.

Chapter 5

being, that he should lie, or a mortal, that he should change his mind," and in 1 Sam 15:29 Samuel says, "the Glory of Israel will not deceive or change his mind, for he is not a mortal that he should change his mind." Compounding the potential difficulty, the Hebrew Bible also attests that Yʜwʜ is a God of truth, as in Ps 31:6, and of faithfulness, as in Deut 32:4. Chisholm has amassed an impressive roster of texts:

> Many passages refer to God's truthfulness in a broad sense. God is true or truthful in the sense that He is a just Judge (e.g., Pss. 89:14; 96:13; Isa. 65:16), a reliable object of worship (in contrast to the pagan idol-gods, e.g., Jer. 10:10), a faithful Defender of His people's interests (e.g., Gen. 24:27; Exod. 34:6; Deut. 32:4; Pss. 30:9; 31:5; 33:4; 40:11; 54:5; 57:10; 61:7; 71:22; 86:15; Isa. 38:18–19), and a reliable source of fixed and beneficial instructions about how to live (e.g., Pss. 19:9; 25:5, 10; 26:3; 43:3; 86:11; 119:142, 151, 160; Dan. 9:13).[6]

How is one to address this very obvious tension? Or should one address it at all? The Hebrew Bible presents not only Yʜwʜ's subversive and sometimes ominous side but also Yʜwʜ's reliability, constancy, justice, and trustworthiness. Claus Westermann rightly acknowledges that "it is the task of a theology of the Old Testament to describe and view together what the Old Testament as a whole, in all its sections, says about God."[7] How then are readers to address these seemingly incompatible witnesses?

Walter Brueggemann offers a helpful insight. He understands divine deception as one example among others of Israel's "countertestimony."[8] For Brueggemann, the Hebrew Bible contains ancient Israel's core testimony, countertestimony, unsolicited testimony, and embodied testimony. Countertestimony is that which inquires of the core testimony, probing and questioning whether it is adequate and where it may at times be deficient or incomplete. Brueggemann describes Israel's countertestimony this way:

> For Israel, everything depends on the adequacy and reliability of its testimony concerning Yahweh. But clearly, there is within Israel an uneasiness about that marvelously positive testimony. A major point I wish to make at the outset is this: Cross-examination, which may be hostile or supportive, is not something done over against the Old Testament by late and outside detractors. It is remarkable that *the process of cross-examination goes on in the Old Testament itself.* . . . The cross-examination is not intended by Israel to obliterate the core testimony. In the disputatious propensity of Israel, rather, core testimony and cross-examination belong to each other and for each other in an ongoing exchange. . . . As a result,

6. Robert B. Chisholm Jr., "Does God Deceive?" *BSac* 155 (1998) 27.

7. Claus Westermann, *What Does the Old Testament Say about God?* (London: SPCK, 1979) 1. Unfortunately, Westermann does not live up to this ideal in every respect in this particular volume.

8. Walter Brueggemann, *Theology of the Old Testament: Testimony, Dispute, Advocacy* (Minneapolis: Fortress, 1997) 360–62.

it is evident that Israel's countertestimony is not an act of unfaith. It is rather a characteristic way in which faith is practiced.[9]

Brueggemann's description of ancient Israel's countertestimony is instructive about the way that one may fruitfully adjudicate the tension between Yнwн's trustworthiness and Yнwн's complicity in deception. It is not an either/or issue. One is not free to choose between the core or countertestimony, upholding the persuasiveness and authority of one to the detriment of the other. Both are a part of the portrait of God and thus demand serious, open, and honest theological attention. Similarly, core and countertestimony while appearing to be in tension with one another (which they no doubt are) are also involved in a relationship of reciprocity. Thus, the core testimony of Yнwн's trustworthiness is challenged by the countertestimony of Yнwн's practice of deceptive activity, but any attempt to make sense of this complex must honor both as authentic, significant voices with regard to the way ancient Israel renders Yнwн. Readers must engage both theologically as a part of the picture of Yнwн.

Some may still take issue with the claim that God deceives, though I have shown that the biblical text clearly articulates God's involvement in deception at several points. My suggestion, in line with Brueggemann, is that, rather than ignoring or dismissing the unpalatable images simply because readers may deem them problematic or in dissonance with their own contemporary mores—or, perhaps more disconcerting, with Israel's core testimony that God is trustworthy and does not lie—we ought to mine them for their potential theological contributions. Is it possible that these texts may reveal something surprisingly encouraging about God, perhaps even something in line with and contributing to Yнwн's trustworthiness? I have argued that divine deception in the biblical text in fact has a highly theological component and that failure to wrestle with the potential theological profundity of these images misses a significant part of both *who* and *how* Yнwн is in relation to ancient Israel. I suggest that one may discern in the Hebrew Bible what I have dubbed a "theology of deception." This theology maintains that Yнwн's participation in deception can be seen as serving a larger theological purpose: deception employed in the interest of Yнwн's *fidelity* to the covenant and the covenant people.

As I see it, there are four possible ways of addressing this tension, of holding this core testimony and countertestimony together. The first position aims to evade the issue as much as possible, either by simply ignoring it entirely or through a variety of hermeneutical strategies. This approach eliminates deception as an interpretive category relating to Yнwн. Eric Seibert's recent volume *Disturbing Divine Behavior* champions this view.[10] Seibert argues deception is but one problematic aspect of Yнwн's character in

---

9. Ibid., 317, 318 (italics his).
10. See chap. 1, pp. 37–39, for a survey of the relevant aspects of Seibert's work.

the Hebrew Bible, but when juxtaposed with a Christocentric hermeneutic to determine the "actual God," it becomes a nonissue.[11] Readers are able to say, "This is not God." I have already argued that Seibert's proposal is inadequate on a variety of fronts, most notably its failure to take seriously the theological witness of these dissident portraits of God. It is not an either/ or witness but a both/and witness. Are texts depicting divine deception not also loaded with theological freight and worthy of at least a hearing? Is it not possible that divine deception communicates something of theological importance? I advance a positive answer on both fronts. While these texts should not be explained away, as Seibert does, they do need to be explained. The task is not to *eliminate the tension* but to give profound theological voice to it, not to render these texts impotent but to let them speak a word about God. Core testimony and countertestimony must both be permitted a voice.

A second proposal swings to the opposite side of the spectrum, interpreting divine deception dualistically. God possesses within Godself both the loving-kindness often attributed to him and also a demonic, shadow side that has a propensity to creep up and cause disarray and trouble. While this approach may appear persuasive at first, based on the evidence presented, it achieves very little in addressing the actual tension. Dualism is not a compelling theological category for God. Dualism actually does not deal with the tension at all but instead separates the two as extremes between which God may vacillate. What emerges is little more than a bipolar deity. God is either entirely good or entirely bad at any given moment, and there is no hope that these two will ever overlap. This sort of black and white thinking serves, unfortunately, as appropriate fodder for individuals who wish to challenge God's existence or God's justice.[12] To reiterate, the matter is not an either/or but a both/and. Core testimony and countertestimony are involved in relationship with one another.

The third way of reconciling divine deception with divine trustworthiness contends that divine deception is at times both applicable and acceptable behavior that may operate as an extension of Yhwh's truthfulness. One may discern two trends within this approach: seeing divine deception as one way that Yhwh punishes sinners or as a necessary component of warfare. I will discuss each in turn.

---

11. Seibert, *Disturbing Divine Behavior*, 170–71, 185–87.

12. Most recently on this topic, see Paul Copan, *Is God a Moral Monster? Making Sense of the Old Testament God* (Grand Rapids, MI: Baker, 2011). Copan is addressing the various arguments put forward by the New Atheists, wrestling with issues such as divine arrogance in requiring worship, the near-sacrifice of Isaac, misogyny, slavery, and ethnic cleansing within ancient Israel. While he does so with varying degrees of success in my view, Copan's rejoinder to the New Atheists provides a sound and current example of the necessity of avoiding dualistic interpretations in relation to God and God's behavior.

Robert Chisholm and J. J. M. Roberts both advocate the position that divine deception is at times appropriate in that it functions punitively. Chisholm holds that divine deception serves as a mode of judgment on sinners; Yhwh uses deception to facilitate and expedite a sinner's downfall.[13] Texts such as Num 23:19 and 1 Sam 15:28–29 that proclaim Yhwh's trustworthiness must be read, argues Chisholm, within their immediate literary context. These affirmations are not making any sort of universal statements about God but relate to the irrevocability of the word of promise or judgment that immediately follows.[14] They must be understood contextually, not universally. Therefore, Yhwh's trustworthiness is not threatened by texts that depict Yhwh as using deception. Divine deception, says Chisholm, is in fact consistent with the divine sense of justice.[15] Chisholm describes his conclusions as follows:

> God's needy and faithful people will always find Him reliable and truthful, but His enemies may discover He is willing and able to use deception and enticement to evil to hasten their journey down the pathway of destruction they have chosen to travel.[16]

J. J. M. Roberts focuses on Yhwh as the source of false prophecy, treating many of the same texts as does Chisholm, and concluding in quite similar fashion that obedience is a prerequisite for experiencing Yhwh's trustworthiness.[17]

Several difficulties emerge with Chisholm's and Roberts's respective readings. Their survey of instances of divine deception are too narrow, as are the applications of statements about God's trustworthiness. Both Chisholm and Roberts limit their analyses of divine deception to the realm of prophecy when, as the survey of texts in my chap. 1 has already indicated, divine deception is a much more diverse phenomenon. They fail to take into account instances of divine trickery that fall outside the bounds of the prophetic corpus and that consequently seem to be functioning in a much different way than this proposal suggests. Similarly, the Hebrew Bible's witness to Yhwh's truthful and trustworthy character is much more broadly attested. Chisholm and Roberts both recognize this point, offering an impressive litany of texts that speak of Yhwh and his words as truthful and trustworthy.[18] It is difficult to see how Chisholm's overall point that affirmations of divine truthfulness must be linked to a proximate word of promise would hold in each of these contexts. The biblical text has a much

---

13. Chisholm, "Does God Deceive?," 12, 28.
14. Ibid., 26.
15. Ibid., 28.
16. Ibid.
17. J. J. M. Roberts, "Does God Lie? Divine Deceit as a Theological Problem in Israelite Prophetic Literature," in *Congress Volume: Jerusalem, 1986* (ed. John A. Emerton; VTSup 40; Leiden: Brill, 1988) 220.
18. Chisholm, "Does God Deceive?" 26–27; Roberts, "Does God Lie?" 211.

more robust view of Yʜᴡʜ's trustworthiness and truthfulness than these arguments acknowledge.

Other difficulties are evident. Unfortunately, sin is not always present in each text surveyed by Chisholm. For instance, though he "assumes" that Israel's sin must underlie Yʜᴡʜ's inciting David to take a census in 2 Sam 24, he ultimately admits that this is little more than an inference based on the fact that Yʜᴡʜ's "anger burns against Israel" when Israel has sinned.[19] He admits that no sin is overt in the text, and to presume sin where none appears achieves little more than stereotyping ancient Israel and God.

Moreover, focus on the punitive nature of divine deception in relation to human obedience creates three attendant problems. First, it runs the risk of slipping into a sort of tempered dualism that still partitions out Yʜᴡʜ as deceptive from Yʜᴡʜ as trustworthy. Second, it creates a sort of in-group ethic of "us versus them" that is incompatible with the understanding of the ancestral promise and its cosmic implications I have argued for in chap. 1.[20] Third, and perhaps most problematic, it assumes the primacy of a retributive or Deuteronomistic theology, in which Yʜᴡʜ's actions are commensurate with human activity when this particular brand of theology is itself but one way that the Hebrew Bible views the matter. One need think only of the righteous Job and the torturous suffering inflicted on him as the result of little more than a divine wager, or the prophetic confessions of Jeremiah, who suffered on account of the divine word and even accused God of deception.

Ken Esau and Richard Patterson hold another view, which is that divine deception is acceptable in that it functions as a vital and necessary aspect of warfare. Whereas Chisholm and Roberts focus almost exclusively on the prophetic corpus, Esau and Patterson limit their inquiry to Exod 3:18 (discussed in chap. 1 above) and to the Deuteronomistic History, respectively. Both conclude that divine deception must be understood in the appropriate context of warfare; Patterson labels this a form of a *ruse de guerre*.[21] According to their views, there are certain situations—war being one of them—in which the ethical code governing Israelite life is suspended. While this approach again provides one particular answer to the "why" of divine deception, it is also limited by its applicability only to the context of battle.[22] Additionally, this position assumes that deception is a negative quality or character trait that is only valid in extreme circumstances, an

---

19. Chisholm, "Does God Deceive?" 21–23.

20. See chap. 1, pp. 40–44.

21. Richard D. Patterson, "The Old Testament Use of an Archetype: The Trickster," *JETS* 42 (1999) 387.

22. Ken Esau ("Divine Deception in the Exodus Event?" *Directions* 35 [2006] 15) notes the limited applicability of his argument in regard to the wider attestation of divine deception in the Hebrew Bible.

assumption that I have called into question in chap. 1.[23] The most vexing issue is that permitting divine deception in the context of war achieves very little in terms of reconciling YHWH's trustworthiness to these instances of deception. Is YHWH only trustworthy insofar as context dictates? Does this view not again create the possibility of dualism, seeing YHWH's shadow side as appropriately emerging during wartime, only to rescind in other circumstances?

While I am sympathetic to these myriad of attempts to grapple with the problem, none has fully honored the theological contribution made by the presence of these texts in the Hebrew Bible. True, many scholars have noted the difficulty in isolating theological content from such difficult texts, but I think one can probe more deeply. If God punishes with deception, this raises the question *why* YHWH is punishing. If YHWH shrewdly practices deception in the context of battle, this again raises the question *why* YHWH is intervening. What is at stake? What do these texts contribute to the portrait of God? I propose that the way to reconcile divine deception and divine trustworthiness is deceptively simple, pun intended. The fourth proposal, and the one I wish to advocate, is that YHWH's practice of deception is deeply and intimately bound to YHWH's covenantal fidelity to ancient Israel.

This covenantal relationship serves as the common denominator in all the examples of divine deception cited in chap. 1. It will prove advantageous to return briefly to these texts and show how the idea of YHWH's covenantal fealty undergirds each. First Kings 22 provides a fitting conclusion to a notoriously bad king; from the Deuteronomist's perspective, Ahab failed to live according to the covenant, as 1 Kgs 16:30 makes plain: "Ahab, son of Omri, did evil in the sight of YHWH more than all who were before him," and 21:25–26 elaborates, "There was no one like Ahab, who sold himself to do what was evil in the sight of YHWH, urged by his wife, Jezebel. He acted most abominably in going after idols, as the Amorites had done."[24] It is well known that comments of this sort are covenantal evaluations, and under Ahab the covenantal relationship—indeed, the entire covenant people—live under threat. Ahab's failure to abide by this relationship, as the Deuteronomist has sketched it for us, results in a deadly

---

23. See chap. 1, pp. 39–40.

24. In 1 Kgs 21:27–29, Ahab repents and YHWH instructs Elijah to tell Ahab that YHWH "will not bring the disaster in his days; but, in his son's days, I will bring the disaster on his house." His son, Ahaziah, is equally wicked and reigns only 2 years. From Ahab to the Assyrian attack, there are 11 kings and more than 130 years. One may address this incongruity by recognizing that for the Deuteronomist even the kings with mixed evaluations ultimately failed. Additionally, one could quite easily see this as yet *another* deceptive word—relayed through the prophet—to Ahab, perhaps explaining what has inspired his confidence in chap. 22, so that he is duped not only into thinking that he will be met with success at Ramoth-gilead but also into thinking that he will avert disaster.

deception perpetrated by Yᴴᴡᴴ, yet a deception that is in the interest of restoring Israel.

Earlier in the Deuteronomistic History, the covenant—particularly the promise of land—appears to be at the fore. All of these texts occur in the context of battle with the express concern of keeping and protecting the promised land. Yᴴᴡᴴ's use of trickery is in line with the fulfillment of the promise of land. These battles for the land stem from Yᴴᴡᴴ's covenantal promise that this particular land will belong to ancient Israel. Just as Abraham is promised a child who will advance the promise—the success of which is directly attributed to Yᴴᴡᴴ at the expense of another, Ishmael—so too Yᴴᴡᴴ promises the land to ancient Israel at the expense of another, the Canaanites, and participates in deception to make certain that the promise attains fulfillment.

Ezekiel 14:9–11 makes the connection between deception and covenant explicit. Yᴴᴡᴴ proclaims that he is responsible for the deception of a hypothetical prophet who will suffer punishment for a particular purpose: "so that the house of Israel may no longer go astray from me, nor defile themselves any more with all their transgressions. Then they shall be my people, and I will be their God" (v. 11). Yᴴᴡᴴ's purposes here are quite transparent. The goal of this divine deception is to restore wayward Israel to God and to covenantal fidelity. The final line of v. 11, "then they shall be my people, and I will be their God," amplifies the covenantal connection by means of the obvious echo stemming from the way that Yᴴᴡᴴ describes the covenant relationship in Exodus. And the Exod 3:16–22 text similarly arises out of Yᴴᴡᴴ's covenantal fidelity, evident in the divine insistence that Moses preface his recounting of Yᴴᴡᴴ's plan to ancient Israel by identifying Yᴴᴡᴴ as "the God of your ancestors, the God of Abraham, of Isaac, and of Jacob," a God who has seen and heard what has been done to Israel in Egypt and, as a result of the promise to the ancestors, acts accordingly.

One may at this point demur, suggesting that the Jeremiah texts do not fit this mold. In Jer 4:10, 15:18, and 20:7, the prophet accuses Yᴴᴡᴴ of deceiving the people into thinking that all is well when destruction is looming, and the prophet's life itself has become torturous from the burden of being unable *not* to utter the prophetic word. Taking Jeremiah's words at face value, I argue, conversely, that in these texts one may discern the other side of the same coin that we have been looking at all along. These deceptions of which Yᴴᴡᴴ stands *accused* are ultimately in accordance with the covenantal relationship. They highlight that the Israelites also may be the object of divine deception when they have transgressed the covenant relationship. Divine deception appears as a necessary component of the relationship that (although it will become soaked with blood) looks forward to a renewed and restored Israel. Put simply, the covenant relationship is at stake in Jeremiah. Jeremiah's failure as a prophet would mean a covenantal failure. The success of the prophet amidst the accusation of deception has covenantal implications as well. In this vein, it is surely not inconsequential that Jer 31:31 speaks of a "new *covenant*" that YHWH will enter into with Israel. Divine deception is the vehicle that will lead to the renewal of Israel and the flourishing of the covenant relationship.

This brief survey has shown that in the Hebrew Bible the idea of divine deception cannot be separated from the notion of YHWH's covenantal fidelity. The divine purpose since the beginning, since Genesis, has been tied up with the protection and perpetuation of the promise and the people of the promise. Divine deception occurs for manifold reasons: to assist in ancient Israel's escape from Egypt, to protect Israel in the wilderness from enemy nations and as they fight for the promised land, to punish a false prophet, to kill a wicked Israelite king, as an accusation from a suffering prophet, or as a method of fulfilling the ancestral promise in the life of the patriarch who will become Israel. Yet in all of these examples, one hears covenantal overtones. What I have challenged is the presupposition that deception is inherently negative, that it is behavior that God does not participate in, and that it cannot inform genuine theological inquiry. In the Hebrew Bible, the divine word of promise functions as the "ultimate good" for YHWH. YHWH's tampering with *our* conventional mores testifies not only to YHWH's steadfastness but also to the divine freedom to transgress any limits for the sake of the covenant relationship.

Taken in toto, the evidence points not to a contradiction between divine deception and divine trustworthiness, between core testimony and countertestimony, but to mutuality. Divine deception is not inimical to but is an *extension of* the trustworthiness of YHWH and the divine word of promise. Perhaps divine deception is a minority witness in the Hebrew Bible, a true countertestimony. But it remains a testimony nonetheless, and therefore a part of the portrayal of God with which one must struggle to make sense. It is not adequate to the biblical witness to say simply that God is good more often than God is bad, or that divine deception is not the primary mode of operation for God, as though one could (or should) quantify the divine characteristics. Both YHWH's trustworthiness and engagement in deception require equal attention. The results of this detailed study on the Jacob cycle, along with an overview of other examples of divine deception show that when God plays the role of trickster it is in the interest of the covenant relationship and people and thus, by extension, a testament to YHWH's covenantal fidelity.

This proposal has the advantage of addressing the issue in a way that is mindful of the theological complexity of the Hebrew Bible and its portrait of YHWH. This proposal does not evade, ignore, or argue the tension away, nor does it accept the polarities of a dualistic interpretation of God. Both traditional and unsettling claims about God are upheld, but neither decimates the other. The core testimony is not allowed to overpower the countertestimony, nor does the countertestimony lose its unsettling aspect.

Moreover, this proposal appreciates the diverse examples and functions of divine deception in the Hebrew Bible and takes them all into consideration.

While this view may sound familiar to Chisholm's discussed above, there are important and noticeable differences. Chisholm identifies God's trustworthiness with a specific and proximate divine word of promise, yet divine deception for him has no relation or bearing on this word of promise. Conversely, I maintain that God is trustworthy to the divine word of promise but that this word of promise is at several places bound up with divine deception. Core testimony and countertestimony operate with very similar concerns. Put most simply, divine deception is but one of a myriad of different ways that the Hebrew Bible, paradoxically, witnesses to Yhwh's unique and unwavering covenantal fealty.

The Hebrew Bible enjoins its readers not to resolve the tensions in God's character in any easy or dismissive way. Value and meaning reside in this tension.[25] Yhwh is a God of tension, or perhaps more accurate to the witness of the Hebrew Bible and the Jacob cycle, a God *in tension*. But this conflicted portrait need not force one to pick and choose between or dismiss what appear to be unpalatable portrayals of God. Instead, they should push readers to probe even more deeply, to read even more closely, and to be receptive to surprising new ways that Yhwh is imagined in the Hebrew Bible. Failure to do so misses the rich theological freight that suffuses disturbing divine behavior, particularly divine deception, and consequently misses the potential foundation for a theology of deception in the Hebrew Bible. The Jacob cycle lays the foundation for this theology and assists in illuminating not only how one may more honestly read divine deception elsewhere in the Hebrew Bible but also how the tension between divine trustworthiness and divine deception is held together and affirmed.

Prospects for Further Study

Although the conversation on divine deception in the Hebrew Bible is still in its infancy with much productive conversation to come, this book also opens avenues for research in additional areas. Here I isolate three that may further discussion on the topic, though they by no means exhaust the possibilities.

Yhwh as Deceiver in the Context of Ancient Near Eastern Gods as Deceivers

In chap. 1, I isolated a number of texts from the ancient Near East that depict various deities as acting deceptively. Given the prevalence of this motif in the milieu of ancient Israel's nascence and development, how

---

25. John W. Rogerson (*Old Testament Theology: Cultural Memory, Communication, and Being Human* [Minneapolis: Fortress, 2010] 50) has recently made a very similar point: "[I]n the Old Testament it is the diversity of voices and their discordances that enable profound insights about the reality to be articulated."

might conceptions outside Israel have influenced and affected Israel's own construction and understanding of Yʜᴡʜ as divine deceiver? Does the image in the Hebrew Bible appear to correspond to or react against images from other ancient Near Eastern peoples? Investigation of how ancient Israel appropriates this tradition may touch on a number of other pertinent topics, including international relations and questions of social identity.

Yʜᴡʜ as Divine Deceiver in Sociohistorical Context

The foregoing chapters have offered an unabashedly literary-theological reading of the entirety of the Jacob cycle, consciously and intentionally bracketing out questions of history. Now, with this interpretive bedrock laid, it would prove worthwhile to situate this reading in a specific historical context, in effect attending to a historical question of another kind: "the communicative purpose of the final Hebrew text."[26] The underlying operative assumption is that literary hermeneutics may inform sociological considerations and realities on the ground.

The contributions of Chris Heard and Mark Brett are formative in this regard for their attention to the predominance of deception in Genesis and its socioliterary implications.[27] Comparing the contributions of Brett and Heard, however, produces fascinating findings. The two volumes were published within one year of each other. Both place Genesis in the Persian period and put the final message of this book in conversation with the policies of Ezra and Nehemiah, both employ a literary hermeneutic toward sociological ends, and both interpret nearly the same texts and adduce much of the same scholarly literature. Their conclusions, however, could not be more different. For Brett, Genesis becomes a type of resistance literature, challenging the exclusivity latent in the endogamy advocated by Ezra and Nehemiah—a challenge that Brett sees as deriving from the confluence of deception and marriage in the Jacob cycle.[28] However, for Heard, Genesis supports this exclusivity by affirming endogamy as the only method for sustaining identity. The same literature, historical context, evidence, and time of writing produce polar opposite conclusions! This notice may testify to the inconclusiveness of the Genesis text on the point of endogamy/exogamy.

The literary phenomenon of a divine trickster raises a litany of new questions. In what historical context does this image fit best? When would it have proven most meaningful? What can one say about the social reality and religious ethos of ancient Israel in light of this reading? And how might

---

26. Mark G. Brett, *Genesis: Procreation and the Politics of Identity* (Old Testament Readings; London: Routledge, 2000) 11.

27. See R. Christopher Heard, *Dynamics of Diselection: Ambiguity in Genesis 12–36 and Ethnic Boundaries in Post-exilic Judah* (Semeia Studies; Atlanta: Society of Biblical Literature, 2001) 171–84; Brett, *Genesis*, 137–46.

28. Ibid., 92, 93, 107–8.

the notion of divine deception in the Jacob cycle inculcate hope in the period during which the cycle and the book of Genesis reach their final form?

Divine Deception in Relation to the Other Ancestral Stories of Genesis

Having examined divine deception in the Jacob cycle and its tie to the
ancestral promise, one may rightly ask whether this reading is endemic
only to the Jacob cycle. Do similar examples of deception linked to the
promise occur in the ancestral stories of Abraham, Isaac, and Joseph, and if
so, how do they compare with the theology of deception in the Jacob cycle?
As a matter of suggestion, the wife-sister narratives (Gen 12, 20, 26) provide
a sound place to begin. In Gen 12:14–20 and especially 20:1–18, Abraham
deceives a foreign ruler into thinking that Sarah is his sister, which leads
to her being taken from him. On both occasions, Yhwh quickly intervenes;
there can be no child of the promise without the mother of the promise. As
a result, Abraham is sent on his way and obtains from (is rewarded by?) the
foreign ruler wealth and property. How might a literary reading of the multiple occurrences of this type scene contribute to a theology of deception
in the Abraham or Isaac narratives? It may also be beneficial to give attention to Gen 50:20, a dying Joseph's retrospective comment on providence
governing his entire life and resulting in his and his family's settling in
Egypt. One should remain mindful that Jacob arrives in Egypt as a result of
his brothers' deception (37:29–35) and achieves a place of prominence in
the Egyptian administration as a result of the deception of Potiphar's wife
(39:1–23). Throughout the Joseph narrative, the text continually affirms
that Yhwh is in control of history and the experiences of this chosen family
(39:2, 3, 5, 21, 23; 41:16, 25, 28, 32; 42:28; 43:23; 45:5, 7, 8, 9; 48:9, 11, 15;
50:20, 24). What does a theology of deception in the Joseph narratives look
like, and how might it compare with a theology of deception in the Abraham or Jacob cycle? Is Genesis perhaps united by a theology of deception?

Concluding Thoughts

Yhwh functions throughout the Jacob cycle as a trickster par excellence.
Through participation in and with Jacob's many deceptions, an under-
appreciated theological portrait of God emerges, one in which Yhwh's
cunning matches and at times exceeds that of the patriarch. This divine
unscrupulousness, while not entirely benign, is the mechanism by which
Yhwh tenaciously works toward the divine purpose. By means of deception,
Yhwh makes advances toward the "great nation" that will become Israel,
toward blessing for the entire cosmos through Israel, and toward a return
to the promised land. In the Jacob cycle, therefore, one observes not an
aberrant, devious God but a divine trickster who will go to any lengths for
the sake of the ancestral promise. In the Jacob cycle, one may discern a true
theology of deception.

Bibliography

Ackerman, Susan. "The Deception of Isaac, Jacob's Dream at Bethel, and Incubation on an Animal Skin." Pages 92–120 in *Priesthood and Cult in Ancient Israel*. Edited by Gary A. Anderson and Saul M. Olyan. Journal for the Study of the Old Testament Supplement 125. Sheffield: Sheffield Academic Press, 1991.

Agyenta, Alfred. "When Reconciliation Means More than the 'Re-Membering' of Former Enemies: The Problem of the Conclusion to the Jacob-Esau Story from a Narrative Perspective (Gen 33, 1–17)." *Ephemerides theologicae Lovanienses* 83 (2007) 123–34.

Albright, W. F. "The Names 'Israel' and 'Judah' with an Excursus on the Etymology of Tôdâh and Tôrâh." *Journal of Biblical Literature* 46 (1927) 151–85.

Alter, Robert. *The Art of Biblical Narrative*. New York: Basic Books, 1981.

———. *Genesis: Translation and Commentary*. New York: Norton, 1996.

Andersen, Francis I. "Note on Gen 30:8." *Journal of Biblical Literature* 88 (1969) 200.

Anderson, John E. "Jacob, Laban, and a Divine Trickster? The Covenantal Framework of God's Deception in the Theology of the Jacob Cycle." *Perspectives in Religious Studies* 36 (2009) 3–23.

———. "Review of Eric A. Seibert, *Disturbing Divine Behavior*." *Review of Biblical Literature* (2011). http://www.bookreviews.org.

Arnold, Bill T. *Genesis*. New Cambridge Bible Commentary. Cambridge: Cambridge University Press, 2008.

Backon, Joshua. "Jacob and the Spotted Sheep: The Role of Prenatal Nutrition on Epigenetics of Fur Color." *Jewish Bible Quarterly* 36 (2008) 263–65.

Barr, James. "Is God a Liar? (Genesis 2–3)—and Related Matters." *Journal of Theological Studies* 57 (2006) 1–22.

Barthes, Roland. "Wrestling with the Angel: Textual Analysis of Genesis 32:23–33." Pages 246–60 in *The Semiotic Challenge*. Edited by Roland Barthes. Translated by Richard Howard. Oxford: Blackwell, 1988.

Bar-Efrat, Shimon. *Narrative Art in the Bible*. Journal for the Study of the Old Testament Supplement 70. Sheffield: Almond, 1989.

Bauer, Johannes B. "Jakobs Kampf mit dem Dämon (Gen 32, 23–33)." Pages 17–22 in *Die Väter Israels: Beiträge zur Theologie der Patriarchenüberlieferungen im Alten Testament*. Edited by A. R. Müller and M. Görg. Stuttgart: Katholisches Bibelwerk, 1989.

Berlin, Adele. *Poetics and the Interpretation of Biblical Narrative*. Bible and Literature Series 9. Sheffield: Almond, 1993. Reprinted Winona Lake, IN: Eisenbrauns, 1994.

Blum, Erhard. *Die Komposition der Vätergeschichte*. Wissenschaftliche Monographien zum Alten und Neuen Testament 57. Neukirchen-Vluyn: Neukirchener Verlag, 1984.

————. *Studien zur Komposition des Pentateuch*. Beihefte zur Zeitschrift für die alttestamentliche Wissenschaft 189. Berlin: de Gruyter, 1990.

————. "Genesis 33,12–20: Die Wege Trennen Sich." Pages 227–38 in *Jacob: Commentaire à plusieurs voix de Gen 25–36: Melanges offerts à Albert de Pury*. Monde de la Bible 44. Edited by J. D. Macchi and T. Römer. Geneva: Labor et Fides, 2001.

Böhl F. M. T. "Volksetymologie en Woordspeling in de Genesis-Verhalen." *Mededeelingen der Koninklijke Akademie van Wetenschappen*. Afdeeling Letterkunde Deel 59, Serie A/3 (1925) 49–79.

Bowen, Nancy R. *The Role of Yahweh as Deceiver in True and False Prophecy*. Ph.D. Dissertation. Princeton Theological Seminary, 1994.

Brett, Mark. *Genesis: Procreation and the Politics of Identity*. Old Testament Readings. London: Routledge, 2000.

Briggs, Richard S. *The Virtuous Reader: Old Testament Narrative and Interpretive Virtue*. Studies in Theological Interpretation. Grand Rapids, MI: Baker Academic, 2010.

Brinton, Daniel. *The Myths of the New World*. Philadelphia: McKay, 1868.

Brodie, Louis T. "Jacob's Travail (Jer. 30.1–13) and Jacob's Struggle (Gen 32.22–32): A Test Case for Measuring the Influence of the Book of Jeremiah on the Present Text of Genesis." *Journal for the Study of the Old Testament* 19 (1981) 31–60.

Brown, Norman O. *Hermes the Thief: The Evolution of a Myth*. Madison: University of Wisconsin Press, 1947.

Brueggemann, Walter. *Cadences of Home: Preaching among Exiles*. Louisville: Westminster John Knox, 1997.

————. *Genesis*. Interpretation. Atlanta: John Knox, 1982.

————. "Of the Same Flesh and Bone (Gn 2,23a)." *Catholic Biblical Quarterly* 32 (1970) 532–42.

————. "A Shape for Old Testament Theology, I: Structure Legitimation." *Catholic Biblical Quarterly* 47 (1985) 28–46.

————. "A Shape for Old Testament Theology, II: Embrace of Pain." *Catholic Biblical Quarterly* 47 (1985) 395–415.

————. *Theology of the Old Testament: Testimony, Dispute, Advocacy*. Minneapolis: Fortress, 1997.

————. *An Unsettling God: The Heart of the Hebrew Bible*. Minneapolis: Fortress, 2009.

Buccellati, Giorgia. "Adapa, Genesis, and the Notion of Faith." *Ugarit Forschungen* 5 (1973) 61–70.

Burrows, Reynold Z. "Deception as a Comic Device in the Odyssey." *Classical World* 59 (1965) 33–36.

Carr, David M. *Reading the Fractures of Genesis: Historical and Literary Approaches*. Louisville: Westminster John Knox, 1996.

————. "Untamable Text of an Untamable God: Genesis and Rethinking the Character of Scripture." *Interpretation* 54 (2000) 347–62.

Childs, Brevard S. *Old Testament Theology in a Canonical Context*. Philadelphia: Fortress, 1985.

Chisholm, Robert B. "Does God Deceive?" *Bibliotheca Sacra* 155 (1998) 11–28.

Clark, W. Malcolm. "A Legal Background to the Yahwist's Use of 'Good and Evil' in Genesis 2–3." *Journal of Biblical Literature* 88 (1969) 266–78.

Clifford, Richard J. "Genesis 25:19–34." *Interpretation* 45 (1991) 397–401.

———. "Genesis 38: Its Contribution to the Jacob Story." *Catholic Biblical Quarterly* 66 (2004) 519–32.

Clines, David J. A. *The Theme of the Pentateuch*. 2nd ed. Journal for the Study of the Old Testament Supplement 10. Sheffield: Sheffield Academic Press, 1997.

Coats, George W. *Genesis, with an Introduction to Narrative Literature*. Forms of the Old Testament Literature. Grand Rapids, MI: Eerdmans, 1983.

———. "Strife without Reconciliation: A Narrative Theme in the Jacob Traditions." Pages 82–106 in *Werden und Wirken des Alten Testament: Festschrift für Claus Westermann zum 70. Geburtstag*. Edited by Rainer Albertz. Göttingen: Vandenhoeck & Ruprecht, 1980.

Cohen, Jeffrey M. "The Jacob-Esau Reunion." *Jewish Bible Quarterly* 21 (1993) 159–63.

———. "Struggling with Angels and Men." *Jewish Bible Quarterly* 31 (2003) 126–28.

Cohn, R. L. "Narrative Structure and Canonical Perspective in Genesis." *Journal for the Study of the Old Testament* 25 (1983) 3–16.

Collins, John J. "Modern Theology." Pages 196–214 in *Reading Genesis: Ten Methods*. Edited by Ronald Hendel. Cambridge: Cambridge University Press, 2010.

Coote, Robert. "The Meaning of the Name Israel." *Harvard Theological Review* 65 (1972) 137–42.

Copan, Paul. *Is God a Moral Monster? Making Sense of the Old Testament God*. Grand Rapids, MI: Baker, 2011.

Crenshaw, James L. *Defending God: Biblical Responses to the Problem of Evil*. Oxford: Oxford University Press, 2005.

———. *A Whirlpool of Torment: Israelite Traditions of God as an Oppressive Presence*. Overtures to Biblical Theology. Philadelphia: Fortress, 1984.

Crüsemann, Frank. [Translated by Carl S. Ehrlich.] "Dominion, Guilt, and Reconciliation: The Contribution of the Jacob Narrative in Genesis to Political Ethics." *Semeia* 66 (1994) 67–77.

———. "Die Gotteskämpferin: Genesis 30,8." Pages 41–45 in *Für Gerechtigkeit straiten: Theologie im Alltag einer bedrohten Welt*. Edited by Dorothee Sölle. Gütersloh: Chr. Kaiser, 1994.

Curtis, Edward M. "Structure, Style, and Content as a Key to Interpreting Jacob's Encounter at Peniel." *Journal of the Evangelical Theological Society* 30 (1987) 129–37.

Dafni, Evangelia G. "RWH SQR und falsche Prophetie in I Reg 22." *Zeitschrift für die alttestamentliche Wissenschaft* 112 (2000) 365–85.

Daube, David, and Reuven Yaron. "Jacob's Reception by Laban." *Journal of Semitic Studies* 1 (1956) 60–62.

Davies, Eryl W. *The Immoral Bible: Approaches to Biblical Ethics*. London: T. & T. Clark, 2010.

Davis, Ellen F. "Job and Jacob: The Integrity of Faith." Pages 203–24 in *Reading between Texts: Intertextuality and the Hebrew Bible*. Edited by Danna Nolan Fewell. Louisville: Westminster John Knox, 1992.

Diamond, J. A. "The Deception of Jacob: A New Perspective on an Ancient Solution to the Problem." *Vetus Testamentum* 34 (1984) 211–13.

Dickson, Keith M. "Enki and Ninhursag: The Trickster in Paradise." *Journal of Near Eastern Studies* 66 (2007) 1–32.

Dillmann, August. *Genesis Critically and Exegetically Expounded*. Volume 2. Edinburgh: T. & T. Clark, 1897.

Dolzani, Michael. "The Ashes of the Stars: Nothrop Frye and the Trickster-God." *Semeia* 89 (2002) 59–73.

Doty, William G. "A Lifetime of Trouble-Making: Hermes as Trickster." Pages 46–65 in *Mythical Trickster Figures: Contours, Contexts, and Criticisms*. Edited by William J. Hynes and William G. Doty. Tuscaloosa: University of Alabama Press, 1993.

Driver, S. R. *The Book of Genesis*. Westminster Commentaries. London: Methuen, 1915.

Edelman, Diana. *You Shall Not Abhor an Edomite for He Is Your Brother: Edom and Seir in History and Tradition*. Archaeology and Biblical Studies 3. Atlanta: Scholars Press, 1995.

Eichrodt, Walther. *Theology of the Old Testament*. 2 Volumes. Translated by J. A. Baker. Philadelphia: Westminster, 1961.

Eising, Hermann. *Formgeschichtliche Untersuchung zur Jakobserzählung der Genesis*. Emsdetten, 1940.

Elliger, Karl. "Der Jakobskampf au Jabbok: Gen 32:33ff. als hermeneutisches Problem." *Zeitschrift für Theologie und Kirche* 48 (1951) 1–31.

Esau, Ken. "Divine Deception in the Exodus Event?" *Directions* 35 (2006) 4–17.

Evans, C. D. "The Patriarch Jacob: An Innocent Man." *Bible Review* 2 (1986) 32–37.

Exum, J. Cheryl, and J. William Whedbee. "Isaac, Samson, and Saul: Reflections on the Comic and Tragic Visions." Pages 272–308 in *Beyond Form Criticism: Essays in Old Testament Literary Criticism*. Edited by Paul R. House. Sources for Biblical and Theological Study 2. Winona Lake, IN: Eisenbrauns, 1992.

Finkelstein, J. J. "An Old Babylonian Herding Contract and Genesis 31:38f." *Journal of the American Oriental Society* 88 (1968) 30–36.

Fishbane, Michael A. "Composition and Structure in the Jacob Cycle (Gen. 25:19–35:22)." *Journal of Jewish Studies* 26 (1975) 15–38.

Fletcher, Judith. "A Trickster's Oaths in the 'Homeric Hymn to Hermes.'" *American Journal of Philology* 129 (2008) 19–46.

Floß, Johannes P. "Wer schlägt wen: Testanalytische Interpretation von Gen 32:23–22." *Biblische Notizen* 20 (1983) 92–132.

———. "Wer schlägt wen: Testanalytische Interpretation von Gen 32:23–22." *Biblische Notizen* 21 (1983) 66–100.

Fokkelman, J. P. *Narrative Art in Genesis: Specimens of Stylistic and Structural Analysis*. Eugene, OR: Wipf & Stock, 1991.

Fontaine, Carole. "The Deceptive Goddess in Ancient Near Eastern Myth: Inanna and Inaraš." *Semeia* 42 (1988) 84–102.

Foster, Benjamin R. *Before the Muses: An Anthology of Akkadian Literature*. 3rd ed. Bethesda: CDL, 2006.

Freedman, Amelia Devin. *God as an Absent Character in Biblical Hebrew Narrative: A Literary-Theoretical Study*. Studies in Biblical Literature 82. New York: Peter Lang, 2005.

Fretheim, Terence E. *The Pentateuch*. Interpreting Biblical Texts. Nashville, TN: Abingdon, 1996.

————. "The Jacob Traditions: Theology and Hermeneutic." *Interpretation* 26 (1972) 419–36.

————. "Which Blessing Does Isaac Give Jacob?" Pages 279–91 in *Jews, Christians, and the Theology of the Hebrew Scriptures*. Edited by Joel S. Kaminsky and Alice Ogden Bellis. Society of Biblical Literature Symposium Series. Atlanta: Society of Biblical Literature, 2000.

Friedman, Richard E. *The Disappearance of God: A Divine Mystery*. Boston: Little, Brown, 1995.

Frolov, Serge. "The Other Side of the Jabbok: Genesis 32 as a Fiasco of Patriarchy." *Journal for the Study of the Old Testament* 91 (2000) 41–59.

Fuchs, Esther. "For I Have the Way of Women: Deception, Gender, and Ideology in Biblical Narrative." *Semeia* 42 (1988) 68–82.

————. "Structure, Ideology and Politics in the Biblical Betrothal Type-Scene." Pages 273–81 in *A Feminist Companion to Genesis*. Edited by Athalya Brenner. Sheffield: Sheffield Academic Press, 1993.

Gammie, John G. "Theological Interpretation by Way of Literary and Traditional Analysis: Genesis 25–36." Pages 117–34 in *Encounter with the Text*. Edited by M. J. Buss. Philadelphia: Fortress, 1979.

Geller, Stephen A. "The Struggle at the Jabbok: The Uses of Enigma in a Biblical Narrative." *Journal of the Ancient Near Eastern Society* 14 (1982) 37–60.

Geoghegan, Jeffrey C. "Jacob's Bargain with God (Genesis 28:20–22) and Its Implications for the Documentary Hypothesis." Pages 23–36 in *Milk and Honey: Essays on Ancient Israel and the Bible in Appreciation of the Judaic Studies Program at the University of California, San Diego*. Edited by Sarah Malena and David Miano. Winona Lake, IN: Eisenbrauns, 2007.

Gerstenberger, Erhard. *Theologies in the Old Testament*. Translated by John Bowden. Minneapolis: Fortress, 2002.

Gese, Hartmut. "Jakob, der Betrüger." Pages 33–43 in *Meilenstein: Festgabe für Herbert Donner zum 16. Februar 1995*. Edited by M. Weippert and S. Timm. Wiesbaden: Harrassowitz, 1995.

Gevirtz, Stanley. "Of Patriarchs and Puns: Joseph at the Fountain, Jacob at the Ford." *Hebrew Union College Annual* 46 (1975) 33–54.

Gillmayr-Bucher, Susanne. "Begegnungen am Brunnen." *Biblische Notizen* 75 (1994) 48–66.

————. "Genesis 24: Ein Mosaik aus Texten." Pages 521–31 in *Studies in the Book of Genesis: Literature, Redaction and History*. Edited by A. Wénin. Leuven: Leuven University Press, 2001.

Golka, Friedmann. "Bechorah und Berachah: Erstgeburtsrecht und Segen." Pages 133–44 in *Recht und Ethos im Alten Testament—Gestalt und Wirkung: Festschrift für Horst Seebass zum 65. Geburtstag*. Edited by Stefan Beyerle,

Günter Mayer, and Hans Strauss. Neukirchen-Vluyn: Neukirchener Verlag, 1999.

Gonzales, Robert R., Jr. *Where Sin Abounds: The Spread of Sin and the Curse in Genesis with Special Focus on the Patriarchal Narratives.* Eugene, OR: Wipf & Stock, 2009.

Good, E. M. "Deception and Women: A Response." *Semeia* 42 (1988) 117–32.

Gordon, Robert P. "The Ethics of Eden: Truth-Telling in Genesis 2–3. Pages 11–33 in *Ethical and Unethical in the Old Testament: God and Humans in Dialogue.* Edited by K. J. Dell. Library of Hebrew Bible/Old Testament Studies 528. New York: T. & T. Clark, 2010.

Grottanelli, Cristiano. "Tricksters, Scapegoats, Champions, Saviors." *History of Religion* 23 (1983) 117–39.

Grüneberg, Keith N. *Abraham, Blessing, and the Nations: A Philological and Exegetical Study of Genesis 12:1–3 in Its Narrative Context.* Beihefte zur Zeitschrift für die alttestamentliche Wissenschaft 332. Berlin: de Gruyter, 2003.

Gunkel, Hermann. *Genesis.* Translated by Mark E. Biddle. Mercer Library of Biblical Studies. Macon, GA: Mercer University Press, 1997.

Hallo, William W., ed. *The Context of Scripture,* vol. 1: *Canonical Compositions from the Biblical World.* Leiden: Brill, 1997.

Hamilton, Victor P. *The Book of Genesis: Chapters 18–50.* New International Commentary on the Old Testament. Grand Rapids, MI: Eerdmans, 1995.

Hamori, Esther J. "The Spirit of Falsehood." *Catholic Biblical Quarterly* 72 (2010) 15–30.

Harris, R. L., and G. L. Archer, Jr., eds. *Theological Wordbook of the Old Testament.* 2 Volumes. Chicago: Moody, 1980.

Hauge, Martin Ravndal. "The Struggles of the Blessed in Estrangement I." *Studia Theologica* 29 (1975) 1–30.

Heard, R. Christopher. *Dynamics of Diselection: Ambiguity in Genesis 12–36 and Ethnic Boundaries in Post-exilic Judah.* Semeia Studies. Atlanta: Society of Biblical Literature, 2001.

Hendel, Ron. *The Epic of the Patriarch: The Jacob Cycle and the Narrative Traditions of Canaan and Israel.* Harvard Semitic Monograph 42. Atlanta: Scholars Press, 1987.

Holladay, William L. *Jeremiah 1: A Commentary on the Book of the Prophet Jeremiah, Chapters 1–25.* Hermeneia. Philadelphia: Fortress, 1986.

Holmgren, Fredrick Carlson. "Holding Your Own against God: Genesis 32:22–32 (in the Context of Genesis 31–33)." *Interpretation* 44 (1990) 5–17.

Honeyman, A. M. "*Merismus* in Biblical Hebrew." *Journal of Biblical Literature* 71 (1952) 11–18.

Houtman, Cornelis. "Jacob at Mahanaim: Some Remarks on Genesis xxxii 2–3." *Vetus Testamentum* 28 (1978) 37–44.

Humphreys, W. Lee. *The Character of God in the Book of Genesis: A Narrative Appraisal.* Louisville: Westminster John Knox, 2001.

Hynes, William J., and William G. Doty. "Introducing the Fascinating and Perplexing Trickster Figure." Pages 1–12 in *Mythical Trickster Figures: Contours, Contexts, and Criticisms.* Edited by William J. Hynes and William G. Doty. Tuscaloosa: University of Alabama Press, 1993.

————, eds. *Mythical Trickster Figures: Contours, Contexts, and Criticisms*. Tuscaloosa: University of Alabama Press, 1993.

Jacob, Benno. *The First Book of the Bible: Genesis*. Translated by Ernest I. Jacob and Walter Jacob. New York: Ktav, 1974.

Jacobs, Mignon R. *Gender, Power, and Persuasion: The Genesis Narratives and Contemporary Portraits*. Grand Rapids, MI: Baker Academic, 2007.

Jacobsen, Thorkild. *Treasures of Darkness: A History of Mesopotamian Religion*. New Haven, CT: Yale University Press, 1976.

Jeansonne, Sharon Pace. "Genesis 25:23: The Use of Poetry in the Rebekah Narratives." Pages 145–52 in *The Psalms and Other Studies on the Old Testament: Presented to Joseph I. Hunt*. Edited by Jack C. Knight and Lawrence A. Sinclair. Nashotah, WI: Nashotah House Seminary, 1990.

————. *The Women of Genesis: From Sarah to Potiphar's Wife*. Minneapolis: Fortress, 1990.

Kaiser, Otto. "Deus Absconditus and Deus Revelatus: Three Difficult Narratives in the Pentateuch." Pages 73–88 in *Shall Not the Judge of All the Earth Do What Is Right? Studies on the Nature of God in Tribute to James L. Crenshaw*. Edited by David Penchansky and Paul L. Redditt. Winona Lake, IN: Eisenbrauns, 2000.

Kaminski, Carol M. *From Noah to Israel: Realization of the Primaeval Blessing after the Flood*. Journal for the Study of the Old Testament Supplement 413. London: T. & T. Clark, 2004.

Kaminsky, Joel S. "Humor and the Theology of Hope: Isaac as a Humorous Figure." *Interpretation* 54 (2000) 363–75.

————. "Reclaiming a Theology of Election: Favoritism and the Joseph Story." *Perspectives in Religious Studies* 31 (2004) 135–52.

————. *Yet I Loved Jacob: Reclaiming the Biblical Concept of Election*. Nashville, TN: Abingdon, 2007.

Kass, Leon. *The Beginning of Wisdom: Reading Genesis*. New York: Free Press, 2003.

Kautzsch, E., ed. *Gesenius' Hebrew Grammar*. Translated by A. E. Cowley. 2nd ed. Oxford: Clarendon, 1910.

Knohl, Israel. "Does God Deceive? An Examination of the Dark Side of Isaiah's Prophecy." Pages 275–91 in *Mishneh Todah: Studies in Deuteronomy and Its Cultural Environment in Honor of Jeffrey H. Tigay*. Edited by N. S. Fox, D. A. Glatt-Gilad, and M. J. Williams. Winona Lake, IN: Eisenbrauns, 2009.

Kodell, Jerome. "Jacob Wrestles with Esau (Gen 32:23–32)." *Biblical Theology Bulletin* 10 (1980) 65–70.

Koehler, L., W. Baumgartner, and J. J. Stamm. *The Hebrew and Aramaic Lexicon of the Old Testament*. Translated and edited under the supervision of M. E. J. Richardson. 4 vols. Leiden: Brill, 1994–99.

Koepping, Klaus Peter. "Absurdity and Hidden Truth: Cunning Intelligence and Grotesque Body Images as Manifestations of the Trickster." *History of Religions* 24 (1985) 191–214.

Korte, Anne-Marie. "Significance Obscured: Rachel's Theft of the Teraphim: Divinity and Corporeality in Gen 31." Pages 157–82 in *Begin with the Body: Corporeality, Religion and Gender*. Edited by J. Bekkenkamp and M. de Haardt. Leuven: Peeters, 1998.

Kraft, R. A. "A Note on the Oracle of Rebecca (Gen xxv. 23)." *The Journal of Theological Studies* 13 (1962) 318–20.

Kristensen, William Brede. "De goddelijke bedrieger." Pages 63–88 in *Mededeelingen der Koninklijke Akademie van Wetenschappen.* Afdeeling Letterkunde 66, Serie B/3. Amsterdam: Müller, 1928.

Kugel, James L. *The Ladder of Jacob: Ancient Interpretations of the Biblical Story of Jacob and His Children.* Princeton: Princeton University Press, 2006.

Lane, Nathan C. *The Compassionate, but Punishing God.* Eugene, OR: Pickwick, 2010.

Lesser, Harry. "'It's Difficult to Understand': Dealing with Morally Difficult Passages in the Hebrew Bible." Pages 292–302 in *Jewish Ways of Reading the Bible.* Edited by George J. Brooke. Journal of Semitic Studies Supplement 11. Oxford: Oxford University Press, 2000.

Levenson, Jon D. *The Death and Resurrection of the Beloved Son: The Transformation of Child Sacrifice in Judaism and Christianity.* New Haven, CT: Yale University Press, 1993.

Lipton, Diana. *Revisions of the Night: Politics and Promise in the Patriarchal Dreams of Genesis.* Journal for the Study of the Old Testament Supplement 288. Sheffield: Sheffield Academic Press, 1999.

Lohr, Joel N. *Chosen and Unchosen: Conceptions of Election in the Pentateuch and Jewish-Christian Interpretation.* Siphrut: Literature and Theology of the Hebrew Scriptures 2. Winona Lake, IN: Eisenbrauns, 2009.

Longmann, Tremper, III. *How to Read Genesis.* Downers Grove, IL: InterVarsity Press Academic, 2005.

Mabee, Charles. "Jacob and Laban: The Structure of Judicial Proceedings (Genesis XXXI 25–42)." *Vetus Testamentum* 30 (1980) 192–207.

Mandolfo, Carleen. "'You Meant Evil against Me': Dialogic Truth and the Character of Jacob in Joseph's Story." *Journal for the Study of the Old Testament* 28 (2004) 449–65.

Marböck, Johann. "Heilige Orte im Jakobszyklus: Einige Beobachtungen und Aspekte." Pages 211–24 in *Die Väter Israels: Beiträge zur Theologie der Patriarchenüberlieferungen im Alten Testament.* Edited by A. R. Müller and M. Görg. Stuttgart: Katholisches Bibelwerk, 1989.

Marcus, David. "Traditional Jewish Responses to the Question of Deceit in Genesis 27." Pages 293–305 in *Jews, Christians, and the Theology of the Hebrew Scriptures.* Edited by Joel S. Kaminsky and Alice Ogden Bellis. Society of Biblical Literature Symposium Series. Atlanta: Society of Biblical Literature, 2000.

Martens, Elmer A. *God's Design: A Focus on Old Testament Theology.* Grand Rapids, MI: Baker, 1981.

Mathews, Kenneth A. *Genesis 11:27–50:26.* New American Commentary 1B. Nashville, TN: Broadman & Holman, 2005.

Matthews, Victor H., and Frances Mims. "Jacob the Trickster and Heir of the Covenant: A Literary Interpretation." *Perspectives in Religious Studies* 12 (1985) 185–95.

McKay, Heather A. "Jacob Makes It across the Jabbok: An Attempt to Solve the Success/Failure Ambivalence in Israel's Self-Consciousness." *Journal for the Study of the Old Testament* 38 (1987) 3–13.

McKenzie, Jacob L. "Jacob at Peniel: Gn 32, 24–32." *Catholic Biblical Quarterly* 25 (1963) 71–76.

McKenzie, Steven L. "'You Have Prevailed': The Function of Jacob's Encounter at Peniel in the Jacob Cycle." *Restoration Quarterly* 23 (1980) 225–31.

Meurer, Thomas. "Die Gebarwettstreit zwischen Lea und Rahel: Der Erzäh-laufbau von Gen 29:31–30:24 als testfall der Erzahlerischen geschlossen-heit einer Zusammenhanglos wirkenden einheit." *Biblische Notizen* 107–8 (2001) 93–108.

Miller, Patrick D., Jr. "Syntax and Theology in Genesis XII 3a." *Vetus Testamentum* 34 (1984) 472–76.

Miscall, Peter D. "The Jacob and Joseph Stories as Analogies." *Journal for the Study of the Old Testament* 6 (1978) 28–40.

Moberly, R. W. L. "Did the Interpreters Get It Right? Genesis 2–3 Reconsidered." *Journal of Theological Studies* 59 (2008) 22–40.

———. "Did the Serpent Get It Right?" *Journal of Theological Studies* 39 (1988) 1–27.

———. "Does God Lie to His Prophets? The Story of Micaiah ben Imlah as a Test Case." *Harvard Theological Review* 96 (2003) 1–23.

———. *Genesis 12–50*. Old Testament Guides. Sheffield: JSOT Press, 1992.

———. *The Theology of the Book of Genesis*. Old Testament Theology. Cambridge: Cambridge University Press, 2009.

Molen, Steven. "The Identity of Jacob's Opponent: Wrestling with Ambiguity in Genesis 32:22–32." *Dialogue* 26 (1993) 187–200.

Myers, Jacob M. "The Way of the Fathers." *Interpretation* 29 (1975) 121–40.

Nicholas, Dean Andrew. *The Trickster Revisited: Deception as a Motif in the Pentateuch*. Studies in Biblical Literature 117. New York: Peter Lang, 2009.

Nicol, George. "Story-Patterning in Genesis." Pages 215–33 in *Text as Pretext: Essays in Honour of Robert Davidson*. Edited by Robert P. Carroll. Sheffield: JSOT Press, 1992.

Niditch, Susan. *A Prelude to Biblical Folklore: Underdogs and Tricksters*. Urbana: University of Illinois Press, 1987.

Noegel, Scott B. "Drinking Feasts and Deceptive Feats: Jacob and Laban's Double Talk." Pages 163–80 in *Puns and Pundits: Word Play in the Hebrew Bible and Ancient Near Eastern Literature*. Edited by Scott B. Noegel. Bethesda, MD: CDL, 2000.

———. "Sex, Sticks, and the Trickster in Gen. 30:31–43: A New Look at an Old Crux." *Journal of Ancient Near Eastern Society* 25 (1997) 7–17.

Noth, Martin. *A History of Pentateuchal Traditions*. Translated by B. W. Anderson. Englewood Cliffs, NJ: Prentice-Hall, 1972.

———. *Die israelitischen Personennamen im Rahmen der gemeinsemitischen Namengebung*. Hildesheim: Olms, 1966.

Paganini, Simone. "Wir haben Wasser gefunden: Beobachtungen zur Erzähla-nalyse von Gen 25,19–26,36." *Zeitschrift für die alttestamentliche Wissenschaft* 117 (2005) 21–35.

Pappas, Harry S. "Deception as Patriarchal Self-Defense in a Foreign Land: A Form Critical Study of the Wife-Sister Stories in Genesis." *The Greek Orthodox Theological Review* 29 (1984) 35–50.

Patterson, Richard D. "The Old Testament Use of an Archetype: The Trickster." *Journal of the Evangelical Theological Society* 42 (1999) 385–94.

Pearson, Douglas. "A Mendelian Interpretation of Jacob's Sheep." *Science and Christian Belief* 13 (2001) 51–58.

Pelton, R. D. *The Trickster in West Africa: A Study of Mythic Irony and Sacred Delight.* Berkeley: University of California Press, 1980.

Pemberton, John. "The Yoruba Trickster God." *African Arts* 9 (1975) 20–92.

Perdue, Leo. *The Collapse of History: Reconstructing Old Testament Theology.* Overtures to Biblical Theology. Minneapolis: Fortress, 1994.

Petersen, David L. "Genesis and Family Values." *Journal of Biblical Literature* 124 (2005) 5–23.

Premsagar, P. V. "Theology of Promise in the Patriarchal Narratives." *Indian Journal of Theology* 23 (1974) 112–22.

Propp, William Henry. *Exodus 1–18.* Anchor Bible 2. New York: Doubleday, 1999

Prouser, Joseph H. "Seeing Red: On Translating Esau's Request for Soup." *Conservative Judaism* 56 (2004) 13–20.

Prouser, O. Horn. "The Truth about Women and Lying." *Journal for the Study of the Old Testament* 61 (1994) 15–28.

Pury, Albert de. "The Jacob Story and the Beginnings of the Formation of the Pentateuch." Pages 51–72 in *A Farewell to the Yahwist? The Composition of the Pentateuch in Recent European Interpretation.* Edited by Thomas B. Dozeman and Konrad Schmid. Society of Biblical Literature Symposium Series. Atlanta: Society of Biblical Literature, 2006.

———. *Promesse Divine et Légende Cultuelle dans le Cycle de Jacob: Genèse 28 et les Traditions Patriarcales.* 2 Volumes. Paris: Gabalda, 1975.

Rackman, Joseph. "Was Isaac Deceived?" *Judaism* 43 (1994) 37–45.

Rad, Gerhard von. "The Form-Critical Problem of the Hexateuch." Pages 1–78 in *The Problem of the Hexateuch and Other Essays.* Translated by E. W. Trueman Dicken. London: SCM, 1984.

———. *Genesis: A Commentary.* Old Testament Library. Rev. ed. Translated by John H. Marks. Philadelphia: Westminster, 1973.

———. *Old Testament Theology.* 2 Volumes. Translated by D. M. G. Stalker. New York: Harper & Row, 1962–65.

Radin, P. *The Trickster: A Study in American Indian Mythology.* New York: Bell, 1956.

Park, Song-Mi Suzie. "Transformation and Demarcation of Jacob's 'Flocks' in Genesis 30:25–43: Identity, Election, and the Role of the Divine." *Catholic Biblical Quarterly* 72 (2010) 667–77.

Rendtorff, Rolf. *The Problem of the Process of Transmission in the Pentateuch.* Journal for the Study of the Old Testament Supplement 89. Sheffield: JSOT Press, 1990.

Richardson, Scott. "The Devious Narrator of the 'Odyssey,'" *The Classical Journal* 101 (2006) 337–59.

Roberts, J. J. M. "Does God Lie? Divine Deceit as a Theological Problem in Israelite Prophetic Literature." Pages 211–20 in *Congress Volume: Jerusalem, 1986.* Edited by John A. Emerton. Supplements to Vetus Testamentum 40. Leiden: Brill, 1988.

Rogerson, John W. *Old Testament Theology: Cultural Memory, Communication, and Being Human*. Minneapolis: Fortress, 2010.

Ross, Allen P. *Creation and Blessing: A Guide to the Study and Exposition of Genesis*. Grand Rapids, MI: Baker Academic, 1998.

————. "Jacob's Vision: The Founding of Bethel." *Bibliotheca Sacra* 142 (1985) 224–37.

————. "Jacob at the Jabbok, Israel at Peniel." *Bibliotheca Sacra* 142 (1985) 338–54.

Sarna, Nahum M. *The JPS Torah Commentary: Genesis*. Philadelphia: Jewish Publication Society, 1989.

Savran, George. "The Character as Narrator in Biblical Narrative." *Prooftexts* 5 (1985) 1–17.

Schreiner, Josef. "Das Gebet Jakobs (Gen 32, 10–13)." Pages 287–303 in *Die Väter Israels: Beiträge zur Theologie der Patriarchenüberlieferungen im Alten Testament*. Edited by A. R. Müller and M. Görg. Stuttgart: Katholisches Bibelwerk, 1989.

————. "Segen für Völker in der Verheißung an die Väter." *Biblische Zeitschrift* 6 (1962) 20–34.

Schmid, Konrad. "Die Versöhnung zwischen Jakob und Esau (Gen 33,1–11)." Pages 211–26 in *Jacob: Commentaire à plusieurs voix de Gen 25–36: Melanges offerts à Albert de Pury*. Edited by J. D. Macchi and T. Römer. Le Monde de la Bible 44. Geneva: Labor et Fides, 2001.

Schneider, Tammi J. *Mothers of Promise: Women in the Book of Genesis*. Grand Rapids, MI: Baker Academic, 2008.

Seibert, Eric A. *Disturbing Divine Behavior: Troubling Old Testament Images of God*. Minneapolis: Fortress, 2009.

Sherwood, Stephen K. *Had God Not Been on My Side: An Examination of the Narrative Technique of the Story of Jacob and Laban, Genesis 29:1–32:2*. Europäische Hochschulschriften Reihe 23. Theologie 400. Frankfurt a/M: Peter Lang, 1990.

Skinner, John. *A Critical and Exegetical Commentary on Genesis*. International Critical Commentary 1. Edinburgh: T. & T. Clark, 1930.

Smith, Craig A. "Reinstating Isaac: The Centrality of Abraham's Son in the 'Jacob-Esau' Narrative of Genesis 27." *Biblical Theology Bulletin* 31 (2001) 130–34.

Smith, Mark S. "Remembering God: Collective Memory in Israelite Religion." *Catholic Biblical Quarterly* 64 (2002) 631–51.

Smith, S. H. "'Heel' and 'Thigh': The Concept of Sexuality in the Jacob-Esau Narratives." *Vetus Testamentum* 40 (1990) 464–73.

Speiser, E. A. *Genesis: Introduction, Translation, and Notes*. Anchor Bible 1. New York: Doubleday, 1964.

Spero, Shubert. "Jacob and Esau: The Relationship Reconsidered." *Jewish Bible Quarterly* 32 (2004) 245–50.

Spina, Frank Anthony. "The 'Face of God': Esau in Canonical Context." Pages 3–25 in *The Quest for Context and Meaning: Studies in Biblical Intertextuality in Honor of James A. Sanders*. Edited by Craig A. Evans and Shemaryahu Talmon. Leiden: Brill, 1997.

Steinberg, Naomi. "Israelite Tricksters, Their Analogues and Cross-Cultural Study." *Semeia* 42 (1988) 1–13.

Sternberg, Meir. *The Poetics of Biblical Narrative: Ideological Literature and the Drama of Reading.* Bloomington: Indiana University Press, 1985.

Syrén, Roger. *The Forsaken First-Born: A Study of a Recurrent Motif in the Patriarchal Narratives.* Journal for the Study of the Old Testament Supplement 133. Sheffield: JSOT Press, 1993.

Taschner, Johannes. *Verheissung und Erfüllung in der Jakoberzählung (Gen 25,19– 33,17): Eine Analyse ihres Spannungsbogens.* Herders Biblische Studien 27. Freiburg: Herder, 2000.

Taylor, J. Glen. "Decoding Jacob at the Jabbok and Genesis 32: From Crude Solar Mythology to Profound Hebrew Theology." *La Société Canadienne des Études Bibliques* 3 (2008) 1–25.

Terrien, Samuel. *The Elusive Presence: Towards a New Biblical Theology.* San Francisco: Harper & Row, 1978.

Teugels, Lieve M. "A Matriarchal Cycle? The Portrayal of Isaac in Genesis in the Light of the Presentation of Rebekah." *Bijdragen* 56 (1995) 61–72.

Thompson, Thomas L. "Conflict Themes in the Jacob Narratives." *Semeia* 15 (1979) 5–26.

Trahman, C. R. "Odysseus' Lies (*Odyssey*, Books 13–19)." *Phoenix* 6 (1952) 31–43.

Turner, Laurence A. *Announcements of Plot in Genesis.* Journal for the Study of the Old Testament Supplement 96. Sheffield: JSOT Press, 1990.

———. *Genesis.* Readings: A New Biblical Commentary. 2nd ed. Sheffield: Sheffield Phoenix, 2009.

Van Seters, John. "Divine Encounter at Bethel (Genesis 28.10–22) in Recent Literary-Critical Study of Genesis." *Zeitschrift für die alttestamentliche Wissenschaft* 110 (1998) 503–13.

Vawter, Bruce. *On Genesis: A New Reading.* New York: Doubleday, 1977.

Velde, H. te. "The Egyptian God Seth as a Trickster." *Journal of the American Research Center in Egypt* 7 (1968) 37–40.

———. *Seth, God of Confusion: A Study of His Role in Egyptian Mythology and Religion.* Translated by G. E. van Baaren-Pape. Probleme der Ägyptologie 6. Leiden: Brill, 1977.

Vera, José Loza. "La Berît entre Laban et Jacob (Gn 31.43–54)." Pages 57–69 in *World of the Aramaeans I: Biblical Studies in Honour of Paul-Eugène Dion.* Edited by P. M. Michèle Daviau, John W. Wevers, and Michael Weigl. Sheffield: Sheffield Academic Press, 2001.

Walsh, Jerome T. *Old Testament Narrative: A Guide to Interpretation.* Louisville: Westminster John Knox, 2009.

Walton, Kevin. *Thou Traveller Unknown: The Presence and Absence of God in the Jacob Narrative.* Carlisle: Paternoster, 2003.

Wenham, Gordon J. *Genesis 16–50.* Word Biblical Commentary 2. Dallas: Word, 1994.

———. *Story as Torah: Reading Old Testament Narrative Ethically.* Grand Rapids, MI: Baker Academic, 2004.

Wessner, Mark D. "Toward a Literary Understanding of 'Face to Face' in Genesis 32:23–32." *Restoration Quarterly* 42 (2000) 109–16.

Westermann, Claus. *Blessing: In the Bible and the Life of the Church*. Translated by Keith Crim. Overtures to Biblical Theology. Philadelphia: Fortress, 1978.

―――. *Genesis 12–36*. Translated by John J. Scullion. Continental Commentary. Minneapolis: Fortress, 1985.

―――. *What Does the Old Testament Say about God?* London: SPCK, 1979.

Whybray, R. N. *The Making of the Pentateuch: A Methodological Study*. Journal for the Study of the Old Testament Supplement 53. Sheffield: JSOT Press, 1987.

Williams, Michael James. *Deception in Genesis: An Investigation into the Morality of a Unique Biblical Phenomenon*. Studies in Biblical Literature 32. New York: Peter Lang, 2001.

Willi-Plein, Ina. "Genesis 27 als Rebekkageschichte: Zu einem historiographischen Kunstgriff der biblischen Vätergeschichten." *Theologische Zeitschrift* 45 (1989) 315–34.

Williamson, Paul R. *Abraham, Israel and the Nations: The Patriarchal Promise and Its Covenantal Development in Genesis*. Journal for the Study of the Old Testament Supplement 315. Sheffield: Sheffield Academic Press, 2000.

Wirshbo, Eliot. "The Mekeone Scene in the *Theogony*: Prometheus as Prankster." *Greek, Roman and Byzantine Studies* 23 (1982) 101–10.

Yoreh, Tzemah. "Jacob's Struggle." *Zeitschrift für die alttestamentliche Wissenschaft* 117 (2005) 95–97.

Zakovitch, Yair. "Inner-Biblical Interpretation." Pages 92–118 in *Reading Genesis: Ten Methods*. Edited by Ronald Hendel. Cambridge: Cambridge University Press, 2010.

Index of Authors

203

Index of Scripture